INTERACTIVE LEARNING SYSTEMS EVALUATION

Interactive Learning Systems Evaluation

Thomas C. Reeves PhD
John G. Hedberg PhD

Educational Technology Publications
Englewood Cliffs, New Jersey 07632

Library of Congress Cataloging-in-Publication Data

Reeves, Thomas C. (Thomas Charles)
Interactive learning systems evaluation / Thomas C. Reeves, John G. Hedberg.
p. cm.
Includes bibliographical references and index.
ISBN 0-87778-304-7
1. Interactive multimedia–Evaluation. 2. Educational technology–Evaluation. I. Hedberg, John G. II. Title.

LB1028.55.R44 2003
371.33–dc21

2002029998

Printed in the United States of America.

Library of Congress Catalog Card Number:
2002029998.

International Standard Book Number:
0-87778-304-7.

First Printing: May, 2003.

Dedication

To Trisha

and

To Danne

Table of Contents

Preface

Evaluation of interactive learning systems has been a passion for both of us since we were graduate students at Syracuse University a quarter century ago. We share a belief that evaluation activities are critical to effective development of interactive learning systems. We believe that evaluation is often overlooked or shortchanged in the haste to generate a product and deliver it on time. We think that evaluation should guide the creative development process by providing timely and insightful information about the status of the design ideas and the quality of their implementation. We hope that this book will help to raise the quality of how evaluation functions are undertaken. Although we recommend that a skilled evaluator should be part of every team of people involved in designing, producing, and implementing interactive learning systems, we are confident that anyone involved in the development process can apply the ideas and tools in this book.

— WEB LINK —
The Web site for this book can be found at http://it.coe.uga.edu/~treeves/ilse.html

The book is structured around the provision of information generating activities related to stages in the design and development of interactive educational products such as multimedia DVD's, Web-based training, electronic performance support systems, and e-learning solutions. We have sought to link specific design activities to evaluation procedures and tools that will help the novice (as well as experienced) evaluator plan, conduct, and report better evaluations. Many of the tools can be used for multiple functions. A Web site associated with this book links functions and tools and provides further examples of how to use them.

The structure of the book follows the design, development, and implementation process or journey through which interactive learning systems come to be. The first chapter of the book introduces the starting point for evaluation, which wc bclicvc is to inform decision-making at all stages of the product development. The chapter also clarifies what we mean by interactive learning systems and how they have evolved over time as learning theories and technologies have also changed.

Chapter Two locates the evaluation process within an appropriate model of inquiry. Without clearly knowing how your values and methods match the questions and goals of an evaluation, you may just be "painting-by-numbers" instead of skillfully applying evaluation strategies.

The third chapter links the roles that evaluation can play with each stage of the interactive product development process. If done well, evaluation data is often the key element to completing each product development stage. We contend that documenting development activities is critical to every step in the instructional design process. As described in Chapter Three, creating effective systems to collect and organize documentation data along the way is an important element in the success of any development project.

Planning and managing the evaluation component of each project is a special skill in itself, as addressed in Chapter Four. In the evaluation courses and workshops we teach, preparing an evaluation plan is a starting assignment to get participants to the first stage of understanding how evaluation works. This critical planning task reinforces the role that good documentation plays in providing reliable sources of informed insights to guide decision-making.

Chapter Five — concept review — describes the first stage in our six stage model. Review is based upon the idea of a project concept or the initial idea about why and what might be undertaken. Review helps you seek out the sometimes serendipitous information that might provide the rationale for why an interactive product should be produced in the first place. As an interactive learning system project gets started and before too many resources have been expended, you need to review delivery options and existing resources.

Chapter Six describes needs assessment, which usually signals the formal start of a development project. Needs assessment seeks to identify exactly what is required for what reason. It analyzes the rationale for various approaches to resolving performance problems or generating effective learning environments. Needs assessment also helps you and other members of your team to clarify design parameters that might have been suggested or imposed by funding or client constraints.

Chapter Seven focuses on formative evaluation — evaluation intended to enhance a product as it is being developed. Formative evaluation is essential as you and your team seek to translate goals and objectives into a working, effective interactive learning product. Here issues such as the usability of the product are tested, and the resulting modifications are made to streamline the cognitive demands of the interface and ensure that the product achieves its educational goals. Interface, navigation, and visual design components are critical elements in the final product that need to be addressed as the product is formulated. Otherwise, it can be very costly to have to rework and recast graphic design elements once full scale production or implementation is underway.

Chapter Eight deals with effectiveness evaluation. This stage involves strategies for evaluating the interactive learning system in action to determine how it is working in the context for which it is intended. During this stage, issues such as assessing student learning from the completed product and the ease of integration within classrooms or other learning contexts become dominant issues.

Chapter Nine is all about impact evaluation. This function examines the integration of an interactive learning system within an organization's structure and specifies how a product supports the organization's goals. Over time, this area might form the basis for decisions about adopting a product, scrapping it, or identifying cost-effective outcomes that might predispose the organization to future use of other interactive learning technologies.

Chapter Ten covers maintenance evaluation, a neglected area which is a critical part of any product's renewal cycle. It seeks to answer questions such as does the product or system still achieve the learning goals for which it was originally designed, and how is it holding up as technology advances?

Chapter Eleven focuses on several issues about how evaluation studies are reported to clients and other stakeholders. Key issues that are addressed include how to inform evaluation audiences in ways that guarantee that the efforts you make as an evaluator have an impact on decisions in a timely manner. If the information is not fed into the process in an effective manner, then the data will result in little action.

Chapter Twelve seeks to explore how you and other evaluators might contribute to the overall advancement of interactive learning systems design in substantial ways beyond the immediate context of any given development initiative. We recommend a new approach that would enable the design lessons learned through evaluations to become more visible and contribute to a body of literature that could inform the overall field of educational technology, especially with respect to the design of interactive learning systems.

This book has been carefully crafted over several years, a project that has taken us back and forth to the far corners of the globe numerous times in the search for and refinement of the evaluation ideas that are contained in it. We trust you will find the book and the associated Web site practical as well as inspirational.

We have both shared earlier drafts of this book in our evaluation courses and workshops, using the feedback from participants to improve the ideas and tools, and especially to enhance the relevance of our ideas. Of course, any errors or problems are ours alone.

Along the way we have also been helped by many of our colleagues, such as Bill Aggen, Shirley Alexander, Christine Brown, Kent Gustafson, Barry Harper, Joe Henderson, Jan Herrington, Jim King, Geraldine Lefoe, Mary Marlino, Carmel McNaught, Mary L. Miller, Mary R. Miller, Jim Okey, Ron Oliver, Geoff Ring, Murray Tillman, and Stanley Varnhagen, among others. Trisha Reeves has been especially generous in proofreading several drafts of the book, using up several red pens in the process. We appreciate the assistance of our editor, Larry Lipsitz, and his associates at Educational Technology Publications, Inc. We also wish to thank the many clients who have hired us to conduct evaluations, thus providing us with rich opportunities for professional development. Most of all, we wish to acknowledge our graduate students who have compelled us to write this book in the first place and who have provided us with invaluable feedback along the way.

Tom Reeves
John Hedberg
January 2003

Interactive Learning Systems Evaluation

CHAPTER 1

A Pragmatic Rationale for Evaluation

Objectives

After reading Chapter One, you should be able to:

- state a pragmatic rationale for evaluating interactive learning systems for education and training that emphasizes the utilization of information by a wide range of people to improve decision making;
- distinguish among various forms, architectures, and theories of interactive learning; and
- distinguish among various technological delivery vehicles for interactive learning.

A decision-oriented, pragmatic rationale for evaluation

Throughout the last decade, interactive learning systems have been the subject of much attention, ranging from enthusiastic advocacy (Perelman, 1992; Pittinsky, 2003) to heavy skepticism (Cuban, 2001; Oppenheimer, 1997). The complexities of interactive learning derive from competing theoretical foundations (such as behavioral versus cognitive psychology) and an often bewildering array of technological delivery options. Similarly, the field of evaluation has evolved into a contentious one with many competing models and several conflicting paradigms. In the face of these complexities, we have written this book to promote a pragmatic perspective for evaluating interactive learning systems in which the primary aim of evaluation is the collection of information to support day-to-day decision making by people just like yourself: project managers, instructional designers, and implementers of interactive learning systems.

When selecting a site for a restaurant, it is commonplace to say that the three most important criteria are "Location, Location, Location." Similarly, in the process of evaluating interactive learning, it can be said that the three most important criteria are "Decisions, Decisions, Decisions." In short, your primary focus should be on the decisions that evaluation must influence. As a developer, manager, or implementer of interactive learning systems, you must make decisions, similar to those of other professionals. Before rendering a diagnosis, a physician collects the medical history of the patient, conducts a thorough examination, and runs various tests. Before building a case for the defense, a criminal lawyer interviews the client, reviews police records, and conducts private investigations. In fact, the quality and reputation of a physician or lawyer are determined largely by how skillful he or she is in conducting "evaluative" acts such as interviewing, testing, and examining.

If you are serious about developing or managing interactive learning systems, you must become skilled at conducting various evaluation activities before making decisions. For example, in the process of producing a Web-based training program, you likely will ask content experts to review draft scripts, observe trainees using prototype versions of the program, and subject the program to thorough usability testing (Nielsen, 2000). None of these activities (interviewing, observing, or usability testing) is especially complicated in and of itself. In fact, most evaluation activities, whether medical, legal, or instructional, involve activities that are relatively simple in concept. However, all of these procedures require skillful application at appropriate times. The major purposes of this book are to describe practical evaluation activities that you can carry out to improve decision making and to provide you with the basic tools to make your evaluative efforts more effective.

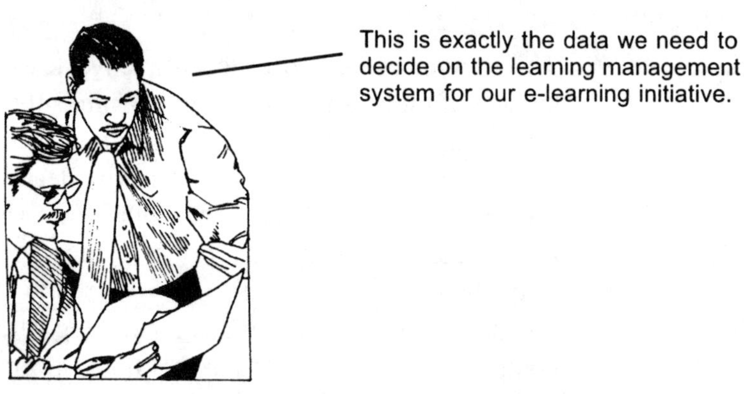

To put it another way, this book is based on a simple premise: Decisions informed by sound evaluation are better than those based on habit, ignorance, intuition, prejudice, or guesswork. Our experience indicates that far too often people make poor decisions about the design and implementation of interactive learning systems because they lack pertinent information. Frankly, we would not have spent our time writing this book if we were not convinced that evaluation, done well, will help you and your clients make better decisions and improve the quality of learning outcomes.

Interactive learning: Forms, architectures, and theories

In Gustave Flaubert's *Madame Bovary*, the narrator muses: "Language is a cracked kettle on which we tap out crude rhythms for bears to dance to while we long to make music that will melt the stars." Certainly, proponents of interactive learning systems have long struggled to find terminology to suggest, much less capture, the exciting potential of this approach to education and training. In a field burdened by a history of disappointing instructional innovations (e.g., programmed instruction, teaching machines, and computer-assisted instruction) (Cuban, 1986, 2001), newer buzzwords for interactive learning (e.g., e-learning, m-learning, and virtual reality) inspire enthusiasts and exasperate skeptics.

Of course, all learning is interactive in the sense that learners interact with content to process, tasks to accomplish, and problems to solve. Who would disagree that highly interactive learning occurs when a French tutor coaches a pupil to develop better enunciation skills? However, in this book, we define interactive learning specifically as a process involving some form of digital mediation between a teacher or designer and a learner. From this perspective, an interactive learning system requires a digital device equipped with a microprocessor (e.g., a computer) and at least one human being (a learner). The steel worker completing mandatory safety training via a multimedia CD-ROM, the undergraduate playing the role of a gorilla in a Web-based simulation of primate behavior, and the three-year-old practicing color-matching skills with Big Bird via a *Sesame Street* DVD program are all engaged in interactive learning.

The meaning of the term "interactivity" is the subject of considerable debate (Rose, 1999; Sims, 2000), especially now that the optimistic prediction that intelligent tutoring systems would dominate education and training by the year 2000 has been proven false (Lajoie, 2000). In our judgment, the essence of what makes a learning system interactive is the task in which the learner is engaged (Herrington, Oliver, & Reeves, 2002). Forms and levels of interactivity are influenced by many aspects of the design of interactive learning systems, but none is more important than the task the learner is trying to accomplish or the problem he or she is trying to solve.

Forms of interactive learning

An early and influential attempt to describe forms of interactive learning was Taylor's (1980) classic model of the roles of computers in education as "tutor, tool, and tutee." In the tutor role, the computer is considered to act as a surrogate teacher. As a tool, the computer is used by learners to do things that would be too laborious, slow, or complex to do without it, for example, writing papers with a word processor, calculating budgets with a spreadsheet, or organizing taxonomies of phenomena with a database program. And when the computer is a tutee, the learner enhances his or her own knowledge by programming it to do something unique, for example, display an original graphic or run an algorithm to model a business process. Numerous educators, trainers, and commercial entrepreneurs have predicted that computers would revolutionize teaching and learning through one or more of these roles. Unfortunately, none of these approaches has lived up to its promise. We attribute much of this dismal record to a lack of appropriate and timely evaluation as well as poor educational research aimed at gathering supportive data for flawed applications of technology (Reeves, 2000).

Consider the tutor role wherein the computer is supposed to instruct the learner, usually via a predefined "interactive lesson." The results of these interactive lessons have been found to be positive, albeit somewhat modest (Coley, Cradler, & Engel, 1997; Hannafin, Hannafin, Hooper, Rieber, & Kini, 1996). Even the staunchest proponents of computer-based instruction (CBI) and intelligent tutoring systems (ITS) must acknowledge the lack of impact these computer-as-tutor applications have had on mainstream education and training (Lajoie, 2000; Lajoie & Derry, 1993; Shlechter, 1991). Part of this failure stems from an overly restrictive perspective of students as passive perceivers or recipients of educational communications, a perspective that has dominated instructional designs for interactive tutors. Another factor contributing to the lack of success of intelligent tutoring systems has been the technical difficulties inherent in building student models and facilitating human-like communications. These challenges have been underestimated by proponents of the "tutor" model (Shute & Psotka, 1996).

The computer-as-tool approach has also disappointed many of its proponents, although there have been some successes when tools have been embedded within innovative pedagogy, such as a whole language approach to literacy development (Bruce & Rubin, 1993). In many cases, software tools such as word-processing, spreadsheet, and database programs have failed to improve teaching and learning significantly because they have not been integrated with an appropriate instructional design. Goodlad (1984) describes the teacher-directed, textbook, and workbook-dominated curriculum that has characterized educational practice for decades. Instead of being employed as "cognitive tools" (Jonassen, 1999; Jonassen & Reeves, 1996; Lajoie, 2000) to solve challenging problems, pursue personal learning goals, or accomplish authentic tasks, computer tools have often been regarded as objects for study themselves and subjected to direct, formal instruction.

For example, consider computer-aided design (CAD) software, which has revolutionized professional practices and dramatically increased productivity in engineering, architecture, and other design fields. Industrial arts teachers (now called "technology educators") enthusiastically adopted CAD software into their classrooms, but instead of engaging students in authentic tasks, they have tended to "teach" students the command sets for the software outside of any meaningful contexts. Not surprisingly, students ended up failing to perceive the relevance and value of such programs within the design professions. As pointed out by Salomon, Perkins, and Globerson (1991), "No important impact can be expected when the same old activity is carried out with a technology that makes it a bit faster or easier; the activity itself has to change" (p. 8).

— WEB LINK —
Seymour Papert's site is: http://papert.www.media.mit.edu/people/papert/

Additional links about Papert's work can be found at: http://www.papert.com

Despite the religious fervor with which the computer-as-tutee role has been embraced in some circles (Papert, 1980, 1993), the results of this method have been much less spectacular than promised. According to proponents of the computer-as-tutee approach, students develop higher-order thinking skills and creativity by teaching the computer to perform tasks (e.g., draw a flower) through the use of "friendly" programming languages such as Logo (Papert, 1980). Studies of the effects of Logo (Pea & Kurland, 1987) have failed to demonstrate the cognitive advantages promised by Papert and others. Defenders of this approach maintain that the implementations of Logo investigated in most studies were too brief and unfocused. Indeed, many applications of Logo and other microworlds described in the literature appear to lack the "mindful engagement" that Salomon and Globerson (1987) argue is necessary for learning. Intensive Logo applications that have engaged students in meaningful tasks over longer periods of time have demonstrated stronger effects (Harel, 1991; Kafai, 1995).

There is a new perspective on interactive learning that has developed within the context of computer-mediated learning environments such as Web-based instruction and training (Khan, 1997; 2001). This perspective is supported by evidence that interactions between learners through online discussion forums, chat rooms, and other technologies can enable authentic learning opportunities that are more powerful than those conceived of within traditional interactive formats such as the aforementioned "tutor, tool, and tutee" models (Kearsley, 2000). These rapidly evolving technologies circumvent travel, time zone, and geography limits allowing learners located at different sites within a global company to share knowledge bases and collaborate to solve complex problems. Through such instructional designs and technologies, the dreams of the "learning organization" can be realized (Hedberg, Brown, Larkin, & Agostinho, 2001; Senge, 1992). The interactivity inherent in this approach is derived from the authentic dialogue that occurs when real people work together to solve difficult problems or accomplish complex tasks. This type of interactivity is not limited to the corporate world. For example, high school and college students from different cultures who are separated by many miles can engage in rich discourse and collaboration that can lead to profound learning (Cummins & Sayers, 1995).

Architectures for interactive learning

— WEB LINK —
Roger Schank's Web site can be found at: http://socraticarts.com/

A powerful contemporary perspective on interactive learning is provided by Roger Schank, founder of the Institute for the Learning Sciences at Northwestern University, and now with Carnegie Mellon University. Figure 1.1 summarizes the five teaching architectures Schank has defined for interactive learning systems. An interactive introduction to Schank's provocative ideas and software descriptions can be found on the Web, and additional material can be found in his books, including *Virtual Learning: A Revolutionary Approach to Building a Highly Skilled Workforce* (1997) and *Coloring Outside the Lines: Raising a Smarter Kid by Breaking All the Rules* (2000).

According to Schank and Cleary (1995), the "transmission-of-content" approach to education "flies in the face of everything scientists have discovered about children's natural learning mechanisms, which are primarily experimentation and reflection — in other words, learning by doing." Schank and his team have developed interactive learning environments for each of the teaching architectures in his model.

For example, for "Simulation-Based Learning by Doing," they developed an English language simulator called "Dustin" to help new employees at Accenture (formerly called Andersen Consulting) who are not native speakers of English. Dustin allows employees to enhance their English skills within the context of the actual environment they will encounter when they attend business meetings at the company's U.S. training center near Chicago.

Dustin includes a series of video scenarios (clearing customs at O'Hare airport, checking into a hotel, and ordering food) that all new employees will encounter. When a trainee keys in his or her responses to the scenarios, the computer parses the language to judge a response. If the trainee is successful with a given scenario, he or she goes on to the next. But if the trainee is unsuccessful, he or she still learns. In fact, "failing" is quite valuable within Schank's model:

> Failure is a key element in Dustin. Students realize what they need to do to learn in a very direct way. They fail at a task and become interested in finding out what they need to know to succeed. In some sense, then, they instruct themselves by seeking the information they need to complete the task. (Schank & Cleary, 1995, p. 82)

Simulation-Based Learning by Doing	This architecture aims to have students learn every possible skill through learning by doing. Because the doing of the task is what prepares the student for real life, it is important that the student be able to actively engage in such tasks. Simulations of all kinds can be built, although the challenge of designing high-fidelity simulations should not be underestimated. The Simulation-Based Learning by Doing Architecture is critical when the subject matter to be learned is experiential at heart. Of course, much of natural learning is the accumulation of experience.
Incidental Learning	Not everything is fun to learn. In fact, some things are terribly boring to learn. But people do habitually learn a variety of information that is quite dull, without being completely bored by it. Often, they do this by picking up the information "in passing," without intending to learn the information at all. The Incidental Learning Architecture is based on the creation of tasks whose end results are inherently interesting, and which can be used to impart dull information.
Learning by Reflection	Sometimes a student doesn't need to be told something, but rather needs to know how to ask about it. It could be that the student has a vague plan he/she wishes to mull over. Or perhaps the student has a problem and needs to figure out a way to approach it. Or maybe the student has finished a project and wishes to think back on how the project could have been done better. In such cases, a teacher's job is to open the student's eyes to new ways of thinking about the situation, to help the student articulate the situation and generate ways of moving forward.
Case-Based Teaching	This architecture depends upon these two ideas: experts are repositories of cases, and good teachers are good storytellers. The task of this architecture is to tell students exactly what they need to know when they need to know it. When students are learning by doing, they experience knowledge failures, times when they realize that they need new information in order to progress. These are the times when Case-Based Teaching can provide the knowledge that students need. Isolated facts are difficult for students to integrate into their memories; useful knowledge is typically best presented in the form of stories.
Learning by Exploring	The previous architectures deal with the difficult problems of getting students involved in their own learning and letting them learn through performing tasks that they care about. Students naturally generate questions, and they are ready to learn from those questions. An important method of teaching is to answer a student's questions and carry on a conversation about the issues in the questions, answering whatever follow-up questions the student generates. The Learning by Exploring architecture is intended to provide such answers in a conversational format.

Figure 1.1. The five teaching architectures defined by Schank and Cleary (1995).

— **WEB LINK** —
Information about the popular Carmen Sandiego educational software can be found at: http://www.carmensandiego.com/

For the second architecture, "Incidental Learning," Schank's team invented intrinsically motivating simulations such as "Road Trip." The "Road Trip" program helps young students learn geography by using maps to negotiate their way around the U.S. in search of video clips of interest to them, such as sports or music. (A similar architecture underlies the popular "Carmen Sandiego" software series in which students "incidentally" learn geography, history, and other subjects while chasing international thieves.) In "Road Trip," students do not study maps, but they do use them to find the videos they desire. According to Schank and Cleary (1995), evaluations of "Road Trip" with fourth graders found that the most important outcome was that students learned to plan road trips using an atlas. In addition, students who knew very little geography significantly improved their scores on standardized tests, and all levels of students reported the simulation to be highly appealing.

"Learning by Reflection," the third teaching architecture in Schank's model, is closely related to "metacognition," that is, the ability to think about, evaluate, and modify one's own learning processes (Short & Weissberg-Benchell, 1989). Research has demonstrated that better learners ask themselves questions, explain examples to themselves and others, and change learning strategies based upon their needs. Schank's "Sounding Board" program is designed to help a learner solve problems or accomplish tasks by asking a series of critical questions. (The program appears similar to therapy simulators that have been developed to mimic the interactions a patient might have with a psychologist.) The "structured brainstorming" that results from "Sounding Board" is especially effective when the learner is trying to create something new, such as a sales strategy. Similar software has also been designed to help students reflect upon books, films, and artworks.

To exemplify the fourth architecture, "Case-Based Teaching," Schank and his team produced "Creanimate," a program that allows children to design animals with unusual features such as a frog with wings. The program asks open-ended questions such as "Why would your frog want to fly?" It also shows pertinent videos such as a "flying fish" video. By posing questions about the rationale behind a learner's design decisions, and the impact the decisions would have upon the animal's survival, "Creanimate" enables the student to learn important biology concepts. Three critical parts of the case-based learning architecture are having numerous appropriate cases related to the subject, providing a complex task for the learner to pursue, and enabling flexible indexing so that the cases are accessible when the learner can best learn from them. Schank and Cleary (1995) state that students interact with programs such as "Creanimate" differently depending upon their unique learning styles.

The last, but certainly not least, of the teaching architectures in Schank's model is "Learning by Exploring." To help learners learn by exploring, Schank argues that it is more important for them to be engaged in a meaningful dialogue about the information they find than to spend most of their time finding information. He and his colleagues have developed what they call "ASK Systems" to help learners find needed information as quickly as possible and to engage them in a simulated dialogue about that information. One example of an "ASK System" was designed for the U.S. military to help officers learn to schedule transportation for personnel and supplies during a crisis such as the Gulf War. The officer selects a role, a task, and a specific problem from the options in the "ASK System," and then is provided with stories that help the officer/learner complete the logistics plan. The interface has been designed to enable the learner to ask questions in many different ways while possible solutions to a problem are explored.

Schank and his colleagues do not represent their teaching architectures as the final word in how to design interactive learning, but as a work in progress. One of the hallmarks of their work at the Institute for the Learning Sciences at Northwestern University was that their design efforts were guided by rigorous research and evaluation studies. Most recently, Schank has focused his energies on the development of a new "e-learning" company called Socratic Arts.

— **WEB LINK** —
More information about Jasper Woodbury is at http://peabody.vanderbilt.edu/ctrs/lsi/

Other architectures (or instructional models) have resulted in award-winning examples of education software. For example, the work by the Cognition and Technology Group at Vanderbilt University has produced the Jasper Woodbury series of problem-based learning resources (Bransford, Brown, & Cocking, 1999). The Vanderbilt "anchored instruction" approach revolves around situating (anchoring) the learning within an authentic context, and thus the elements of the context motivate teams of students to solve the problems posed (Cognition and Technology Group at Vanderbilt, 1992). For example, to develop pragmatic (as opposed to inert) math skills, students collaborate to build a playground supported by a high-fidelity multimedia simulation.

— **WEB LINK** —
More information about StageStruck is at: http://www.immll.uow.edu.au/immll/stagestruck.htm

Interactive multimedia software has extended innovative learning architectures even to creative disciplines such as drama. The award-winning CD-ROM, *StageStruck*, from the Interactive Multimedia Learning Laboratory at the University of Wollongong in Australia, enables students to direct performances based on scenes from professional playwrights or to write their own scenes. The context is sufficiently realistic to require the same decision-making issues in the simulated theater as required in real-world production.

Theories underlying interactive learning

Since the earliest days of teaching machines, behavioral learning theory has had a pervasive influence on the design of interactive learning systems. Debunking behavioral psychology has become fashionable, but behaviorism continues to be the underlying psychology for many forms of interactive learning. According to classical behavioral psychology (Skinner, 1968), the important factors in learning are not internal states that may or may not exist, but behaviors that can be directly observed. From the behaviorist perspective, instruction consists primarily of shaping desirable behaviors through the scientific arrangement of stimuli, responses, feedback, reinforcement, and other contingencies. First, a stimulus is provided, often in the form of a short presentation of content. Second, a response is demanded, often by asking a question. Third, feedback is given regarding the accuracy of the response. Fourth, positive reinforcement is given for accurate responses. Fifth, inaccurate responses result in either a repetition of the original stimulus or a modified (often simpler) version of it, and the cycle begins again.

During the last decade, many scientists and educational researchers have suggested that we are experiencing a "cognitive" revolution in learning theory (Bransford, Brown, & Cocking, 1999; Brown, Collins, & Duguid, 1989; Clark & Mayer, 2003; Jonassen, 1999; Papert, 1993; Schank & Cleary, 1995). Whether this movement is revolutionary or not, it confronts many obstacles, not the least of which is the dominant "instructivist" pedagogical paradigm that is used to justify the production of interactive learning systems that transmit a standardized curriculum to every student.

Constructivist learning theory has been proposed as an alternative to the traditional "instructivist" or "transmissionist" approach to education and training (Duffy & Jonassen, 1992). Constructivism is concerned with the cognitive processes whereby we construct meaning and knowledge in the world as well as with the results of the constructive process (Phillips & Early, 2000). How we construct knowledge depends upon what we already know, our previous experiences, how we have organized our experiences into knowledge structures such as schema and mental models, and the beliefs we use to interpret the objects and events we encounter. Fosnot (1996) offers a definition of constructivism:

> Constructivism is a theory about knowledge and learning; it describes both what "knowing" is and how one "comes to know." ... the theory describes knowledge as temporary, developmental, nonobjective, internally constructed, and socially and culturally mediated. Learning from this perspective is viewed as a self-regulatory process of struggling with the conflict between existing personal models of the world and discrepant new insight, constructing new representations and models of reality as a hu-

> man meaning-making venture with culturally developed tools and symbols, and further negotiating such meaning through cooperative social activity, discourse, and debate. Although constructivism is not a theory of teaching, it suggests taking a radically different approach to instruction....a constructivist view of learning suggests an approach to teaching that gives learners the opportunity for concrete, contextually meaningful experience through which they can search for patterns, raise their own questions, and construct their own models, concepts, and strategies. The classroom in this model is seen as a minisociety, a community of learners engaged in activity, discourse, and reflection. The traditional hierarchy of teacher as the autocratic knower and learner as the unknowing, controlled subject studying to learn what the teacher knows begins to dissipate as teachers assume more of a facilitator's role and learners take on more ownership of the ideas. Indeed, autonomy, mutual reciprocity of social relations, and empowerment become the goals. (p. ix)

Radical constructivists such as von Glaserfeld (1989) maintain that the ultimate nature of reality or whether it even exists does not matter as much as our unique and shared constructions of reality. According to constructivism, teachers are doomed to fail in attempts to map their own interpretations of the world onto learners because they do not share a set of common experiences and interpretations. Reality (or at least what we know and understand of it) resides in the mind of each knower, who interprets the external world according to his or her own experiences, beliefs, and knowledge. Learners are able to comprehend a variety of interpretations and to use them in arriving at their own unique interpretations of the world. The mind filters input from the world in making its interpretations, and therefore we each conceive of the external world somewhat differently. Fortunately, we are able to share our unique interpretations through language, art, and other communication channels, so that we are not completely isolated in our own special worlds. Constructivists regard multimedia as an especially powerful channel for self-expression and communication, as well as an appropriate vehicle for interactive learning (Jonassen, 1999).

In traditional instruction, "active" refers to stimulus, response, feedback, and reinforcement conditions that help students mirror accepted views of reality whereas in constructivist learning environments, "active" learners interact with the surrounding environment (including both the technology-mediated aspects and the support provided by other learners) to create their own interpretations of reality. While early computer-based tutorials utilized a transmissionist pedagogy grounded in behavioral psychology (Skinner, 1968), contemporary interactive learning environments are designed to implement constructivist pedagogy based upon cognitive learning theories (Wilson, 1996). Rather than working their way through problems and solutions that have been predefined by teachers and instructional designers, learners engaged in constructivist approaches to interactive learning define and refine the nature of a problem they have identified, reconstruct their knowledge to solve that problem, and represent their solution in multimedia formats (Lehrer, 1993).

Throughout this book, we present examples of interactive learning systems that we have evaluated in a variety of contexts. Some of these programs are decidedly "instructivist" in nature, and others are examples, at least in part, of constructivist learning theory. Although the particular type of interactive learning system you want to evaluate may not be represented exactly in these examples, the variety of systems we have included is such that we believe you can find adequate models for your specific needs.

Interactive learning: Systems for delivery and collaboration

In addition to examining the theoretical aspects of interactive learning, it is important to consider the array of options for linking learners to learning opportunities and resources. Imagine a simulation designed to help adults learn a second language by immersing them in a foreign scenario. There are a variety of technological options for this interactive learning environment, including CD-ROM, Digital Video Disc (DVD), and the World Wide Web. Although each of these delivery systems is different, the programs could have similar mixes of pedagogical strategies; for example, the learner could be interacting within the context of a real task (e.g., checking into a hotel), listening to a native speaker, selecting responses from a menu of choices, receiving feedback, and branching out to remedial instruction as indicated by his or her success or failure in the simulation. Using technologies such as the Web can also enable human-to-human levels of interaction (Kearsley, 2000). For example, whereas at a basic level the learner might interact with a prepared set of resources, if connectivity is provided, the learner can ask questions of an online tutor located anywhere in the world or seek feedback from peers.

The proliferation of delivery systems for interactive learning is sometimes overwhelming. From the early days of B. F. Skinner's teaching machines, we have progressed to virtual reality immersion systems and teacher holograms. How long will it be before interactive learning systems regularly involve 3-D full-immersion video? To make matters even more complicated, the many acronyms (e.g., CAI, CBI, CAL, CBE, DVD, IMM, WBLE, etc.) used to designate various technology options are used inconsistently in different parts of the world. We cannot provide a comprehensive list of all of them here, and anything we could produce would soon be out-of-date, as newer technologies are developed every few months.

— WEB LINK —
The Masie Center is a good source for information about interactive delivery system options: http://www.masie.com/

In lieu of a comprehensive list of technology options for interactive learning, we have listed some of the primary technologies in use today (Figure 1.2). The list is presented in more or less chronological order to reflect the time when these various technologies were introduced. Some delivery systems with which you might be familiar may not appear in Figure 1.2 (e.g., digital video interactive or DVI) because these technologies either vanished from the interactive market soon after their appearance or because we consider them to be too similar to other technologies already on our list. Of course, we expect that there will be new delivery options by the time this book goes into print. For example, companies are already producing interactive multimedia courseware for personal digital assistants (PDAs) such as Palm Pilots, and it may be that the buzzword "m-learning" (m = mobile) will catch on (Gayeski, 2002). The challenge of keeping up with the delivery options for interactive learning involves reading journals and commercial magazines, attending conferences and trade shows, and surfing the Web on a regular basis.

From time to time, various authorities call for standardization of delivery systems for interactive learning, but we view these demands as unrealistic. Large computer and electronics corporations invest millions and millions of dollars in research and development for new technologies, and these types of investments are unlikely to stop. Calling for standardization of delivery systems is a lost cause because change is the name of the game. Indeed, the "chaos" that new technologies caused for big business from time to time in the 20th century (e.g., the widespread adoption of television in the 1950s or personal computers in the 1980s) is more likely to be the norm in what Hock (1999) calls the "chaordic age" of the 21st century.

You don't have to look back very far within the history of interactive learning systems to see similar changes. Just as soon as corporate trainers thought that CD-ROM was the ideal delivery option for interactive education and training, along came the Web. As experienced developers of interactive learning systems, we recommend that you get used to living in an unpredictable world where the ultimate delivery system will never exist. Of course, as an evaluator of interactive learning and performance support systems, you must keep up with the latest technical developments in order to evaluate individual projects in an informed manner.

Older Technologies

Magnetic Media	In the past, most interactive learning programs (such as computer-based training) were delivered on diskettes or loaded onto a hard-drive server and accessed over a local area network. Most computers around the globe today include modems and CD-ROM drives, and thus the days when interactive learning is delivered via computer diskettes or other magnetic media have virtually come to an end.
Interactive Videodisc (IVD)	IVD involves the integration of an optical disc storing video frames and a computer program providing interactive routines. Interactive videodiscs were popular because of the high quality of the video they provided, but IVD programs are rarely produced today, and soon will be museum artifacts.
CD-I	Compact Disc Interactive (CD-I) is an optical technology that integrates a variety of media on a single compact disc such as audio, images, and up to an hour of full-screen motion video. CD-I requires only a CD-I player (a self-contained disc player and microprocessor) and any video monitor or TV. CD-I players went out-of-production in 1999.

Current Technologies

CD-ROM	CD-ROM (compact disc-read only memory) became a standard peripheral on most microcomputers sold in the 1990s, and they are a major component of the installed base of computers available today. CD-ROM is an optical medium that can store 660 megabytes of media including text, graphics, sound, and video. Many popular interactive "edutainment" programs are delivered via CD-ROM. Today, CD-ROM drives are being replaced with DVD drives that play most of the available CD-ROMs as well as the new DVD programs. CD-ROM is also being used as a hybrid medium with the Web to reduce the bandwidth requirements of multimedia programs.
World Wide Web (Web)	The World Wide Web is a network of files on computers all over the world. The computers are accessed using modems and phone lines via "links" using software browsers available from companies such as Netscape or Microsoft. Publicly accessible Web-based interactive learning examples abound, and many corporations provide training and performance support to their employees via restricted sites called "intranets." Larger Web "pipelines" (e.g., cable and digital satellite systems) are gaining popularity because of the faster access they provide to end-users. Increasingly, the need to have direct wired connections to the Web is becoming less necessary because wireless connections are becoming widely available. The Web as a communications technology is an interestingly different form of technology to the laser disk technologies in that it can be structured in multiple ways to link learners with each other as well as to dynamic resources.
DVD	Digital Video Disc (DVD) combines the data intensity of CD-ROM with the video quality of videodisc into an interactive format that requires a special player that works with any video monitor or TV. It has more than seven times the capacity of a CD-ROM, and can show full-screen, full-speed video.

Figure 1.2. Popular delivery systems for interactive learning.

— WEB LINK —
For information about various initiatives to set courseware standards:
http://www.adlnet.org/
http://www.microsoft.com/net/
http://aicc.org/
http://www.imsproject.org/

Although delivery modes for interactive learning may never be standardized, there are efforts to establish technical standards for the courseware that will be delivered via present and future technologies. Whether you are developing or simply using various e-learning formats such as Web-based training (WBT) or Web-based learning environments (WBLE), you should be aware of the Advanced Distributed Learning (ADL) initiative and other efforts to promote technical specifications for sharing instructional content and learning management systems (LMS) over the Internet or across various intranets. For example, the U.S. Department of Defense is promoting the Sharable Content Object Reference Model (SCORM) via the ADL initiative. Other entities developing their own set of standards for courseware include Microsoft Corporation, the Aviation Industry CBT Committee, and EDUCAUSE (Bush, 2002).

Aside from the technology options discussed above, there are two terms used in reference to interactive learning today that deserve additional clarification. The first term is multimedia. (An earlier draft of this book was titled *Evaluating Interactive Multimedia*, but we ultimately decided to broaden the focus of this volume to all forms of interactive learning systems.) Multimedia at its simplest is the integration of visual, aural, textual, and data displays within one learning environment. The second term is distance learning, a poorly understood phenomenon with implications for all levels of education and training. Nowadays, distance learning and related terms (e.g., online learning or e-learning) focus on options for breaking or modifying the physical links between instructor and student, either by place or time, and also on ways in which learning can be facilitated by the instructor and through supportive technologies. Both multimedia and distance learning have captured the interests of the public around the globe, and as such are given special attention throughout this volume.

Multimedia

The terminology used to describe multimedia and related software can be confusing. "Interactive multimedia," "hypermedia," and simply "multimedia" are used interchangeably by some and very distinctly by others. For example, Locatis, Letourneau, and Banvard (1989) prefer the term "hypermedia," defining it as "a computer-based approach to information management in which data is stored in networks of nodes connected by links. Nodes can contain text, graphics, audio, video, source code, or other data..." (p. 65). The IBM Corporation (1991), on the other hand, proffers a more inclusive definition of multimedia: "The concept of multimedia makes accessible full-motion video, photographic still images, animation, stereo sound, and text and graphics – giving users the ability to weave a limitless number of stories for a universe of applications."

Fischer and Mandl (1990) claim that hypermedia can be distinguished from multimedia by "the depth and richness of the information contained" and by the degree to which "the learner decides how much of this virtual database he or she wants to use." They imply that hypermedia is a higher-order learning system than multimedia because of its complexity and accessibility. Gygi (1990) also makes a distinction between hypermedia and multimedia, and chastises those who "persist in believing that multimedia is inherently motivating" (p. 281). She maintains that the critical element in the dynamic power of hypermedia is the user's ability to alter the medium, not the presence of multiple presentation formats (e.g., animation, graphics, sound, text, and video).

Despite the confusion, subtle distinctions have evolved in the use of the two terms. The commercial world and the general public definitely prefer the term multimedia. Apple Computer, Inc., the IBM Corporation, and the Microsoft Corporation each continue to make major investments in multimedia technologies. The online bookseller, Amazon.com, lists more than a thousand books with multimedia in the title (and fewer than a hundred with hypermedia). However, many in the academic world still prefer the term hypermedia. For example, recent books on hypermedia by academics include *From Web to Workplace: Designing Open Hypermedia Systems* (Gronbaek & Trigg, 1999) and *Adaptive Hypermedia and Adaptive Web-Based Systems* (Brusilovsky & Stock, 2000).

For those who specifically use the term hypermedia, the central tenet of the definition seems to be chiefly the concept of linked nodes. For those who use the term multimedia, the central tenet seems to rest mainly in the concept of a system consisting of a combination of text, graphics, still pictures, video, and sound. We prefer the term multimedia to describe the types of programs we most often design, implement, and evaluate. The term hypermedia seems less useful because the term "hyper" is often used in a negative sense in Western society to describe someone, especially a child, unable to control his or her behavior sufficiently to meet the expectations of structured environments such as a classroom. Further, we define multimedia as an interactive database that allows users to access information in multiple forms, including text, graphics, video, and audio. From an instructional viewpoint, we define interactive multimedia as any combination of media and pedagogical dimensions that support learning, commonly through simulated experience.

Classic examples of interactive multimedia for education include: Broderbund's *Just Grandma and Me*, IBM's *Illuminated Books*, Apple Computer's *The Visual Almanac*, and the awarding winning *Investigating Lake Iluka* and *Exploring the Nardoo* simulations developed at the University of Wollongong in Australia. Notable interactive multimedia programs for training include Apple Computer's *Macintosh Funda-*

mentals course and IBM's *Management Training* series. Today, interactive multimedia is increasingly used for e-learning, point-of-sales, information kiosks, and museum applications as well as for entertainment. Multimedia is also incorporated into electronic performance support systems (EPSS) (Gery, 1991; Winslow & Bramer, 1994).

— **WEB LINK** —
Information about currently available multimedia authoring tools can be found at:

iShell from Tribeworks http://tribeworks.com/

HyperStudio from Knowledge Central http://www.hyperstudio.com/

Toolbook from http://www.click2learn.com/

Flash from http://www.macromedia.com/

SuperCard from http://www.SuperCard.us/

One of the most promising uses of multimedia occurs when students are encouraged to construct their own representations of knowledge using multimedia construction programs such as *HyperStudio, Toolbook, or Flash* (Jonassen & Reeves, 1996). Based upon Perkins's (1985) "knowledge as design" pedagogy, learners undertake a task or solve a problem, using multimedia as a cognitive tool to support their problem-solving processes and ultimately to present their solutions to others. Lehrer (1993) describes the results of a study involving eighth graders who used a multimedia construction tool called *HyperAuthor* to design their own lessons about the American Civil War. This study exemplifies the principle that: "Cognitive tools empower learners to design their own representations of knowledge rather than absorbing knowledge representations preconceived by others." This is not only a highly motivating process, but there is also good evidence that authorship results in ownership of the ideas in the representations (Jonassen & Reeves, 1996).

Distance learning

Another important area of interactive mediated learning is more commonly referred to as distance learning or distance education (Moore & Kearsley, 1995). Traditionally, distance learning was delivered via media that were asynchronous and unidirectional, such as mailed print materials and radio and television broadcasts. However, new technologies and faster telecommunications capabilities are providing robust interactive tools for distance learning. Among the primary characteristics of these technologies are enhanced interactivity and both synchronous and asynchronous communications among teachers and learners.

One long-established approach to delivering interactive learning at a distance is called audiographics. With audiographics, teaching and learning are achieved through two discrete telecommunications links. One link connects computers and another link provides audioconferencing through telephone communications (see Figure 1.3). Standard telephone connections are used to connect students and a teacher with two-way voice and graphic communication. The teacher and students view the same information on their computer screens. Any party can edit and change the displayed image under control of the teacher. The two-way audio communication provides a "classroom" environment for instruction and related activities, such as classroom management. A fax machine for transmitting teaching materials and student assignments between sites is another piece of technology that may be included in an audiographics environment.

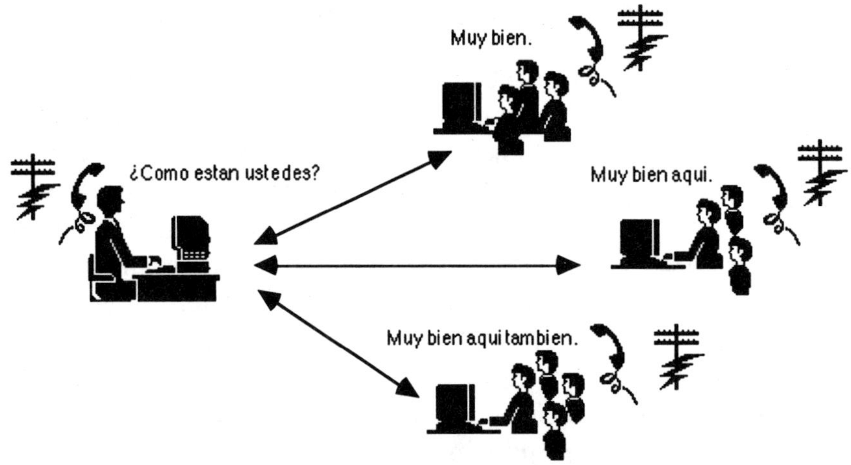

Figure 1.3. Illustration of typical audiographics system.

Audiographics (also called telematics) is used in Australian, Canadian, and South African schools as a means to cost-effectively increase the curriculum offerings to children in rural schools. It is especially popular as a medium for delivering LOTE (Languages Other Than English). Rural schools often have too few students and qualified staff to offer LOTE locally. Telematics link students from several remote schools in a virtual class of 15 to 20 students from several remote schools and a LOTE teacher who delivers a formal course. More than 170 rural schools in Western Australia use telematics to support subjects as diverse as Japanese and computer science (Oliver & Reeves, 1996).

Today, the Web is being promoted as the ultimate delivery system for distance learning, and many projects have integrated the Web into various types of education or training programs (Khan, 1997, 2001). Several other Internet tools are available to support interactive learning at a distance, such as chat rooms, MUDs, MOOs, and listservs. However, the slow speed of access to the Web over existing telephone modems limits the Web for delivery of interactive distance learning when high bandwidth is required. Several projects have used the hybrid system of CD-ROM and Web browsers to provide instant access to multimedia materials (immediacy) with online topicality (currency). As new, faster "pipelines" to the Web become more commonplace (e.g., digital cable and DSL), the proliferation of distance learning opportunities on the Web is expected to be enormous. Before long, wireless networks will improve access to the Web, thereby enabling widespread access to interactive learning environments. In developing countries, wireless systems such as mobile phones and access to the Internet are providing opportunities for connectivity at a much cheaper cost than traditional terrestrial networks. Buzz-words for these trends are e-learning and m-learning (Rosenberg, 2000). Many training departments are using the Web to provide updates and short courses to keep their employees up-to-date with new products and company directions. However, most e-learning solutions still provide a one-way experience whereby "content" is delivered to the learner. True interactivity in terms of collaboration and dialogue, while technically possible, is still largely ignored. With better evaluations of interactive learning technologies and appropriate authoring tools, this may change over the next few years.

One trend is clear: Distance learning is not just for remote learners anymore. Increasingly, people enrolling in distance learning programs may live or work near traditional educational institutions, but choose "distance" options because they value the flexibility and convenience these alternatives can provide over instruction that is offered at a fixed place and time. Students may be enrolled concurrently in distance and traditional courses. Interestingly, distance learning as a term appears to be declining in usage in favor of terms such as flexible delivery, flexible learning, e-learning, and blended learning, all of which reflect the convergence of various interactive learning technologies. If sufficient attention is given to the instructional design of these flexible learning systems, learners may eventually choose them for quality reasons as well as convenience. In the end, we expect that distinctions between place and time of learning will become less and less relevant. Interactive learning environments are evolving, and creative designers can combine new forms of technology with people, tasks, and tools to ensure that people collaborate and learn. But the importance of rigorously evaluating interactive learning systems should not be underestimated.

Summary

This chapter began by presenting a pragmatic, down-to-earth rationale for evaluation as a systematic process that should be focused on the decisions that must be made during the design and use of interactive learning systems. It also includes some important distinctions among types of interactive learning and vehicles for their delivery. In the next chapter, we present four major inquiry paradigms that influence evaluation practice today and describe several noteworthy evaluation models.

References

Bransford, J. D., Brown, A. L., & Cocking, R. R. (Eds.). (1999). *How people learn: Brain, mind, experience, and school.* Washington, DC: National Academy Press.

Brown, J. S., Collins, A., & Duguid, P. (1989). Situated cognition and the culture of learning. *Educational Researcher*, *18*(1), 32-41.

Bruce, B., & Rubin, A. (1993). *Electronic quills: A situated evaluation of using computers for writing in classrooms.* Hillsdale, NJ: Lawrence Erlbaum Associates.

Brusilovsky, P., & Stock, O. (2000). *Adaptive hypermedia and adaptive Web-based systems.* New York: Springer-Verlag.

Bush, M. D. (2002). Connecting instructional design to international standards for content reusability. *Educational Technology*, 42(6), 5-13.

Clark, R. C., & Mayer, R. E. (2003). *E-learning and the science of instruction: Proven guidelines for consumers and designers of multimedia learning.* San Francisco: Jossey-Bass/Pfeiffer.

Cognition and Technology Group at Vanderbilt. (1992). The Jasper experiment: An exploration of issues in learning and instructional design. *Educational Technology Research and Development*, *40*(1), 65-80.

Coley, R. J., Cradler, J., & Engel, P. K. (1997). *Computers and classrooms: The status of technology in U. S. schools.* Princeton, NJ: Educational Testing Service.

Cuban, L. (1986). *Teachers and machines: The classroom use of technology since 1920.* New York: Teachers College Press.

Cuban, L. (2001). *Oversold and underused: Computers in the classroom.* Cambridge, MA: Harvard University Press.

Cummins, J., & Sayers, D. (1995). *Brave new schools: Challenging cultural illiteracy through global learning networks.* New York: St. Martin's Press.

Duffy, T. M., & Jonassen, D. H. (Eds.). (1992). *Constructivism and the technology of instruction: A conversation.* Hillsdale, NJ: Lawrence Erlbaum Associates.

Fischer, P. M., & Mandl, H. (1990). Introduction: Toward a psychophysics of hypermedia. In D. H. Jonassen & H. Mandl (Eds.), *Designing hypermedia for learning* (pp. 19-25). Heidelberg, Germany: Springer-Verlag.

Fosnot, C. T. (1996). *Constructivism: Theory, perspectives, and practice*. New York: Teachers College Press.

Gayeski, D. (2002). *Learning unplugged: Using mobile devices for learning and performance improvement*. New York: AMACOM.

Gery, G. (1991). *Electronic performance support systems*. Boston: Weingarten.

Goodlad, J. I. (1984). *A place called school: Prospects for the future*. New York: McGraw-Hill.

Gronbaek, K., & Trigg, R. H. (1999). *From Web to workplace: Designing open hypermedia systems*. Cambridge, MA: MIT Press.

Gygi, K. (1990). Recognizing the symptoms of Hypertext...and what to do about it. In B. Laurel (Ed.), *The art of human-computer interface design* (pp. 279-287). New York: Addison-Wesley.

Hannafin, M. J., Hannafin, K. M., Hooper, S. R., Rieber, L. P., & Kini, A. S. (1996). Research on and research with emerging technologies. In D. H. Jonassen (Ed.), *Handbook of research on educational communications and technology* (pp. 378-402). New York: Macmillan.

Harel, I. (Ed.). (1991). *Children designers: Interdisciplinary constructions for learning and knowing mathematics in a computer-rich school*. Norwood, NJ: Ablex Publishing.

Hedberg, J. G., Brown, C., Larkin, J. L., & Agostinho, S. (2001). Designing practical Web sites for interactive training. In B. H.. Khan (Ed.), *Web-based training* (pp. 257-269). Englewood Cliffs, NJ: Educational Technology Publications.

Herrington, J., Oliver, R., & Reeves, T. C. (2002). Patterns of engagement in authentic online learning environments. In A. Williamson, C. Gunn, A. Young, & T. Clear. (Eds.), *Proceedings of the 19th Annual Conference of the Australian Society for Computers in Learning in Tertiary Education (ASCILITE)* (pp. 279-286). Auckland, New Zealand: UNITEC.

Hock, D. (1999). *Birth of the chaordic age*. San Francisco: Berrett-Koehler.

International Business Machines Corporation. (1991). *IBM multimedia: Personalize the information revolution* (brochure). Atlanta: IBM.

Jonassen, D. H. (1999). *Computers as mindtools for schools: Engaging critical thinking*. Englewood Cliffs, NJ: Prentice-Hall.

Jonassen, D. H., & Reeves, T. C. (1996). Learning *with* technology: Using computers as cognitive tools. In D. H. Jonassen (Ed.), *Handbook of research on educational communications and technology* (pp. 693-719). New York: Macmillan.

Kafai, Y. B. (1995). *Minds in play: Computer game design as a context for children's learning*. Hillsdale, NJ: Lawrence Erlbaum Associates.

Kearsley, G. (2000). *Online education: Learning and teaching in cyberspace*. Belmont, CA: Wadsworth/Thomson Learning.

Khan, B. H. (Ed.). (1997). *Web-based instruction.* Englewood Cliffs, NJ: Educational Technology Publications.

Khan, B. H. (Ed.). (2001). *Web-based training*. Englewood Cliffs, NJ: Educational Technology Publications.

Lajoie, S. P. (Ed.). (2000). *Computers as cognitive tools: No more walls.* Mahwah, NJ: Lawrence Erlbaum Associates.

Lajoie, S. P., & Derry, S. J. (Eds.). (1993). *Computers as cognitive tools.* Hillsdale, NJ: Lawrence Erlbaum Associates.

Lehrer, R. (1993). Authors of knowledge: Patterns of hypermedia design. In S. P. Lajoie & S. J. Derry (Eds.), *Computers as cognitive tools* (pp. 197-227). Hillsdale, NJ: Lawrence Erlbaum Associates.

Locatis, C., Letourneau, G., & Banvard, R. (1989). Hypermedia and instruction. *Educational Technology Research and Development, 37*(4), 65-77.

Moore, M. G., & Kearsley, G. (1995). *Distance education: A systems view.* Belmont, CA: Wadsworth.

Nielsen, J. (2000). *Designing Web usability: The practice of simplicity.* Indianapolis, IN: New Riders Publishing.

Oliver, R., & Reeves, T. C. (1996). Dimensions of effective interactive learning with telematics for distance education. *Educational Technology Research and Development, 44*(4), 45-56.

Oppenheimer, T. (1997, July). The computer delusion. *The Atlantic Monthly*, 45-62.

Papert, S. (1980). *Mindstorms: Children, computers, and powerful ideas.* New York: Basic Books.

Papert, S. (1993). *The children's machine: Rethinking school in the age of the computer.* New York: Basic Books.

Pea, R. D., & Kurland, D. M. (1987). On the cognitive effects of learning computer programming. In R. D. Pea & K. Sheingold (Eds.), *Mirrors of minds: Patterns of experience in educational computing* (pp. 147-177). Norwood, NJ: Ablex Publishing.

Perelman, L. J. (1992). *School's out: Hyperlearning, the new technology, and the end of education.* New York: William Morrow.

Perkins, D. N. (1985). *Knowledge as design: Critical and creative thinking for teachers and learners.* Hillsdale, NJ: Lawrence Erlbaum Associates.

Phillips, D. C., & Early, M. (Eds.). (2000). *Constructivism in education: Opinions and second opinions on controversial issues.* Chicago: University of Chicago Press.

Pittinsky, M. S. (Ed.). (2003) *The wired tower: Perspectives on the impact of the Internet on higher education.* Upper Saddle River, NJ: Prentice-Hall

Reeves, T. C. (2000). Socially responsible educational technology research. *Educational Technology, 40*(6), 19-28.

Rose, E. (1999). Deconstructing interactivity in educational computing. *Educational Technology, 39*(1), 43-49.

Rosenberg, M. J. (2000). *E-learning: Strategies for delivering knowledge in the digital age.* New York: McGraw-Hill.

Salomon, G., & Globerson, T. (1987). Skill may not be enough: The role of mindfulness in learning and transfer. *International Journal of Educational Research, 11*, 623-638.

Salomon, G., Perkins, D. N., & Globerson, T. (1991). Partners in cognition: Extending human intelligence with intelligent technologies. *Educational Researcher, 20*(3), 2-9.

Schank, R. C. (1997). *Virtual learning: A revolutionary approach to building a highly skilled workforce.* New York: McGraw-Hill.

Schank, R. C. (2000). *Coloring outside the lines: Raising a smarter kid by breaking all the rules.* New York: HarperCollins.

Schank, R. C., & Cleary, C. (1995). *Engines for learning.* Hillsdale, NJ: Lawrence Erlbaum Associates.

Senge, P. M. (1990). *The fifth discipline: The art and practice of the learning organization.* New York: Doubleday.

Shlechter, T. M. (Ed.). (1991). *Problems and promises of computer-based training.* Norwood, NJ: Ablex Publishing.

Short, E. J., & Weissberg-Benchell, J. A. (1989). The triple alliance for learning: Cognition, metacognition, and motivation. In C. B. McCormick, G. Miller, & M. Pressley (Eds.), *Cognitive strategy research: From basic research to educational applications* (pp. 33-63). New York: Springer-Verlag

Shute, V. J., & Psotka, J. (1996). Intelligent tutoring systems: Past, present, and future. In D. H. Jonassen (Ed.), *Handbook of research for educational communications and technology* (pp. 570-600). New York: Macmillan.

Sims, R. (2000). An interactive conundrum: Constructs of interactivity and learning theory. *Australian Journal of Educational Technology, 16*(1), 45-57.

Skinner, B. F. (1968). *Technology of teaching.* New York: Meredith Publishing.

Taylor, R. (Ed.). (1980). *The computer in the school: Tutor, tool, tutee.* New York: Teachers College Press.

von Glaserfeld, E. (1989). An exposition of constructivism: Why some like it radical. In R. B. Davis, C. A. Maher, & N. Noddings (Eds.), *Constructivist views on the teaching and learning of mathematics.* Athens, GA: JRME Monographs.

Wilson, B. G. (Ed.). (1996). *Constructivist learning environments: Case studies in instructional design.* Englewood Cliffs, NJ: Educational Technology Publications.

Winslow, C. D., & Bramer, W. L. (1994). *FutureWork: Putting knowledge to work in the knowledge economy.* New York: The Free Press.

CHAPTER 2

Inquiry Paradigms and Evaluation Models

Objectives

After reading Chapter Two, you should be able to:

- describe four major inquiry paradigms that influence contemporary evaluation practice;
- describe several evaluation models that are relevant to evaluating interactive learning systems; and
- identify strengths and weaknesses of competing paradigms and models of evaluation.

Evaluation: The state-of-the-art

— WEB LINK —
A wealth of up-to-date information about evaluation can be found at the ERIC Clearinghouse on Assessment and Evaluation site: http://erlcae.net/

Contemporary conceptions of evaluation range from an absolute "measurement" perspective to a completely relativistic "constructivist" perspective (Scriven, 1993). The former is characterized by the motto: "If anything exists, it can be measured." Advocates of the measurement perspective believe that there is an objective reality existing apart from the beliefs of those who seek to reveal its nature. Measurement proponents seek better and better instruments (e.g., tests) to calibrate the nature of that ultimate reality (Thorndike, 1971). Their search for finer and finer measures is based on the belief that it is only human weakness that blocks perception of the unchanging natural laws that govern all phenomena, from the motions of planets to the processes of human learning. Isaac Newton's precise, mechanistic universe is the preferred model of how the world works for evaluators who emphasize the measurement perspective.

In sharp contrast, the constructivist perspective is characterized by the words of Egon Guba and Yvonna Lincoln (1989), who wrote: "it [constructivist evaluation] takes the position that evaluation outcomes are not descriptions of the 'way things really are' or 'really work,' or some 'true state of affairs,' but instead represent meaningful constructions that individual actors or groups of actors form to 'make sense' of the situations in which they find themselves" (p. 8). Constructivists generally view measurement as a futile act because they contend that the act of measuring always affects what is being measured. Constructivists seek better and better ways of sharing understandings of the world, but ultimately view as irrelevant the prediction and control so integral to the measurement perspective. Guba and Lincoln (1989) go so far as to maintain that: "To accept the basic premises undergirding responsive constructivist evaluation is virtually to abandon hope that solutions to social problems can ever be found" (p. 47).

Fortunately, in between these two radically different perspectives, one overly optimistic about prediction and control, the other viewing these goals as irrelevant, exist other conceptions of evaluation (Patton, 1997; Shadish, Cook, & Leviton, 1991). For example, one influential evaluation authority, Michael Scriven (1993), argues that evaluations must ultimately yield judgments of what has value and worth. Scriven writes, "Evaluation is what separates astronomy from astrology, good explanations from bad ones, good experimental designs – or bridge designs – from inferior ones, good scientists, engineers and technologists from run-of-the-mill ones" (p. 30). Another evaluation "guru," Elliot Eisner (1985), calls for the training of evaluators who will serve as connoisseurs of what is "good" in education and training.

We believe that most developers and managers of interactive learning systems fail to conduct evaluations at all, or focus on evaluating delivery systems per se rather than the actual pedagogical or instructional design aspects of the systems being evaluated (Clark, 1994, 2001). They can hardly be blamed for this because evaluation as a form of professional practice itself has evolved (some might say devolved) into a contentious field with many competing models and several conflicting paradigms. The various ways that different evaluators use similar terms to mean different things can be especially frustrating to the uninitiated (Hopson, 2000). The proliferation of evaluation paradigms and models is confusing for people new to the field, but we believe that this complexity also enriches the options available for disciplined evaluation. It is important to review the breadth and nature of these paradigms and models, and that is the purpose of this chapter.

Conflicting paradigms

Although popularly used in recent years to describe everything from a change of philosophy to a change of clothing styles, "paradigm," in the scientific sense, represents a well-established, clearly-delineated approach to conducting inquiry in a field. The status of evaluation within the context of interactive learning is hardly "well-established" or "clearly-delineated," and yet evaluation practitioners are influenced by inquiry paradigms, whether consciously or not (Schubert & Schubert, 1990; Soltis, 1992).

According to the *International Encyclopedia of Educational Evaluation* (Walberg & Haertel, 1990), the predominant usage of "paradigm" refers to the explicit and tacit assumptions that guide inquiry within a field. In *The Structure of Scientific Revolutions*, Thomas Kuhn (1962) described how paradigms change within fields; for example, how the shift from Newtonian to quantum physics required fundamental changes in the philosophy, assumptions, theories, and methodology of research in the "purest" of sciences. According to Kuhn, the dominant mode of inquiry within a field at any given time depends upon complex interrelationships among theories, measurement assumptions, research methods, and analytical procedures. Kuhn's "revolution" thesis holds that as a mode of inquiry is practiced over time, anomalies accumulate concerning the assumptions within a field and thus reconceptualization is required. Eventually, a new paradigm emerges.

The prospect of a new paradigm for inquiry emerging from time to time in a field is very powerful. However, within the context of interactive learning, this process is not likely to occur. Evaluation has been so infrequently and inconsistently applied that anomalies have had few opportunities to be revealed, and reconceptualization has rarely been required. Much more effort is put into creating new methods of evaluation (usually called models) than into applying them, and thus there is no real resolution of the effectiveness of one paradigm in comparison to another. Not surprisingly, the field of evaluation is replete with alternative, some would say incompatible, paradigms and diverse models (Rogers, Hacsi, Petrosino, & Huebner, 2000; Shadish, Cook, & Leviton, 1991). In the following pages, we attempt to delineate four major paradigms related to the evaluation of interactive learning.

Analytic-Empirical-Positivist-Quantitative Paradigm

The "Analytic-Empirical-Positivist-Quantitative Paradigm" represents the most established of the paradigms that guide evaluation in education and the social sciences. The "analytic" aspect of this paradigm reflects a belief in a mechanistic, deterministic reality whereby parts can be separated from wholes, and cause and effect relationships among parts can be revealed. The "empirical" aspect refers to the goals of inquiry as being the definition, prediction, control, and explanation of physical phenomena as revealed through experience (induction) and experiments (deduction). The "positivist" aspect represents a faith in scientific progress and the perfectibility of humanity. Finally, the "quantitative" aspect stems from a reliance on measuring variables and analyzing the relationships among them with descriptive and inferential statistics.

Subscribers to the "Analytic-Empirical-Positivist-Quantitative Paradigm" believe in a separate, material reality that exists apart from the beliefs of individuals, groups, or societies. Following E. L. Thorndike and other early measurement theorists, they believe that for anything to be said to exist, it must be able to be measured. They seek to explain changes in variable aspects of reality (e.g., learning or performance) through controlled experimentation. Detachment from the phenomena under study is preferred to maintain objectivity. Mathematical analysis and statistical significance are held in the highest regard.

The "Analytic-Empirical-Positivist-Quantitative Paradigm" is the most widely used evaluation paradigm within both education and training (Kirkpatrick, 1998), and not surprisingly, it also is most often employed when evaluations of interactive learning systems are conducted. The reliance upon this paradigm stems partly from the desire to determine the comparative effectiveness of one program or product over another. Often, the first question asked about an innovative interactive learning program is: "Is this interactive learning program better than competing programs, be they other innovations or the 'traditional' programs or products?" Classical experimental or quasi-experimental methods are frequently the preferred method of determining the comparative superiority of one program over another (Campbell & Stanley, 1966).

The dominance of this paradigm also derives strength from the degree to which it is entrenched in the universities where many novice evaluators learn their craft. Most members of the tenured generation of educational psychology and instructional technology faculty, who dominate the teaching of evaluation as well as instructional design methods, were schooled in positivist, quantitative methods, and as a result, they tend to teach these same approaches. In addition, they may be unfamiliar with or uncomfortable with alternative paradigms. This situation may be changing as more graduate students enroll in courses focused on alternative paradigms such as qualitative methodologies and critical theory taught by faculty outside evaluation and instructional design departments.

It is common within the instructional design literature to divide evaluation into two types, formative (conducted to "improve" whatever is evaluated) and summative (conducted to "prove" the effectiveness or worth of whatever is evaluated). The application of experimental methods within the context of designing interactive learning systems is limited by several factors, especially by the time and resources usually required by this approach. Carey and Dick (1991) sum up the limited utility of experimental methods as follows:

> Such experimental studies are rarely employed in summative evaluation field trials for lengthy instruction because it is almost impossible to hold constant all factors in the design, much less those in the instruction. The list of study limitations often exceeds the list of study questions. (p. 300)

Carey and Dick recommend alternatives to the experimental evaluation approach, including expert judgments and detailed analyses of the relationships among implementation and outcome variables. Heller (1996) also maintains that "it is difficult to design experiments for summative evaluation because experiments require that all aspects of the application, save one or two, are held constant" (p. 76). However, Heller recommends small-scale quasi-experimental methods as a formative evaluation strategy, especially with respect to investigating specific questions such as whether to label icons with text in a multimedia kiosk. Pearrow (2000) even suggests that experimental methods can be used within the context of testing the usability of Web sites.

Constructivist-Hermeneutic-Interpretivist-Qualitative Paradigm

If the "Analytic-Empirical-Positivist-Quantitative Paradigm" represents the most established of the paradigms that can guide evaluation, the "Constructivist-Hermeneutic-Interpretivist-Qualitative Paradigm" can be described as first among the up-and-coming alternatives. Interest in qualitative evaluation methodologies in education has grown steadily during the past twenty years. One small but telling indicator is that the 1993-94 president of the American Educational Research Association (AERA), a group associated with experimental approaches to investigating education since 1915, was Elliot W. Eisner, a long-time proponent of qualitative evaluation and educational criticism (Eisner, 1977, 1985).

The "constructivist" aspect of the "Constructivist-Hermeneutic-Interpretivist-Qualitative Paradigm" reflects the belief that humans individually and collectively construct reality. The "hermeneutic" aspect of this paradigm has its original meaning in the analysis of religious texts, especially in reference to different scholarly interpretations of the Bible. More recently, hermeneutics has come to mean the analysis of curriculum in the broadest sense and instructional programs and products in a more focused sense, including attempts to expose the values underlying these phenomena (Schubert & Schubert, 1990). The "interpretivist" aspect stresses the need to put analyses in context, presenting the interpretations of many, sometimes competing, groups (often called stakeholders) interested in an evaluation's outcomes. The "qualitative" aspect represents the emphasis on the human being as the primary evaluation instrument, rejecting the mathematical modeling of phenomena upon which the quantitative paradigm depends so heavily.

Proponents of the "Constructivist-Hermeneutic-Interpretivist-Qualitative Paradigm" have sharply divergent views about the nature of reality from those of proponents of the quantitative paradigm. They believe that "Truth is a matter of consensus among informed and sophisticated constructors, not correspondence with an objective reality" (Guba & Lincoln, 1989, p. 44). Further, they are concerned with understanding the nature of this constructed reality from multiple perspectives, emphasizing the roles of culture, gender, context, and other factors in the construction of "reality." With regard to evaluation methodology, they have adopted many anthropological methods of inquiry, especially human observation. Not surprisingly, immersion in the context of an evaluation is highly preferred over the detachment of the classical laboratory scientist.

The emphasis on observation as an evaluation strategy is especially relevant to evaluations of interactive learning. Observational methods are among the most effective strategies for collecting formative evaluation information during the development of an interactive learning program, including highly formalized observations such as usability tests (Nielsen, 2000; Pearrow, 2000). As noted above, formative evaluation is focused on finding ways of improving a program under development. According to Flagg (1990), "Formative evaluators employ a wide range of data collection measures, drawn mainly from four categories of methods: self-report, observation, tests, and records or documents" (p. 149). Masters of observational methods for evaluating instructional programs include the creators of "Sesame Street" at the Children's Television Workshop (Schauble, 1990) and operators of software usability testing labs at companies such as Bell Laboratories and the IBM Corporation (Hix & Hartson, 1993; Nielsen, 1993, 2000).

Critical Theory-Neomarxist-Postmodern-Praxis Paradigm

Whereas proponents of the quantitative paradigm proclaim their objectivity and believers in the qualitative paradigm revel in their subjectivity, advocates of the "Critical Theory-Neomarxist-Postmodern-Praxis Paradigm" wear the label "social activists" with pride. Critical theorists condemn the "Analytic-Empirical-Positivist-Quantitative Paradigm" as reactionary and criticize the "Constructivist-Hermeneutic-Interpretivist-Qualitative Paradigm" as unengaged. In fact, members of the Neomarxist faction of this paradigm view themselves as the forces of liberation engaged in an on-going conflict with the powers of oppression.

The "critical theory" aspect of the "Critical Theory-Neomarxist-Postmodern-Praxis Paradigm" relates to a concern "with questions of power, control, and epistemology as social constructions with benefits to some and not to others" (Muffoletto, 1993, p. 4). The "neomarxist" aspect of this paradigm is derived from the liberation education movement led by Paulo Freire (1970) and Ivan Illich (1970). Neomarxist evaluators seek to expose the "hidden curriculum" underlying instructional technology and other educational reforms. The "postmodern" perspective questions the conception of instructional technology "as neutral or as leading inevitably to progress" (Hlynka & Yeaman, 1992, p. 2). Postmodernists deconstruct the "texts" inherent in the products and programs developed by instructional designers, seeking to reveal contradictions and the exclusion of minority interests. Deconstruction, which has its roots in literary analysis as a process of revealing the hidden meanings of texts, is a primary strategy within this paradigm. The "praxis" aspect represents a desire to abandon the search for "truth" as sought by empiricists or "understanding" as desired by interpretivists in favor of seeking "little truths which are situationally appropriate" (Anderson, 1993, p. 1).

From the perspective of the evaluation of interactive learning systems, the "Critical Theory-Neomarxist-Postmodern-Praxis Paradigm" may be difficult to conceive, much less apply. After all, why would proponents of this anti-authoritarian paradigm seek to serve an instructional design process that has its roots in systems models developed for large-scale weapons production by the military-industrial complex (Noble, 1991)? Nonetheless, evaluators should be aware of the "critical theory" perspective if only because it encourages evaluators and instructional designers to question again and again the cultural, political, and gender assumptions underlying an instructional product or program. Skepticism and questioning are the basic tenets of this paradigm. In fact, Michel Foucault, a major figure in this movement, demands "that we question everything, including law, science, religion, and Western philosophy" (Anderson, 1993, p. 1). At the risk of stating the obvious, it is clear that not everyone will be comfortable with this paradigm.

The primary modes of inquiry for followers of this paradigm are criticism and deconstruction. For postmodernists, the basic notion of evaluation as a quasi-scientific process is secondary to the practice of criticism. Hlynka and Yeaman (1992) regard evaluation as a strategy for improving the effectiveness and efficiency of instructional design and the innovations it develops, whereas they promote criticism as having the more important role of "constantly rethinking and deconstructing our beliefs, tools, and technology" (p. 2).

Eclectic-Mixed Methods-Pragmatic Paradigm

Our last "paradigm" for evaluation cannot be found in any traditional analysis of paradigms for inquiry in education (Schubert & Schubert, 1990; Soltis, 1992). Nonetheless, it is perhaps the most important of the four paradigmatic orientations because it is the one approach capable of handling the complexity (some would say chaos) that is the hallmark of contemporary society and technology (Casti, 1994; Pascale, Millerman, & Gioja, 2000; Sedgwick, 1993). It is also the paradigm we espouse in the rest of this volume.

The concept of complexity is exceedingly relevant to evaluation within the context of instructional design. Sedgwick (1993), in an article titled "The Complexity Problem," maintains that: "It is becoming increasingly clear that the comfort of a good fit between man and machine is largely absent from the technology of the information age" (p. 96). A similarly pessimistic observation can be made about the fit among instructors, learners, and the interactive learning programs resulting from systematic instructional design (ID). According to Leshin, Pollock, and Reigeluth (1992), the major problem with ID models is that "they have totally ignored guidance as to what makes good instruction" (p. 1). Leshin *et al.* (1992) also maintain that traditional ID models can be followed rigorously and still yield poor instruction.

At least part of the poor success record of systematic instructional design stems from the inadequate, simplistic evaluation methods incorporated within most ID models (Reeves, 1989). Evaluation activities are often carried out without clearly specifying the many decisions that must be made during the ID process. Ultimately, the failure of instructional innovations to transform practice in education and training can be partially attributed to a failure to anticipate critical decisions about the design, implementation, and maintenance of interactive learning systems. The failure to incorporate evaluation focused on critical decisions is one of the reasons instructional design is under attack in some sectors (Gordon & Zemke, 2000).

The "eclectic" aspect of the "Eclectic-Mixed Methods-Pragmatic Paradigm" refers to its openness to borrowing the methods of the other three paradigms to collect information and solve a problem. The "mixed methods" aspect relates to the recognition that multiple perspectives are necessary to "triangulate" or "bracket" information and conclusions regarding complex phenomena. The "pragmatic" aspect reflects the practical orientation that, although ultimate prediction and control may never be achieved in the design and implementation of interactive learning systems for education and training, things can get better.

Proponents of the "Eclectic-Mixed Methods-Pragmatic Paradigm" rarely concern themselves with ultimate conceptions of reality, preferring to deal with the practical problems that confront them as educators and trainers. They view modes of inquiry as tools to better understanding and more effective problem solving, and they do not value one tool over another any more than a carpenter would value a hammer over a saw. They recognize that a tool is only meaningful within the context in which it is to be used. Mark, Henry, and Julnes (2000) exemplify this perspective in their conceptualization of evaluation as "sense-making." Pragmatists accept their interconnectivity with the phenomena they seek to understand and change (Bruce & Rubin, 1992). They also recognize the weaknesses of their tools, and struggle against great odds to ensure that evaluation will affect decision making more than will politics, ignorance, intuition, habit, and prejudice. Finally, they are honest with themselves and their audiences about the tentative and probabilistic nature of the recommendations they make.

There are few indications that instructional design theorists or evaluators in general recognize the importance of an eclectic approach to evaluation within instructional design (Mark & Shotland, 1987). An exception to this trend is Johnson (1989), who describes the complex problems that instructional designers face amid a world of "chaos, connectivity, and computers" (p. 182), and argues for applying the science of chaos within instructional design. The more common approach in the instructional design literature is to fall back on traditional notions of formative and summative evaluation (Briggs, Gustafson, & Tillman, 1991; Leshin, Pollock, & Reigeluth, 1992). Some experts seek to build new tools that can support instructional designers or completely automate the instructional design process (Merrill, Li, & Jones, 1990), but how these systems will encompass evaluation is unclear.

Fortunately, a few contemporary instructional design theorists recognize the need for enhanced approaches to instructional design (Seels, 1993). For example, Gustafson (1993) calls for a major examination and renewal of the fundamentals of instructional design. Instructional systems design has been severely criticized in some sectors (Gordon & Zemke, 2000), and reform may be overdue. Regardless of how the field of instructional design evolves, better evaluation methods, especially enhanced formative designs and strategies, must play a major role in the development of interactive learning systems (Maslowski & Visscher, 1999). Indeed, we view decision-oriented evaluation as the most important aspect of the entire ID process.

– WEB LINK –
An evaluation handbook with a pragmatic focus is at: http://cleo.murdoch.edu.au/projects/cutsd99/handbook/handbook.htm

From the perspective of the evaluation of interactive learning systems, we will argue throughout this volume that the "Eclectic-Mixed Methods-Pragmatic Paradigm" has the most potential for enhancing interactive learning systems and providing evidence of their effectiveness and worth. We do not wish to convey that the other paradigms lack merit, but simply that they sometimes place blinders on their proponents that a more receptive and open stance may reduce or eliminate.

Competing models

Whereas paradigms refer to a general orientation toward inquiry, models are much more specific and prescriptive in nature. Although some authorities trace the roots of contemporary evaluation practice back thousands of years to ancient China (Popham, 1974), most experts acknowledge the development of scores of evaluation models since the 1930s. We do not intend to provide a comprehensive review of all the evaluation models that have been developed; instead, we refer you to other sources for this information (Owen & Rogers, 1999; Shadish, Cook, & Leviton, 1991; Worthen, Sanders, & Fitzpatrick, 1996). Nevertheless, it is useful to review a few of the models that have been employed for evaluating interactive learning systems.

Instructional designers and evaluators usually concern themselves with discrete models rather than paradigms. Alkin and Ellett (1990) maintain that "Evaluation models either describe what evaluators do or prescribe what they should do" (p. 15). Prescriptive models are more specific than descriptive models with respect to procedures for planning, conducting, analyzing, and reporting evaluations. According to Alkin and Ellett, descriptive models are more general in that they describe the theories that undergird prescriptive models. In this regard, descriptive, theory-based models are akin to inquiry paradigms. There are dozens of prescriptive evaluation models, but descriptive models are relatively rare.

Tylerian Objectives-Based Evaluation Model

No description of evaluation models would be complete without including the seminal contributions of Ralph W. Tyler and his many followers (Smith & Tyler, 1942; Tyler, 1949). According to Alkin and Ellett (1990), the essence of the Tylerian model is that "evaluation should judge that a program is good if, and only if, its objectives are achieved" (p. 16). Tyler changed the focus of evaluation from assessment of the inputs into an educational program to a comparison between a program's objectives as stated and as achieved.

Tyler's emphasis upon the importance of objectives has influenced many aspects of education, including the design of interactive learning systems. The specification of objectives is a major factor in virtually all instructional design (ID) models (Gustafson, 1991). A major benefit touted for specifying objectives during ID is that they provide the basis for the development of measurement procedures and instruments that can be used to evaluate the effectiveness of instruction. Indeed, it is difficult to imagine how ID might proceed very far without some attempt to delineate the objectives of the development effort.

Tyler's approach is deceptively simple: Establish goals, derive specific behavioral objectives from the goals, tailor instruction and performance measures to the objectives, collect performance data on the objectives, and finally judge the effectiveness of a program based upon the learners' achievement of the objectives. If only it were that simple, there would be no need for this book.

The first problem with Tyler's approach is that many goals cannot be specified in terms of easily measured behavioral objectives, e.g., the goal of preparing children to be good citizens. Second, measurement of even the most behavioral of objectives is often a difficult process involving complex issues of feasibility, reliability, and validity. Third, programs often have unintended outcomes that may be more important than the stated goals of a program, either positively or negatively. Moreover, focusing on the specific objectives of a program may obscure what critical theorists call the "hidden curriculum." Fourth, focusing on whether objectives have been attained does not address the worth of the objectives themselves (Scriven, 1974). For these and other reasons, the Tylerian evaluation model has been supplanted by other models.

Experimental Evaluation Model

The experimental (or more often, quasi-experimental) model is a widely accepted and frequently employed approach to evaluation and research within education and training. Not surprisingly, it has had, and continues to have, many proponents (Campbell & Stanley, 1966; Rossi & Freeman, 1989; Tate, 1990). The most familiar version of this approach is represented in Figure 2.1.

	Time			
		1 (pre)		2 (post)
Experimental Group	R	O	X	O
Control Group	R	O		O

R = Random Assignment O = Observation X = Treatment

Figure 2.1. The true control group, pretest-posttest evaluation design.

House (1991) identifies Suchman as one of the originators and strongest advocates of the experimental approach to evaluation:

> The logic of this design is foolproof. Ideally, there is no element of fallibility. Whatever differences are observed between the experimental and control groups, once the above conditions are satisfied, must be attributed to the program being evaluated. (Suchman, 1967, pp. 95-96; cited in House, 1991, p. 7)

It is difficult to argue with authorities who speak in terms of their approach being foolproof or infallible. It is also difficult to oppose an approach that is deeply entrenched in the minds and actions of so many educators. However, there is a distinct contrast between the advocacy of experimental methods by many evaluators and academics (Fitz-Gibbon & Morris, 1987; Gage, 1989; Schrag, 1992) and the rejection of these methods by contemporary philosophers of science (Casti, 1989; House, 1991; Phillips, 1987). Phillips remarks on this irony:

> New approaches to the design of evaluations of educational and social programs are being formulated that make the "true experiment" seem like a lumbering dinosaur, yet some folk persist in thinking that dinosaurs are wonderful creatures. (p. viii)

What are some of the problems with experimental and quasi-experimental approaches to evaluation? First, the control of treatment variables, as required by experimental methodologies, is impractical in most contexts where interactive learning systems are implemented. Decades of implementation studies clearly indicate that there are substantive differences between the designs of innovative programs and products and their actual implementation (Berman & McLaughlin, 1978; Cuban, 1986). Second, the emphasis on measuring educational outcomes via tests in this approach is rarely matched by a concomitant effort to establish the reliability and validity of those measures. In addition, the tests themselves are often poor indicators of the important outcomes of instructional programs (Stake, 1990). Third, the experimental approach can only support or fail to support pre-stated hypotheses; it cannot discover unexpected effects of a product within an instructional context. Fourth, randomized experiments are extremely difficult to conduct and can be unethical in some situations. The distinguishing feature between true experimental and quasi-experimental studies is the lack of randomization in the assignment of subjects to treatments in the latter.

Not surprisingly, the vast majority of evaluations conducted with this model are "quasi-experimental," a compromise that introduces many difficulties with respect to the analysis and interpretation of findings. As a result, evaluators operating within the experimental model frequently fall back upon designs that can be most easily managed, focus on variables that are easiest to measure, apply statistical methods without meeting the assumptions underlying their use, and draw conclusions that have little or no practical application (Schwab, 1970). Readers interested in a more extensive critique of experimental and quasi-experimental approaches to evaluation are referred to Cronbach (1980), Guba and Lincoln (1989), House (1991), and Lagemann (2000).

Patton's Qualitative Evaluation Model

Although the earliest efforts to define qualitative methods for educational evaluation originated in Great Britain (Hamilton, 1976), a major contributor to this movement has been an American scholar, Michael Quinn Patton (1980, 1987, 1990, 1997). Patton (1987) stresses that qualitative methods are "particularly useful for studying variations in program implementation" (p. 13). He also emphasizes the value of qualitative methods, especially observations, if the intent of an evaluation is formative, i.e., focused on improving a program or product.

Patton (1980, 1987) describes several different methods of qualitative evaluation, including observations, case studies, interviews, and document analysis. He also stresses rigorous training for qualitative evaluators. Quantitative evaluators and researchers are often subjected to a regimen of statistics and research methodology courses before they can undertake inquiry. Patton maintains that disciplined training and careful preparation are required for qualitative evaluators as well.

Critics of the qualitative approaches advocated by Patton (1987) and others claim that they are too subjective and that the results of qualitative studies lack generalizability (Cizek, 1995). Opponents also maintain that qualitative evaluators have a bias against the precision and accuracy of numerical data. Patton, however, claims that the numbers derived from quantitative methods are seductive because they "convey a sense of precision and accuracy even if the measurements which yielded the numbers are relatively unreliable, invalid, and meaningless" (pp. 165-66). Patton says that he is not anti-numbers, but pro-meaning.

Instructional designers conversant with the formative evaluation methods described by Flagg (1990) will find support and guidance in the writings of Patton (1980, 1987, 1990, 1997). Dick and Carey (1991) also promote the value of early one-on-one observations and field trial observations within ID projects. Reeves (1992) suggests that qualitative methods are particularly appropriate in instructional design projects within school settings where more formal, controlled methods are unfeasible. Much of the six-phase evaluation model we describe later in this book is based upon the application of a variety of qualitative methods.

Fourth Generation Evaluation Model

The constructivist aspect of the "Constructivist-Hermeneutic-Interpretivist-Qualitative Paradigm" described above is perhaps best characterized by the model that Guba and Lincoln (1989) call "Fourth Generation Evaluation." Guba and Lincoln (1989) present seven principles that underlie their model:

1) evaluation is a sociopolitical process;
2) evaluation is a joint, collaborative process;
3) evaluation is a teaching/learning process;
4) evaluation is a continuous, recursive, and highly divergent process;
5) evaluation is an emergent process;
6) evaluation is a process with unpredictable outcomes; and
7) evaluation is a process that creates reality.

A primary outcome of "Fourth Generation Evaluation" is "rich, thick" description based upon extended observation and careful reflection. Constructivists seek more effective ways of sharing understandings of the world, but ultimately regard the prediction and control so integral to the quantitative measurement perspective as irrelevant. As noted at the beginning of this chapter, Guba and Lincoln (1989) express a pessimistic perspective about the possibilities of evaluations actually leading to the ultimate resolution of social problems. They recommend substituting "local understanding for generalized explanation" (p. 48).

Guba and Lincoln's (1989) gloomy (they would say realistic) outlook plays right into the hands of the critics of the Fourth Generation Evaluation model. Advocates of the quantitative, positivist paradigm who believe in the ultimate perfectibility of humanity criticize the lack of emphasis on generalizability within this model. Critical theorists who believe in social action and political commitment criticize the hopelessness of Guba and Lincoln's perspective. Constructivists would respond to their critics that the burden of generalizability and action should be placed on the consumers of an evaluation rather than the evaluators themselves.

A common element in both Fourth Generation Evaluation as an evaluation model and instructional design as a process is the importance of negotiation. Guba and Lincoln (1989) recommend negotiation strategies for reaching consensus about the purposes, methods, and outcomes of evaluation. Similar negotiation strategies can also be used by instructional designers attempting to develop instructional innovations such as e-learning solutions and electronic performance support systems within the constraints of limited time, money, and personnel. Although hard-core positivists will almost certainly find the relativism espoused by Guba and Lincoln disconcerting, this constructivist approach has the potential to help instructional designers deal realistically with the complexities they will inevitably face in developing interactive learning systems for education and training.

Eisner's Art Criticism Evaluation Model

Elliot W. Eisner, a former art teacher, coined the term "educational connoisseurship" to describe the first of two primary facets of his art-based evaluation model (1977, 1985). Just as there are connoisseurs in the worlds of literature, drama, and art, Eisner argues that education should have its own connoisseurs, individuals with refined tastes and sensitivity to educational phenomena. The second primary facet of Eisner's approach is educational criticism, i.e., the public expression of the connoisseur's observations and appraisals of education.

Educational criticism has three major dimensions: description, interpretation, and assessment. It is the last dimension, assessment, that distinguishes Eisner's approach from traditional qualitative inquiry. As Barone (1990) describes, "...it is also the task of the educational critic to *explicitly* appraise features of the critical object according to personally held educational criteria" (p. 198, emphasis in original). The critic has the responsibility to convey his or her values to the public so that they may judge the worth of the critic's assessment.

Traditional empirical methods are concerned with internal and external validity. Eisner (1985) has described two related processes that he calls "structural collaboration" and "referential adequacy." The former is concerned with the coherence, cohesiveness, and persuasiveness of the criticism. The latter is related to the insights or "psychological generalizability" of the critique. These two processes have the goals of ensuring that the reader finds the critical piece credible and that it moves the reader to some decision or action.

Educational connoisseurship and criticism, as proposed by Eisner (1977, 1985), have not been implemented widely. Opponents of educational criticism claim that it is too subjective. Proponents of this model respond that positivists are also subjective when they formulate research questions, choose instruments, and interpret data, but that their subjectivity is hidden. Educational critics, on the other hand, have an explicit responsibility to disclose the values underlying their subjectivity; they do not suffer from the illusion of objectivity (Barone, 1990).

Another reason for the limited application of Eisner's ideas may be the difficulty in training people to be connoisseurs and a lack of venues for expression of educational criticism, especially in established research journals. Eisner (1985) suggests that anyone involved in education (teacher, student, parent, or administrator) has the right and responsibility to be a critic, but that certain people can be trained in the approach and eventually establish a reputation for the refined tastes and appreciation that are indications of authentic connoisseurship.

Can designers and users of interactive learning systems apply Eisner's ideas to the challenges they face? Certainly, the frequent use of expert reviewers as an evaluation strategy within the instructional design process has something in common with educational connoisseurship and criticism. When employing expert reviewers during formative or summative evaluation, developers of interactive learning systems should seek to clarify the underlying values that influence the experts' judgments. In addition, those interested in the creative aspects of multimedia for interactive learning will find the art-based concepts and ideas that Eisner adopts of considerable interest.

Postmodern Evaluation Model

According to Jencks (1989), postmodernism advocates multiple, often contradictory ways of knowing in contemporary society. The "post" in postmodernism reflects a belief that we are existing in a time beyond the failed modernity of the industrial age. "Modern" is meant pejoratively to refer to the misplaced faith in science, technology, and progress that have left the world with the threat of nuclear holocaust, environmental destruction, and global racism and intolerance (Hlynka & Yeaman, 1992). Hlynka and Belland (1991) present multiple perspectives on postmodernism and related evaluative perspectives such as critical theory. They criticize the field of educational technology for overemphasizing modern technologies and positivist modes of inquiry. They point out that educational technology can be viewed as a series of failed innovations including motion pictures, television, programmed instruction, instructional systems design, computer-based instruction, and intelligent tutoring systems. They recommend the postmodern perspective as an approach to revealing the political agendas hidden in each of these "innovations."

Hlynka and Yeaman (1992) describe how to be a postmodernist:

> 1. Consider concepts, ideas and objects as texts. Textual meanings are open to interpretation.
> 2. Look for binary oppositions in those texts. Some usual oppositions are good/bad, progress/tradition, science/myth, love/hate, man/woman, and truth/fiction.
> 3. "Deconstruct" the text by showing how the oppositions are not necessarily true.
> 4. Identify texts which are absent, groups who are not represented and omissions, which may or may not be deliberate, but are important. (pp. 1-2)

What are the lessons of the postmodernist perspective for designers of interactive learning systems? Basically, instructional designers should not automatically assume that their systems models and instructional technologies are the best methods for establishing conditions for teaching and learning. Further, they should constantly examine and reexamine their motives and methods to ensure that minority perspectives are included. They should attend to critics of educational technology such as Cuban (1986) and Postman (1995). Even reputed "cranks" such as Clifford Stoll (2000) should not be ignored because, in the midst of the hyperbole, an important idea may surface occasionally. In addition, designers of interactive learning systems should invite alternative views that can be used to rethink and deconstruct the programs and products they develop (Cuban, 2001; Yeaman, 1994).

Not surprisingly, critics of the postmodernist model see it as anti-technology, anti-progress, and anti-science. Postmodernists respond that positivism and science have had their chance to perfect the world and have failed miserably. Postmodernists seek to empower the disenfranchised in contemporary society, especially female, third-world, and non-white interests (Anderson, 1994). It is difficult to be postmodernist within the context of instructional design and evaluation because post-modernism largely rejects such systems-oriented modes of development and inquiry. Instructional systems design (ISD) is criticized as a tool of positivists who hold onto the false hope of linear progress. Further, criticism is valued over evaluation because of its emphasis on identifying "dysfunctions as well as functions" (Hlynka & Yeaman, 1992, p. 2). Although the incongruency between instructional design and postmodernism is certainly problematic, there is some value in the postmodernist perspective as a method of checking interactive learning systems for aspects that may be racist, sexist, and/or culturally insensitive.

Stake's Responsive Evaluation Model

Upon first consideration, Stake's (1980) Responsive Evaluation Model might appear to fit within the qualitative paradigm. However, according to Stake (1990), this model does not adhere to one methodology: "There is a common misunderstanding that responsive evaluation requires naturalistic inquiry or qualitative research" (p. 76). Stake claims that the methods for responsive evaluation are negotiated by the "stakeholders" in the evaluation. Sometimes, they will be naturalistic or phenomenological; other times they will be quantitative or goal-oriented. More often, responsive evaluators will attempt to "triangulate" issues and findings using multiple methods.

According to Stake (1990), the key distinction of this model is "that of emphasizing the issues, language, contexts, and standards of stakeholders" (p. 77). Stakeholders are defined as the diverse people who are affected by a program, including administrators, teachers, students, parents, community members, program developers, and representatives of funding sources. The evaluators themselves are also viewed as critical stakeholders, and their judgments are given weight equal to the perspectives of others in evaluation reports. However, the evaluators must endeavor to expose the subjectivity of their own judgments as rigorously as they do those of other stakeholders.

Another essential element of responsive evaluation is the continuous nature of observations and reporting. Responsive evaluators begin to provide feedback to stakeholders as early as possible during an evaluation, fully expecting to please some people and displease others. The questions and methods of evaluation are modified throughout the evaluation in response to the evolving concerns of the stakeholders.

Critics of the Responsive Evaluation Model argue that "too much attention is given to subjective data, for example, the testimony of participants" (Stake, 1990, p. 76). Stake defends the approach by maintaining that subjectivity is inherent in any type of observation or measurement. He claims that responsive evaluators endeavor to expose the origins of their subjectivity, whereas other types of evaluators may disguise their subjectivity by using so-called objective tests and experimental designs. Responsive evaluation can also be criticized because it requires a level of trust and cooperation within an evaluation context that may be unrealistic, especially when the financial or political stakes are high.

The utility of responsive evaluation within the context of design may rest more in the values espoused by Stake (1980, 1990) than in specific methodological aspects of the model. Responsiveness to the multiple audiences likely to be affected by an instructional program or product under development should be a key ingredient of the analysis phase of any ID model. This responsiveness is an ideal rarely attained in many ID projects, and attention to the ideas and values inherent in Stake's Responsive Evaluation Model may improve the degree to which minority issues are considered by designers of interactive learning systems.

Multiple Methods Evaluation Model

In 1987, the American Evaluation Association published an important volume in the New Directions for Program Evaluation Series called *Multiple Methods in Program Evaluation* (Mark & Shotland, 1987). What Mark and Shotland and their co-authors present is not so much a unitary model for evaluation as a set of guidelines for applying an eclectic approach to evaluating instructional inputs, processes, and outcomes. They maintain that the primary benefits of "multiple methods" are addressing different but complementary questions in an evaluation and reducing the misplaced belief in the certainty assumed to be associated with traditional experimental methods.

Using multiple methods is not just a simple matter of two or more methods being better than one. Two poorly designed and sloppily conducted evaluation strategies will yield no better picture of the findings than one poor study. Mark and Shotland (1987) maintain that multiple methods are only appropriate when they are chosen for a particular purpose, such as investigating a particularly complex program that cannot be adequately assessed with a single method.

Key issues in Mark and Shotland's (1987) approach are "triangulation" and "bracketing." Triangulation involves using multiple measures to converge on a more accurate estimate of the "true" value of a variable. For example, if an instructional designer needs to determine the motivation of trainees to engage in Web-based learning, a questionnaire, an interview protocol, and a personality scale might be used in an effort to gain a more precise assessment of their motivation. The triangulation approach assumes that errors in one type of measure are canceled out by errors in another type. According to Mark and Shotland, this is an optimistic view, especially in education and other social sciences.

Bracketing, on the other hand, involves using multiple measures to provide a range of estimates of the value of a variable. This is a subtle but important difference. The instructional designer interested in student motivation might use the same three measures (questionnaire, interview, and personality scale), but the results would be examined differently. Whereas from the triangulation perspective, the designer would assume convergence of the measures toward a more accurate assessment of motivation, the instructional designer employing a bracketing perspective would interpret differences among the measures as reflecting a range of motivation. The data might be used to make an interactive learning system more responsive to learners with different sources and levels of motivation. Mark and Shotland (1987) maintain that the bracketing approach is more practical in evaluation because of the complexity and uncertainly involved in education and other social science contexts.

Probably the most valid criticism of the multiple measures approach is that it is so complex in terms of design, implementation, analysis, and interpretation that few evaluators or instructional designers will be able to apply the approach without the assistance of a team of methodologists and statisticians. However, the benefits of considering the approach and employing aspects of it are considerable. Evaluations focused on the effectiveness of instructional innovations in comparison to other programs have often led to findings of no significant differences (Clark, 1992). Although methodological issues may have invalidated many of these studies, there is also a strong possibility that a single weak outcome measure was used. Bracketing the outcomes of instructional innovations with multiple methods may yield a more realistic portrayal of the outcomes of these systems. Increased emphasis on accountability for the large investments being made in learning technologies in schools and business demand that evaluators consider alternative methods, even when they are complex and challenging.

Summary

This chapter has reviewed the four major paradigms that influence evaluation practice today. In addition, brief descriptions of several noteworthy evaluation models were included. We expressed a preference for an eclectic paradigm, and we are convinced that no single existing evaluation model is sufficiently comprehensive to guide the effective and efficient evaluation of interactive learning systems. In the next chapter, we present our analysis of the functions of evaluation as they relate to the processes of designing and implementing interactive learning.

References

Alkin, M. C., & Ellett, F. S. (1990). Development of evaluation models. In H. J. Walberg & G. D. Haertel (Eds.), *The international encyclopedia of educational evaluation* (pp. 15-21). New York: Pergamon Press.

Anderson, J. (1993, January). *Foucault and disciplinary technology.* Paper presented at the Annual Conference of the Association for Educational Communications and Technology, New Orleans, LA.

Anderson, J. (1994). The rite of right or the right of rite: Moving toward an ethics of technological empowerment. *Educational Technology, 34*(2), 29-34.

Barone, T. E. (1990). Curricular implications of educational connoisseurship and criticism. In H. J. Walberg & G. D. Haertel (Eds.), *The international encyclopedia of educational evaluation* (pp. 197-200). New York: Pergamon Press.

Berman, P., & McLaughlin, M. (1978). *Federal programs supporting education change. A model of education change, Vol. VIII: Implementing and sustaining innovations.* Santa Monica, CA: Rand.

Briggs, L. J., Gustafson, K. L., & Tillman, M. H. (Eds.). (1991). *Instructional design: Principles and applications* (2nd ed.). Englewood Cliffs, NJ: Educational Technology Publications.

Bruce, B., & Rubin, A. (1992). *Electronic quills: A situated evaluation of using computers for writing in classrooms.* Hillsdale, NJ: Lawrence Erlbaum Associates.

Campbell, D. T., & Stanley, J. C. (1966). *Experimental and quasi-experimental designs for research.* Chicago: Rand-McNally.

Carey, L. M., & Dick, W. (1991). Summative evaluation. In L. J. Briggs, K. L. Gustafson, & M. H. Tillman (Eds.), *Instructional design: Principles and applications* (pp. 269-311). Englewood Cliffs, NJ: Educational Technology Publications.

Casti, J. L. (1989). *Paradigms lost: Images of man in the mirror of science.* New York: William Morrow.

Casti, J. L. (1994). *Complexification: Explaining a paradoxical world through the science of surprise.* New York: HarperCollins.

Cizek, G. J. (1995). Crunchy granola and the hegemony of the narrative. *Educational Researcher, 24*(2), 26-28.

Clark, R. E. (1992). Media use in education. In M. C. Alkin (Ed.), *Encyclopedia of educational research* (pp. 805-814). New York: Macmillan.

Clark, R. E. (1994). Media will never influence learning. *Educational Technology Research and Development, 42*(2), 21-29.

Clark, R. E. (Ed.). (2001). *Learning from media: Arguments, analysis, and evidence.* Greenwich, CT: Information Age Publishing.

Cronbach, L. J. (1980). *Toward reform of program evaluation.* San Francisco: Jossey-Bass.

Cuban, L. (1986). *Teachers and machines: The classroom use of technology since 1920.* New York: Teachers College Press.

Cuban, L. (2001). *Oversold and underused: Computers in the classroom.* Cambridge, MA: Harvard University Press.

Dick, W., & Carey, L. M. (1991). Formative evaluation. In L. J. Briggs, K. L. Gustafson, & M. H. Tillman (Eds.), *Instructional design: Principles and applications* (pp. 227-267). Englewood Cliffs, NJ: Educational Technology Publications.

Eisner, E. W. (1977). On the uses of educational connoisseurship and criticism for evaluating classroom life. *Teachers College Record, 78,* 345-58.

Eisner, E. W. (1985). *The art of educational evaluation: A personal view.* London: Falmer.

Fitz-Gibbon, C. T., & Morris, L. L. (1987). *How to design a program evaluation.* Newbury Park, CA: Sage.

Flagg, B. N. (1990). *Formative evaluation for educational technologies.* Hillsdale, NJ: Lawrence Erlbaum Associates.

Freire, P. (1970). *Pedagogy of the oppressed.* New York: Herder & Herder.

Gage, N. L. (1989). The paradigm wars and their aftermath: A "historical" sketch of research on teaching since 1899. *Teachers College Record, 91,* 135-150.

Gordon, J., & Zemke, R. (2000, April). The attack on ISD. *Training, 37*(4), 42-53.

Guba, E. G., & Lincoln, Y. S. (1989). *Fourth generation evaluation.* Newbury Park, CA: Sage.

Gustafson, K. L. (1991). *Survey of instructional development models* (2nd ed.). Syracuse, NY: Syracuse University, ERIC Clearinghouse on Information Resources.

Gustafson, K. L. (1993). Instructional design fundamentals: Clouds on the horizon. *Educational Technology, 33*(2), 27-32.

Hamilton, D. (1976). *Curriculum evaluation.* London: Open Books.

Heller, R. S. (1996). Evaluating interactive multimedia. In J. Thomson (Ed.), *Multimedia resources* (pp. 65-87). Belmont, CA: Wadsworth.

Hix, D., & Hartson, H. R. (1993). *Developing user interfaces: Ensuring usability through product and process.* New York: John Wiley & Sons.

Hopson, R. K. (Ed.). (2000). *How and why language matters in evaluation.* San Francisco: Jossey-Bass.

House, E. R. (1991). Realism in research. *Educational Researcher, 20*(6), 2-9, 25.

Hlynka, D., & Belland, J. C. (1991). *Paradigms regained: The uses of illuminative, semiotic, and post-modern criticism as modes of inquiry in educational technology: A book of readings*. Englewood Cliffs, NJ: Educational Technology Publications.

Hlynka, D., & Yeaman, A. R. J. (1992, September). Postmodern educational technology. *ERIC Digest*.

Illich, I. (1970). *Deschooling society*. New York: Harper & Row.

Jencks, C. (1989). *What is post-modernism?* New York: St. Martin's Press.

Johnson, K. A. (1989). Chaos, connectivity, and computers. In K. A. Johnson & L. J. Foa (Eds.), *Instructional design: New strategies for education and training* (pp. 182-191). New York: Macmillan.

Kirkpatrick, D. L. (1998). *Another look at evaluating training programs*. Alexandria, VA: American Society for Training & Development.

Kuhn, T. S. (1962). *The structure of scientific revolutions*. Chicago: The University of Chicago Press.

Lagemann, E. C. (2000). *An elusive science: The troubling history of educational research*. Chicago: The University of Chicago Press.

Leshin, C. B., Pollock, J., & Reigeluth, C. M. (1992). *Instructional design strategies and tactics*. Englewood Cliffs, NJ: Educational Technology Publications.

Mark, M. M., Henry, G. T., & Julnes, G. (2000). *Evaluation: An integrated framework for understanding, guiding, and improving policies and programs*. San Francisco: Jossey-Bass.

Mark, M. M., & Shotland, R. L. (Eds.). (1987). *Multiple methods in program evaluation*. San Francisco: Jossey-Bass.

Maslowski, R., & Visscher, A. (1999). The potential of formative evaluation in program design models. In J. van den Akker, N. Nieveen, R. M. Branch, K. L. Gustafson, & T. Plomp, (Eds.), *Design methodology and developmental research in education and training* (pp. 137-144). The Netherlands: Kluwer Academic Publishers.

Merrill, M. D., Li, Z., & Jones, M. K. (1990). Second generation instructional design (ID_2). *Educational Technology*, *30*(2), 7-14.

Muffoletto, R. (1993, January). *Schools and technology in a democratic society: Equity and social justice*. Paper presented at the Annual Conference of the Association for Educational Communications and Technology, New Orleans, LA.

Nielsen, J. (1993). *Usability engineering*. Boston: Academic Press.

Nielsen, J. (2000). *Designing Web usability*. Indianapolis, IN: New Riders.

Noble, D. D. (1991). *The classroom arsenal: Military research, information technology, and public education*. New York: The Falmer Press.

Owen, J. M., & Rogers, P. (1999). *Program evaluation: Forms and approaches*. Newbury Park, CA: Sage.

Pascale, R. T., Millerman, M., & Gioja, L. (2000). *Surfing the edge of chaos: The laws of nature and the new laws of business*. New York: Random House.

Patton, M. Q. (1980). *Qualitative evaluation methods*. Newbury Park, CA: Sage.

Patton, M. Q. (1987). *How to use qualitative methods in evaluation.* Newbury Park, CA: Sage.

Patton, M. Q. (1990). *Qualitative evaluation and research methods* (2nd ed.). Newbury Park, CA: Sage.

Patton, M. Q. (1997). *Utilization-focused evaluation: The new century text* (3rd ed.). Thousand Oaks, CA: Sage.

Pearrow, M. (2000). *Web site usability handbook.* Rockland, MA: Charles River Media.

Phillips, D. C. (1987). *Philosophy, science, and social inquiry.* New York: Pergamon Press.

Popham, W. J., (Ed.). (1974). *Evaluation in education: Current applications.* Berkeley, CA: McCutchan Publishing.

Postman, N. (1995). *The end of education: Redefining the value of school.* New York: Alfred A. Knopf.

Reeves, T. C. (1989). The role, methods, and worth of evaluation in instructional design. In K. A. Johnson & L. J. Foa (Eds.), *Instructional design: New strategies for education and training* (pp. 157-181). New York: Macmillan.

Reeves, T. C. (1992). Evaluating schools infused with technology. *Education and Urban Society Journal, 24*(4), 519-534.

Rogers, P. J., Hacsi, T. A., Petrosino, A., & Huebner, T. A. (Eds.). (2000). *Program theory in evaluation: Challenges and opportunities.* San Francisco: Jossey-Bass.

Rossi, P. H., & Freeman, H. E. (1989). *Evaluation: A systematic approach* (4th ed.). Newbury Park, CA: Sage.

Schauble, L. (1990). Formative evaluation in the design of educational software at the Children's Television Workshop. In B. N. Flagg (Ed.), *Formative evaluation for educational technologies* (pp. 51-66). Hillsdale, NJ: Lawrence Erlbaum Associates.

Schrag, F. (1992). In defense of positivist research paradigms. *Educational Researcher, 21*(5), 5-8.

Schubert, W. H., & Schubert, A. L. (1990). Alternative paradigms in curriculum inquiry. In H. J. Walberg & G. D. Haertel (Eds.), *The international encyclopedia of educational evaluation* (pp. 157-162). New York: Pergamon Press.

Schwab, J. J. (1970). *The practical: A language for curriculum.* Washington, DC: National Education Association

Scriven, M. (1974). Standards for the evaluation of educational programs and products. In G. D. Borich (Ed.), *Evaluating educational programs and products* (pp. 5-24). Englewood Cliffs, NJ: Educational Technology Publications.

Scriven, M. (1993). *Hard-won lessons in program evaluation.* San Francisco: Jossey-Bass.

Sedgwick, J. (1993, March). The complexity problem. *The Atlantic*, 96-104.

Seels, B. (1993). Instructional design fundamentals: A review and reconsideration: Introduction to a special issue. *Educational Technology, 33*(2), 7-8.

Shadish, W. R., Cook, T. D., & Leviton, L. C. (1991). *Foundations of program evaluation: Theories of practice.* Newbury Park, CA: Sage Publications.

Smith, E. R., & Tyler, R. W. (1942). *Appraising and evaluating student progress.* New York: Harper.

Soltis, J. F. (1992). Inquiry paradigms. In M. C. Alkin (Ed.), *Encyclopedia of educational research* (pp. 620-622). New York: Macmillan.

Stake, R. E. (1980). Program evaluation, particularly responsive evaluation. In W. B. Dockrell & D. Hamilton (Eds.), *Rethinking educational research.* London: Hodder and Stoughton.

Stake, R. E. (1990). Responsive evaluation. In H. J. Walberg & G. D. Haertel (Eds.), *The international encyclopedia of educational evaluation* (pp. 75-77). New York: Pergamon Press.

Stoll, C. (2000). *High tech heretic: Reflections of a computer contrarian.* New York: Anchor Books.

Suchman, E. A. (1967). *Evaluative research.* New York: Russell Sage.

Tate, R. (1990). Experimental design. In H. J. Walberg & G. D. Haertel (Eds.), *The international encyclopedia of educational evaluation* (pp. 553-561). New York: Pergamon Press.

Thorndike, R. L. (Ed.). (1971). *Educational measurement* (2nd ed.). Washington, DC: American Council on Education.

Tyler, R. W. (1949). *Basic principles of curriculum and instruction.* Chicago: University of Chicago Press.

Walberg, H. J., & Haertel, G. D. (Ed.). (1990). *The international encyclopedia of educational evaluation.* New York: Pergamon Press.

Worthen, B. R., Sanders, J. R., & Fitzpatrick, J. L. (1996). *Program evaluation: Alternative approaches and practical guidelines* (2nd ed.). New York: Addison Wesley/Longman.

Yeaman, A. R. J. (1994). Deconstructing modern educational technology. *Educational Technology, 34*(2), 15-24.

CHAPTER
3

The Functions of Evaluation

Objectives

After reading Chapter Three, you should be able to:

- identify the major functions of evaluation that should drive decision-making during the process of designing and implementing interactive learning systems;
- identify typical activities that are carried out to fulfill each of the major evaluation functions; and
- appreciate the importance of evaluation within the instructional design process.

Evaluation functions within the development process

If you are a designer of interactive learning systems, you probably employ a systematic approach to development, whether it is a classic instructional systems design (ISD) model (Briggs, Gustafson, & Tillman, 1991; Dick & Carey, 1990), a "rapid prototyping" approach (Tripp & Bichelmeyer, 1990), or some hybrid method (Piskurich, 2000). Although ISD models have come under attack recently (Gordon & Zemke, 2000), they remain important processes for developing education and training programs around the world. Despite new developments in automated course development tools and the widespread availability of reusable course components, predictions of the demise of ISD are probably premature (Zemke & Rossett, 2002).

Regardless of the method used, few people design interactive learning systems alone; you are likely to be a member of a team of instructional designers, content experts, programmers, videographers, graphic artists, project managers, evaluators, and others. In our experience, creating interactive learning systems has much in common with film production.

Just as a team representing diverse skills and talents is required to produce motion pictures, few individuals can accomplish all the tasks involved in creating interactive learning systems by themselves.

Figure 3.1 illustrates a typical ISD model that might be used to develop an interactive learning system, especially one involving multimedia. The problem with this and many other representations of ISD is that they make the steps involved in creating an interactive learning system appear entirely too linear. In actuality, the process is much more iterative and much less mechanical than ISD models imply. In addition, creativity is as essential as the application of scientific principles within the process of designing interactive learning systems.

	PROCESS	**TEAM**	**PRODUCT**
ANALYSIS	- Conducting Needs Assessment - Preparing Learner Assessment - Specifying Content & Objectives - Selecting Authoring Systems - Selecting Delivery Systems - Planning Design Project - Planning Evaluation Strategies	- Project Manager - Subject Matter Expert(s) - Instructional Designer(s) - Project Evaluator(s) - Programmer(s)	- Needs Assessment Report - Learner Profile - Content Outline - Learning Hierarchy - Objectives - Authoring System Specs. - Delivery System Specs. - PERT Chart/Project Timetable - Evaluation Plan
DESIGN	- Creating Interface Requirements - Specifying Performance Support - Screen Design - Flowcharting - Prototyping - Formatting Screens - Conducting Formative Reviews	- Project Manager - Subject Matter Expert(s) - Instructional Designer(s) - Project Evaluator(s) - Programmer(s) - Graphic Artist(s) - Video Producer(s)	- Treatment Description - Instructional Archetypes - Flowcharts - Scripts - Format Sheets - ILS Prototypes - Improvement Specifications
PRODUCTION	- Authoring Interactions - Creating Graphics - Preparing Adjunct Materials - Conducting Preproduction - Conducting Production - Conducting Postproduction - Integrating Optical Media & Code - Usability Testing - Mastering Optical Media	- Project Manager - Subject Matter Expert(s) - Instructional Designer(s) - Project Evaluator(s) - Programmer(s) - Graphic Artist(s) - Video Producer(s) - Video Editor(s) - Talent (e.g., actors)	- Interactive Code - Graphics - Adjunct Materials - Program Documentation - Shot Lists - Video/Film - Audio - Edited Video - CD-ROM - ILS Program
EVALUATI0N	- Documenting Project - Testing ILS - Validating ILS - Conducting Impact Evaluation	- Project Manager - Subject Matter Expert(s) - Instructional Designer(s) - Project Evaluator(s) - Programmer(s)	- Project Documentation - Functionally Valid ILS - Instructionally Valid ILS - Formative Eval. Report - Effectiveness Eval. Report - Impact Eval. Report

Figure 3.1. Instructional design model for interactive learning systems.

Perhaps the Walt Disney Corporation best captures the essence of producing interactive learning systems with its creative and patented term, "Imagineering!" One of the major reasons ISD is being questioned is the perception that ISD practitioners are not as creative as developers who follow less structured models (Gordon & Zemke, 2000). In addition, ISD is weakened by the failure of researchers in the instructional technology field to produce robust design principles (Clark & Estes, 1998). Despite the efforts of Gagné (1985), Merrill (2002), and others, there is no grand, unified science of instruction, and frankly we don't think there ever will be. Human learning is simply too complex for complete prediction and control. Lacking comprehensive scientific rules, you and your design team must combine the limited scientific principles and incomplete learning theories that do exist with imagination and common sense to develop interactive learning systems that are effective, efficient, and responsive to learner needs.

Another problem with most graphical representations of the ISD process is that they make evaluation appear to be an activity that is conducted late in the development process when it is, or should be, the key function that literally informs or drives the other functions involved in the process. In Figure 3.2, we present an alternative representation of the relationships between major development functions (conceptualize, design, develop, implement, institutionalize, and re-conceptualize) and the major functions of evaluation (review, needs assessment, formative evaluation, effectiveness evaluation, impact evaluation, and maintenance evaluation).

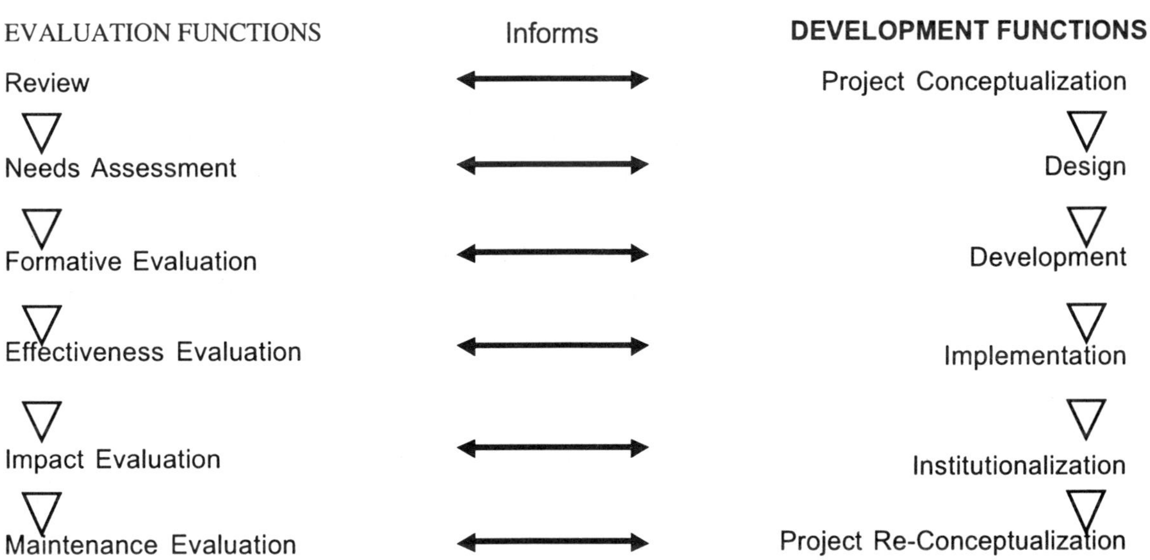

Figure 3.2. Relationships among evaluation and development functions.

Admittedly, the representation in Figure 3.2 is also flawed in that few actual interactive learning projects will follow the idealized path that is represented in this model. Evaluation is rarely implemented to the degree that it should be, perhaps for fear that projects will falter or even come to a complete halt if draft deliverables are evaluated fully. Our illustration intentionally emphasizes the importance of evaluation. As described in Chapter One, our rationale for writing this book is to provide information and tools that will enable you to collect and utilize evaluation data as the basis for informed decision-making throughout the process of developing and implementing interactive learning systems. We don't think the importance of evaluation can be overestimated, but we recognize that some may view this emphasis as impractical.

A case study: *Macintosh Fundamentals*

A case study from our own experience as members of a design team may provide a better portrayal of the typical process of how an interactive learning system comes to be developed and evaluated. When the Macintosh computer was first introduced by Apple Computer, Inc. in 1984, the interfaces for the operating system and the few software programs then available for the novel machine (e.g., MacWrite, MacPaint, and MacDraw) were so simple and intuitive that Apple promoted the idea that no training was necessary to use a Macintosh. However, within a few years, the complexity of the different Macintosh models that became available, accompanied by the proliferation of sophisticated peripheral devices and powerful software packages, changed the situation dramatically. In the face of these changes, the people marketing, selling, supporting, or just using Macintosh computers began to demand more and better training. In response to these needs in the United States, Apple established a network of education centers around the country where new employees, vendors, and users could experience hands-on training with the Macintosh. As Apple sales went up, the demand for basic training increased at the education centers. At the same time, the need for higher level courses was identified as even newer programs and peripherals for the Macintosh came on the scene.

In the face of unrealistic demands on the live trainers at the Apple Education Centers, the training development group at Apple headquarters in Cupertino, California began to explore the idea of developing an interactive learning system to deliver basic Macintosh training. Eventually, a large-scale training package called *Macintosh Fundamentals* was developed under the leadership of Jim Laffey, a multimedia pioneer at Apple Training Support (and now a professor at the University of Missouri). Although it may seem like ancient history to today's e-learning designers, the development of the award-winning *Macintosh Fundamentals* program provides a rare and noteworthy example of the integration of evaluation throughout the ISD process. The initial conceptualization of the interactive learning system included thorough **reviews** of existing interactive training materials as well as a comprehensive literature review. In addition, external evaluators were contracted to conduct a **needs assessment** at Apple Training Centers to identify the key goals and objectives that should be included in this first comprehensive interactive learning system for the Macintosh computer.

Actual design of the training system commenced once the specifications for the delivery platform were identified. The design and development phases of the process were informed by a sequence of alpha, beta, and field tests conducted both in-house at Apple headquarters in California and at three Apple Education Centers in different states. Alpha tests normally involve assemblage of a working version of the interactive learning system so that it can be tested in-house. During beta tests, a relatively complete version of the system is provided to all internal clients as well as to selected external clients. During field tests, well-tested versions of the training system are released to most customers with the understanding that changes may still be made in the program. Numerous other **formative evaluation** activities drove the development effort.

Although it took almost an entire year to complete, and cost nearly a million dollars, *Macintosh Fundamentals* was used by more than 10,000 trainees in the first two years of its use. During the first year of use, **effectiveness evaluations** were conducted by external evaluators at several training centers. After effectiveness was demonstrated, limited **impact evaluations** were conducted. Overall, these evaluations indicated that *Macintosh Fundamentals* was as effective as Apple's leader-led training had been, yielded more consistent results, and had significant long-term impact on the knowledge, skills, and attitudes of the trainees who had used the interactive learning system. Ongoing **maintenance evaluation** activities eventually indicated the need for a major reconceptualization of introductory training for the Macintosh, and a new learning system was developed. The subsequent program did not have to be delivered at Apple Training Centers because it could be distributed via CD-ROM to trainees at their own local sites. (Apple now delivers much of its training over the Web.)

Of course, not everything about the development of *Macintosh Fundamentals* proceeded as smoothly as described above, nor was every decision made solely on the basis of evaluation data. Internal politics as well as design prejudices and other factors influenced some of the decisions made by the project managers and team members, but most of the critical decisions were informed by timely and accurate evaluation data. All six functions of evaluation that we have identified (review, needs assessment, formative evaluation, effectiveness evaluation, impact evaluation, and maintenance evaluation) were represented in this case study. The details about how these functions should be carried out during the development of interactive learning systems are presented in chapters five to ten of this book.

Defining the functions

A chapter is devoted to each of the six functions of evaluation identified in Figure 3.2. However, to give you an overview of those chapters, we define each of the functions in a bit more detail below by identifying its purposes and presenting a hypothetical example of its application.

Review

The function of review is most important during the initial conceptualization for an interactive learning system. There are two primary review activities that are presented in this book, the review of professional literature related to the project and the review of existing interactive learning systems. The overall purpose of the review function is to ensure that you and your team members are as well-informed as possible about the primary options for interactive learning related to a project during its earliest stages of conceptualization.

Suppose that you are the head of a small entrepreneurial company trying to identify a product line that will set your company apart from your competitors. With your background in elementary education, you believe there is a market for remedial multimedia programs for students ages 6-9 in the area of science education. There are several review strategies that you should undertake before preparing a business plan or funding proposal for the development of this product. You would want to review the science education literature with the following questions in mind:

1) What national, state, or local standards or guidelines have been established for science education by groups such as the National Science Foundation or the Department of Education?
2) What do critiques of existing educational software reveal about the quality and effectiveness of these products?
3) What do projections indicate about the home school market for educational software?

If you discover that there are interactive products already on the market that claim to meet the needs you have identified, you will want to conduct a systematic review of these materials addressing questions such as:

1) How well do the objectives of these products align with the national, state, or local standards or guidelines you identified during your literature review?
2) What pedagogical strategies are employed in these materials?
3) What evidence exists that these materials are effective at a reasonable price?

Chapter Five presents activities, procedures, and tools for carrying out systematic reviews of the literature and existing products.

– WEB LINK –
Additional information about Western Governors University can be found at:
http://www.wgu.edu

Needs assessment

Needs assessment is one of the most widely underutilized evaluation functions in the process of developing interactive learning systems. In our experience, most projects are undertaken because of some political decision or in response to a request for proposals (RFP) that is uninformed by sufficient up-front analysis. A case in point is Western Governors University, an online university conceived in 1995 with great fanfare by then Governor Roy Romer of Colorado and Governor Mike Leavitt of Utah. Six years later, the virtual university still had more courses (developed at the cost of millions of dollars) than it had students. A cover story in *The Industry Standard* (Boynton, 2000) about Governor Leavitt describes the initiative:

> But the jewel in Leavitt's crown – as well as the thorn in his side – is the virtual Western Governors University, which he and Colorado Governor Roy Romer concocted in 1995. The idea was for 13 Western states to collaborate on class offerings to ease overcrowding and minimize the expense of educating the children of the baby boomers – which in Utah's case is estimated will add 130,000 students to an already overburdened school system by 2010. The university would also part with certain academic standards as criteria for a degree, in favor of competency in a specific field. Launched with lots of hype in 1998, the university has been a bust. The goal was to have 500 degree-seeking students and 7,000 students in corporate training programs by this year; it currently has only 200 degree-seeking students and hasn't met its other enrollment targets, lacks accreditation and is running at a deficit. (p. 151)

There is little evidence that even a rudimentary needs assessment or market analysis was conducted before launching Western Governors University (Berg, 1998). There was and is, of course, plenty of hype promoting the future of online education and the end of schools and campuses as we know them (Jones, 2000; Perelman, 1992; Pittinsky, 2003), and therefore, the Western Governors and their backers may have felt compelled to get to the market first with virtual degrees. In hindsight, a relatively small expenditure on needs analysis and other evaluation strategies would have been a good investment.

The primary activities carried out under the rubric of needs assessment are task analysis, job analysis, learner analysis, and answering the question, "Why is this project uniquely needed?" (Rossett, 1987, 1998). The overall purpose of needs assessment is to identify the critical needs that the proposed interactive learning system is intended to meet. The results of needs assessment activities are often stated in terms of goals and objectives. Content, delivery system, and authoring system specifications may also be derived from these activities.

Suppose that you work in the training department of a mining company where the number of accidents resulting in injury and death has increased steadily over a five-year period to an alarming level. Management has ordered your department head to develop an interactive multimedia kiosk that will be located at the entrance of each work site to remind workers of safety requirements and the procedures for reporting hazards. You have been appointed to lead the multimedia development team. There is considerable pressure on you to get these kiosks up and running within four months, but you insist on a thorough needs assessment first. You contract with an outside firm to conduct this needs assessment, and after two weeks of interviews, focus groups, observations, and document analysis, the needs assessment report reveals that workers are quite adept at reporting hazards in the workplace. The source of the injuries appears to be the introduction of new high-speed drilling equipment on which the workers have been inadequately trained. It is recommended that, instead of an interactive multimedia kiosk emphasizing the reporting of hazards, what is really needed is better training in the operation of the new drills. Management negotiates with the equipment manufacturer to provide this training, and the manufacturer subsequently awards your department a contract to produce the new training program.

Chapter Six presents activities, procedures, and tools for carrying out job analysis (Hartley, 1999), task analysis (Schraagen, 2000), and other components of needs assessment.

Formative evaluation

The function of formative evaluation is perhaps the most important one in the entire process of developing interactive learning systems. Budget constraints often mean that some evaluation activities must be abbreviated or even eliminated, but formative evaluation should be the least diminished because it often yields the greatest payoff of any function of evaluation. The overall purpose of formative evaluation is to provide information to guide decisions about creating, debugging, and enhancing an interactive learning system at various stages of its development. Some of the primary activities carried out during formative evaluation include expert review, user observations, and usability testing (Flagg, 1990; Hix & Hartson, 1993; Shneiderman, 1997).

Suppose that you are a curriculum director at a state department of education. You have won a federal award to develop an interactive multimedia Web site that will train teachers to recognize and report signs of child abuse. You and your team have prepared a draft treatment and illustrated it with story-boards. Before further development, you conduct a series of focus groups in which you present the treatment to several groups for review, including teachers, school administrators, parents, and health professionals. You also present the treatment to a team of attorneys from the state attorney's office. The reviews indicate that your treatment is generally acceptable, but that you have not sufficiently included opportunities to learn the legal responsibilities and liabilities that teachers have with respect to recognizing and reporting child abuse. Based on this review, the legal aspects of the treatment are clarified, and script development can begin.

Chapter Seven presents activities, procedures, and tools for carrying out observations, expert reviews, alpha and beta tests, usability studies, and other components of formative evaluation (George & Cowan, 1999).

Effectiveness evaluation

The function of effectiveness evaluation is to drive decisions about the marketing and implementation of an interactive learning system. The overall purpose of effectiveness evaluation is to determine whether the interactive learning system accomplishes its objectives within the immediate or short-term context of its implementation. Some of the primary effectiveness evaluation activities include field tests, observations, interviews, and performance assessment.

Suppose that you are a professor of educational technology at a large state university, sometimes serving as an evaluation consultant for the defense industry. A new virtual reality (VR) system has been developed by a military contractor to train soldiers in land navigation, and you have been commissioned to evaluate the effectiveness of this training. Traditionally, soldiers have been trained to navigate with compasses via a combination of leader-led classroom training and field exercises. The VR program puts soldiers into simulated battlefields where they must traverse mine fields and other hazards using a virtual compass.

The military command has requested an experimental study of the effectiveness of the VR program wherein a random sample of 50 soldiers will undergo the traditional training and another random sample of 50 will experience VR training. You request a delay to study the actual use of the VR system in more detail, but the officers and contractors insist that the study proceed immediately. After the training, all soldiers complete a written examination and a performance test wherein they use compasses to negotiate their way across several types of terrain on the south end of the military base. The results for the written tests are comparable for both groups, but the performance tests indicate that the traditionally trained soldiers successfully navigated the course 63% of the time whereas the VR group had a success rate of only 47%. These results are extremely disappointing to both the military command and the outside contractor. Convinced that the VR system would be effective, some of the contractors even question the validity of your evaluation.

Fortunately, you conducted a series of observations during the training implementation that help to explain the poor results. First, you observed that the sergeants conducting the traditional training used slides of the site where the performance tests were conducted to highlight specific navigation strategies, and in doing so inadvertently familiarized their trainees with the test course. Second, you discovered in focus group interviews that 50% of the VR trainees experienced severe nausea while using the VR system, and thus ended up closing their eyes during much of the training to overcome vertigo. A subsequent analysis of the data indicated that of the soldiers who did not suffer nausea, 78% were successful in the field exercise. Your analysis of the training implementation problems indicated the need for an investigation of the physical and psychological effects of the VR training on soldiers.

Chapter Eight presents activities, procedures, and tools for carrying out implementation studies, quasi-experimental studies, participant observations, and other components of effectiveness evaluation.

Impact evaluation

The impact evaluation function is extremely challenging. Not surprisingly, few interactive learning systems have been subjected to a rigorous impact evaluation. The overall purpose of impact evaluation is to determine whether the knowledge, skills, and attitudes learned in the context of instruction transfer to the intended context of use, e.g., the work place. It is not unusual to find that interactive instructional programs that possess immediate effectiveness fail to affect practice "on the job." For example, workers may be able to recite safety procedure rules such as wearing safety goggles, but neglect to follow these rules when performing their jobs. Some of the primary activities carried out during impact evaluations are document analysis, interviews, and observations.

Suppose that you work in the educational services department of a medical school where an innovative interactive multimedia program has been purchased to train senior medical students in the practice of cost-benefit analysis regarding the prescription of pharmaceuticals for flu and cold sufferers. Studies indicate that past graduates of the medical school frequently over-prescribe antibiotics and other drugs for patients at considerable added expense. The program is designed to train physicians to be more aware of the cost-benefit ratios involved in drug regimens, to consider less expensive, off-the-shelf remedies, and to recognize the long-term effects of antibiotics and other pharmaceuticals on their patients and on public health.

An earlier effectiveness evaluation revealed that the medical students accomplish the stated objectives of the multimedia program with a 97% achievement rate. However, you insist that an impact study be carried out to detect whether the program has any impact on the actual performance of the graduating physicians. Subsequently, an analysis of the prescription rates between the previous graduating class and the first class of medical students who experienced the cost-effectiveness training indicates no statistically significant differences in behavior. Interviews with the students in both classes reveal that although the second class was more aware of the cost-effectiveness issues, the pharmaceutical advice of the supervising physicians during their practicums outweighed the recommendations presented in the multimedia program.

Chapter Nine presents activities, procedures, and tools for carrying out observations, interviews, and other components of impact evaluation.

Maintenance evaluation

The function of maintenance evaluation is an increasingly important one in the world of interactive learning systems as more and more software is developed and distributed on wider and wider networks. The enormity of the problem can be sensed if one surfs the Web searching for interactive learning opportunities concerning HTML programming. There are numerous sites available, but their effectiveness and impact remain unexamined, and the currency of their content is often questionable. The overall purpose of maintenance evaluation is to examine the viability of an interactive learning system over time. Some of the primary activities carried out in the name of maintenance evaluation are document analysis, interviews, observations, and automated data collection.

Suppose that you are the Webmaster for an electronics corporation, responsible for developing and maintaining an "Intranet" that provides training and performance support for sales personnel. The Web site provides sales personnel with the latest marketing information about a wide range of products, recommended sales strategies, and tools for calculating sales quotes for customers. The Web site has been operational for nine months, and statistics indicate a steadily declining rate of usage of the site by the sales staff. You decide to investigate, and via a series of telephone interviews with sales personnel, you find that a major missing component of the Web site is performance and price information about products sold by your corporation's major competitors. Subsequently, you add information and tools to the site that arm your sales staff with critical competitive information. Not only do the number of hits on the Intranet increase over the next six months, but there is a rise in sales that management attributes to the enhanced Web site.

Chapter Ten presents activities, procedures, and tools for maintenance evaluation.

Activities, procedures, and tools

For each of the six major evaluation functions in our model, we have identified activities, procedures, and tools to assist you in carrying out the functions. For example, for the formative evaluation function, one activity that is frequently used is expert review, i.e., recruiting experts to review the content, instructional design, and other aspects of your interactive learning system as it is being developed. Expert review is also a frequently used strategy in the development of the user interface for interactive learning systems (Nielsen, 1993; Preece, 1994). When you ask experts to review the human-computer interface for your interactive program, you will usually want to structure this procedure by using a tool such as a user interface rating form. This form is one of the evaluation instruments that we introduce in Chapter Seven.

– WEB LINK –
The official support Web site for this book can be found at: http://it.coe.uga.edu/~treeves/ilse/

The tools we provide in this book should be regarded as templates which can be modified as needed. Electronic versions of these tools can be found on the official Web site for this book. The tools have been developed in common software applications such as word-processing programs (Microsoft Word) and spreadsheets (Microsoft Excel).

Figure 3.3 illustrates the relationships among evaluation functions, activities, procedures, and tools that are presented throughout the following chapters. For each function, we identify a set of critical activities that must be carried out to fulfill the function. For each activity, we describe the specific procedures recommended for carrying it out. Finally, for each procedure, we provide one or more tools to assist in following the procedure.

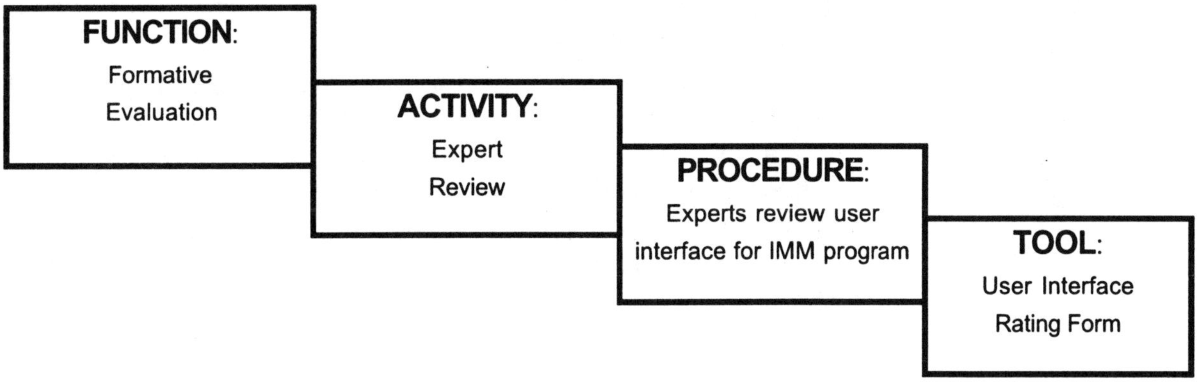

Figure 3.3. Relationship among functions, activities, procedures, & tools.

Summary

This chapter has presented an overview of the six functions of evaluation that we believe are necessary to drive the instructional design (ID) and implementation processes for interactive learning systems. There are, of course, other evaluation approaches that are not as relevant to the evaluation of interactive learning systems. We encourage you to explore the broader evaluation literature (Patton, 1997; Rossi & Freeman, 1999; Scriven, 1993; Shadish, Cook, & Leviton, 1991). We have also highlighted the importance of these evaluation functions within the ID process by presenting scenarios that illustrate the roles evaluation functions fulfill at various stages of the process. In the next chapter, we present guidelines for planning and managing evaluation efforts within the context of the design and use of interactive learning systems.

References

Berg, G. A. (1998). Public policy on distance learning in higher education: California State and Western Governors Association initiatives. *Educational Policy Analysis Archives*, *6*(11). Available: http://epaa.asu.edu/epaa/v6n11.html

Boynton, R. S. (2000). Gateway to high-tech heaven? *The Industry Standard*, *3*(30), 138-141, 144-145, 147, 149, 151, 154, 156, 161, 163, 165.

Briggs, L. J., Gustafson, K. L., & Tillman, M. H. (Eds.). (1991). *Instructional design: Principles and applications* (2nd ed.). Englewood Cliffs, NJ: Educational Technology Publications.

Clark, R. E., & Estes, F. (1998). Technology or craft: What are we doing? *Educational Technology*, *38*(5), 5-11.

Dick, W., & Carey, L. (2000). *The systematic design of instruction* (5th ed.). New York: Addison-Wesley.

Flagg, B. N. (1990). *Formative evaluation for educational technologies.* Hillsdale, NJ: Lawrence Erlbaum Associates.

Gagné, R. M. (1985). *The conditions of learning and theory of instruction* (4th ed.). New York: Holt, Rinehart and Winston.

George, J., & Cowan, J. (1999). *A handbook of techniques for formative evaluation: Mapping the student's learning experience.* London: Kogan Page.

Gordon, J., & Zemke, R. (2000, April). The attack on ISD. *Training, 37*(4), 42-53.

Hartley, D. E. (1999). *Job analysis at the speed of reality.* Amherst, MA: HRD Press.

Hix, D., & Hartson, H. R. (1993). *Developing user interfaces: Ensuring usability through product & process.* New York: John Wiley & Sons.

Jones, G. R. (2000). *Cyberschools: An education renaissance* (2nd ed.). Englewood, CO: Cyber Publishing Group.

Merrill, M. D. (2002). First principles of instruction. *Educational Technology Research and Development, 50*(3), 43-59.

Nielsen, J. (1993). *Usability engineering.* Boston: Academic Press.

Patton, M. Q. (1997). *Utilization-focused evaluation: The new century text* (3rd ed.). Thousand Oaks, CA: Sage.

Perelman, L. J. (1992). *School's out: Hyperlearning, the new technology, and the end of education.* New York: William Morrow.

Piskurich, G. M. (2000). *Rapid instructional design: Learning ID fast and right.* San Francisco: Jossey-Bass.

Pittinsky, M. S. (Ed.). (2003) *The wired tower: Perspectives on the impact of the internet on higher education.* Upper Saddle River, NJ: Prentice-Hall

Preece, J. (1994). *Human-computer interaction.* New York: Addison-Wesley.

Rossett, A. (1987). *Training needs assessment.* Englewood Cliffs, NJ: Educational Technology Publications.

Rossett, A. (1998). *First things fast: A handbook for performance analysis.* San Francisco: Jossey-Bass/Pfeiffer.

Rossi, P. H., & Freeman, H. E. (1999). *Evaluation: A systematic approach* (5th ed.). Thousand Oaks, CA: Sage.

Schraagen, J. M. (2000). *Cognitive task analysis.* Mahwah, NJ: Lawrence Erlbaum Associates.

Scriven, M. (1993). *Hard-won lessons in program evaluation.* San Francisco: Jossey-Bass.

Shadish, W. R., Cook, T. D., & Leviton, L. C. (1991). *Foundations of program evaluation: Theories of practice.* Thousand Oaks, CA: Sage.

Shneiderman, B. (1997). *Designing the user interface: Strategies for effective human-computer interaction* (3rd ed.). New York: Addison-Wesley.

Tripp, S. D., & Bichelmeyer, B. (1990). Rapid prototyping: An alternative instructional design strategy. *Educational Technology Research and Development*, *38*(1), 31-44.

Zemke, R. E., & Rossett, A. (2002, February). A hard look at ISD. *Training*, *39*(2), 26-34.

CHAPTER 4

Planning and Managing Evaluations

Objectives

After reading Chapter Four, you should be able to:

- prepare a plan for evaluating an interactive learning system during design and implementation;
- carry out the activities required to manage the evaluation of an interactive learning system; and
- establish a documentation system for a project to develop or implement an interactive learning system.

Why plan?

Preparing a detailed evaluation plan is essential before you undertake any facet of evaluation. An evaluation plan is usually a written document that spells out the "who, what, when, where, why, and how" of an evaluation effort. Any given plan will likely go through several stages of revision before it is accepted, and it is likely to be modified during its implementation. Negotiating an evaluation plan with team members, clients, and other relevant audiences represents a major part of the effort you will invest in evaluating interactive learning systems. In fact, once you have developed a well-designed plan and a set of reliable and valid evaluation instruments, it is sometimes possible to turn much of the actual data collection over to others. On the other hand, trying to evaluate without a plan almost always will be disastrous.

Beyond the obvious benefits, an evaluation plan has at least two other distinct advantages. First, the process of preparing a plan helps you understand the size and scope of an evaluation project. You need that understanding to establish a meaningful timeline and a reasonable budget for the evaluation. Second, the planning process gives you an opportunity to establish good rapport with your clients (the people paying for the evaluation) and other audiences (any people who may use the information provided by the evaluation for decision making).

An evaluation plan template

Figure 4.1 presents a list of the major components of an evaluation plan. An important aspect of this plan template is that it encourages you to identify in advance decisions that must be made about whatever is being evaluated. After all, unless your evaluation is designed to guide or influence decisions, you probably should not bother with evaluating an interactive learning system in the first place. The strategy seems simple, but it is actually quite challenging. Working with your clients and other relevant audiences, you must try to anticipate as many decisions as possible that might be made about the interactive learning system being developed or implemented. For each decision, you then will identify questions that must be answered to help your clients or others make better decisions. Then and only then should you decide upon an evaluation design or select specific data collection methods for the evaluation.

Evaluation planning often requires political savvy and astute negotiation skills. Just as politicians must engage in persuasion and negotiation to get anything accomplished within legislative bodies, evaluators often find themselves in the position of having to persuade their clients of the value of asking certain questions or addressing certain issues in an evaluation. Unwilling or unable to confront the complexities involved in most evaluation contexts, clients and other audiences for evaluation will demand direct and simple answers to complex questions. Experienced evaluators know that direct and simple answers are extremely rare, and that "it depends" and other conditional statements are part of even the best evaluations. A sound evaluation plan will expose as many of these conditionals as possible up-front, but the trick is doing so without having the clients decide to abandon evaluation altogether.

— WEB LINK —
Go to: http://it.coe.uga.edu/~treeves/ilse/

A copy of the evaluation plan template is included in the Web site that supports this book. Parts of a hypothetical evaluation plan are excerpted in this chapter to illustrate the planning process (see Figures 4.2 – 4.15).

Introduction	Introduces the major sections of the plan as well as the primary people involved in writing the plan.
Background	Describes any information needed to provide the reader with an understanding of the background of the interactive learning being evaluated.
Purposes	Delineates the purposes of the evaluation. A single plan can address a variety of purposes, but all must be delineated clearly. Evaluation is always a political process and all parties must accept the purposes for the evaluation to be successful.
Audiences	Specifies the clients as well as all the primary and secondary audiences or consumers of the evaluation. In general, it is recommended to open up the evaluation to as many people or agencies as the client will allow.
Decisions	Specifies the anticipated decisions that should be influenced by the evaluation. This section is probably the most difficult, but it should be included if the evaluation is to have impact on decision-making. Most developers do not wish to anticipate negative outcomes, but these too must be considered.
Questions	Clarifies the questions to be addressed by the evaluation design and data collection methods. The clearer and more detailed these questions are, the more likely that you will be able to provide reliable and valid answers to them.
Methods	Describes the evaluation design and procedures. There are scores of designs and hundreds of procedures which can be used. The keys to success are matching these options to the purposes and questions of your client and keeping within the budget and timeline of the study.
Sample	Specifies which learners, instructors, and other personnel will participate in the evaluation. A rationale for sample sizes should be included.
Instrumentation	Describes all the evaluation instruments and tools to be used. Actual instruments should be included in appendices for review and approval.
Limitations	Spells out any limitations to the interpretation and generalizability of the evaluation. It should also describe potential threats to the reliability and validity of the evaluation design and instrumentation.
Logistics	Specifies who will be responsible for the various implementation, analysis, and reporting aspects of the evaluation.
Timeline	Presents the schedule for implementation, analysis, and reporting of the evaluation.
Budget	Clarifies the finances for the evaluation. Personnel time is usually the major cost factor. Other significant cost factors are travel, data preparation (e.g., transcribing taped interviews), and document duplication. Unfortunately, many evaluations lack sufficient funding.

Figure 4.1. Components of an evaluation plan.

Introduction

This section introduces the major sections of the plan as well as the primary people involved in writing it. Figure 4.2 provides an example of a typical "Introduction" section. It is a good idea to introduce the reader to the type and amount of information upon which you have based your evaluation planning, both in terms of human input and review of other materials.

Evaluation Plan for "The Science of Amazon Exploration"
Draft of 11 August

Introduction

This document describes the background, purposes, limitations, audiences, decisions, questions, methods, sample, instrumentation, procedures, logistics, and timeline for the evaluation of the Science of Amazon Exploration (SAE) interactive multimedia CD-ROM currently being developed by the Imagination Corporation. The methodology, procedures, and instrumentation included in this plan are based on several meetings between members of the development team (Gwen Glass, Bobbi Burgess, and Lou Landers) and the evaluation team (Tom Reeves and John Hedberg), as well as a review of several draft design documents.

Figure 4.2. Introduction section for an evaluation plan.

Background

This section (illustrated in Figure 4.3) describes any information that is needed to provide the reader with an understanding of the background of the interactive learning system being evaluated. The program or product being evaluated is called the "evaluand." The reader should be given enough information to understand the unique nature of the evaluand, but not so much detail as to become bored. Explain any jargon used in describing the interactive learning system (e.g., e-learning) if the plan will be read by audiences unfamiliar with technical terms or the latest buzzwords. Although most evaluation plans are often rather dry reading, it does not have to be that way. Your evaluation plan can tell a story that is interesting, and you can include screen images from the evaluand. However, if lengthy background materials are needed, put them in an Appendix.

Purposes

This section (see Figure 4.4) thoroughly describes the purposes of the evaluation. An evaluation can address a variety of purposes, but all must be delineated clearly. Because evaluation is a political process, all parties must agree upon its purposes if it is to succeed. Sometimes the purposes stated in a plan will be related to one of the six major functions of evaluation described in Chapter Three, i.e., review, needs assessment, formative evaluation, effectiveness evaluation, impact evaluation, or maintenance evaluation. More often, you will need to plan an evaluation that includes two or more of the major functions of the evaluation model proposed in this book. Given that the nature of the product or program being evaluated is sure to change over time, trying to anticipate all the evaluation functions in advance is difficult, and flexibility is required throughout the process.

Background

The interactive multimedia CD-ROM under development is called "The Science of Amazon Exploration" (SAE). (A second one planned is called "The Technology of Amazon Exploration" (TAE).) While it is obvious that the topic of this CD-ROM will have great appeal in schools and homes, the program is unique in its use of constructivist pedagogy. In traditional science and technology instruction, information is presented in encapsulated formats, often via abstract "teacher talk" and texts, and it largely is left up to the student to generate any possible connections between conditions (such as a problem) and actions (such as the use of knowledge as a tool to solve the problem). There is ample evidence that students who are quite adept at "regurgitating" memorized information on tests rarely retrieve that same information when confronted with novel conditions that warrant its application (Bransford, Sherwood, Hasselbring, Kinzer, & Williams, 1990). In a sense, most knowledge acquired through traditional instruction is "inert" except within the confined structure of traditional tests.

Interactive multimedia programs can be designed to present a focal event or problem situation that will serve as an "anchor" or focus for collaborative efforts among instructors and students to retrieve and construct knowledge (Brown, Collins, & Duguid, 1989; Cognition and Technology Group at Vanderbilt (CTGV), 1992). Perhaps the best known multimedia example of this approach is the "Jasper Problem Solving Series" developed by John Bransford, Susan Goldman, and their colleagues at the Cognition and Technology Group at Vanderbilt University (CTGV, 1992).

Cognitive psychologists involved in the development of "Jasper" call this type of instruction "anchored instruction" (Bransford *et al.*, 1990; CTGV, 1992) because the process of constructing new knowledge is situated or anchored in meaningful and relevant contexts. They maintain that events and problems presented in these types of programs should be designed to be intrinsically interesting, problem-oriented, and challenging. They have evidence that in response to these types of events and problems, students are more highly motivated and that they construct useful as opposed to inert knowledge (Bransford *et al.*, 1990; CTGV, 1992).

The SAE and TAE CDs will provide precisely the types of problem situations that "anchored" interactive learning environments demand. In the "science" CD, the students will be confronted with realistic and challenging problems, e.g., a natural disaster such as a flood, and they must solve the problems that these disasters present for local inhabitants, explorers, fauna, and flora in the region. In the "technology" CD, students would confront the problem of mounting Amazon expeditions in different timeframes, e.g., the 20s, the 50s, now, and in the next century. Within each timeframe, they would have to adapt the technologies available at that time to mount a successful exploration of an unknown region of the Amazon. (For example, in the 50s expedition, they would not have the advantage of the satellite maps available as a result of the NASA programs of the 80s, but they would have improvements in malaria medicines over the medicine used by the 20s explorers because of the medical research done during the Second World War.)

Figure 4.3. Background to an evaluation plan.

Purpose

The overall purpose of this evaluation is to provide decision makers at the Imagination Corporation with the timely, accurate information required to support decisions regarding the enhancement, extension, and/or marketing of the SAE interactive multimedia CD-ROM. A list of anticipated decisions follows. As a result of this evaluation and the decisions and actions stemming from it, the SAE interactive multimedia CD-ROM should be ready for beta testing in selected markets within the fourth quarter of next year.

Specific sub-purposes of this evaluation are:

1) to collect information for improving the SAE interactive multimedia CD-ROM from selected content and instructional experts;
2) to collect information for improving the SAE interactive multimedia CD-ROM from members of the target audience (middle school students and teachers);
3) to establish procedures for the customer beta test of the SAE interactive multimedia CD-ROM; and,
4) to establish procedures for the ongoing collection of information for improving the SAE interactive multimedia CD-ROM after its customer beta test.

Figure 4.4. Purpose section of an evaluation plan.

Audiences

This section specifies all the primary and secondary audiences or consumers of the evaluation. Patton (1997) prefers the term "stakeholders" to designate audiences. In general, it is recommended to share information about an evaluation with as many people as the client will allow. Primary audiences include the people most directly involved in or affected by the evaluation, e.g., the target users of a product. Secondary audiences are any people judged to have a stake in the evaluation and thus a right to know about its methods and results (e.g., members of a state or district school board who review educational materials for certification purposes). As Patton (1997) noted "....stakeholders typically have diverse and often competing interests" (p. 42). Which audiences will receive evaluation reports is often a major focus for negotiation between you and your clients. Figure 4.5 provides a model description of audiences.

Audiences

The primary audiences for the evaluation are the members of the Imagination Corporation design and development team and the managers of Imagination Corporation. Important secondary audiences include other consultants involved in the development effort (e.g., marketing and sales personnel and content experts) as well as the larger educational community. The designers and implementers of this evaluation are Dr. Tom Reeves and Dr. John Hedberg, evaluation specialists from The University of Georgia and the University of Wollongong, respectively.

Figure 4.5. Audiences section of an evaluation plan.

Decisions

This section is the most difficult part of a plan to prepare, but it should be included if the evaluation is to have meaningful impact on decision making. (See Figure 4.6.) Trying to anticipate the decisions which can be influenced by an evaluation takes creativity and trust. Many clients do not wish to anticipate negative outcomes for their efforts, but these too must be considered. Obviously, you cannot create an exhaustive list of all the decisions that will be made about a program or product. Although we recognize that there will always be unanticipated decisions, we encourage you to identify decisions up front because if you don't, your evaluation efforts are unlikely to be as influential as they could be.

Decisions

If this evaluation is to provide timely, accurate information to support decision making, we must anticipate decisions that will be made. It is important to remember that most of these decisions will be made regardless of the quantity and quality of information available to the decision makers. The following decisions are anticipated:

1) Implementation procedures and delivery options for the SAE interactive multimedia CD-ROM will be established.
2) Modifications will be made in the SAE interactive multimedia CD-ROM to improve its effectiveness and appeal.
3) Other topics selected for interactive multimedia will be identified.
4) Advertising and marketing decisions will be made about the SAE CD-ROM by the marketing and sales department of Imagination Corporation.

Figure 4.6. Decisions section of an evaluation plan.

Questions

A key element of a sound evaluation plan is careful specification of the questions to be addressed by the evaluation design and data collection methods. The clearer and more detailed these questions are, the more likely that you will be able to provide reliable and valid answers to them. Whenever decisions are made, questions are asked and alternatives are considered, formally and/or informally. In order to influence the decisions listed in your plan as well as other unanticipated decisions, your evaluation must provide answers to a variety of questions that enable "informed" decision making. Figure 4.7 provides one example.

Another challenge in evaluation planning is limiting the questions to those that are the most relevant to the decisions that must be made without exceeding the amount of time, money, and other resources that are allocated for evaluation. It most cases, there will be far more questions that could be asked than your resources will allow, and therefore some difficult choices must be made about which questions will actually be addressed. You are advised to make these choices in collaboration with your clients and other primary audiences in advance of any data collection for the evaluation.

Questions

The following questions will be addressed during this formative evaluation:

a. What are the logistical requirements for implementing the SAE interactive multimedia CD-ROM?
    - hardware
    - software
    - adjunct materials
    - help and support

b. What are user reactions to the SAE CD-ROM?
    - appeal
    - motivation
    - usability
    - comprehension

c. What are teacher reactions to the SAE CD-ROM?
    - appeal
    - utility

d. What are expert reactions to the SAE CD-ROM?
    - content
    - instructional design
    - human-computer interface
    - aesthetics

e. What corrections must be made to the SAE CD-ROM?

f. What enhancements can be made to the SAE CD-ROM?

Figure 4.7. Questions section of an evaluation plan.

Methods

The "Methods" section (illustrated in Figure 4.8) describes the overall evaluation design and data collection strategies to be employed in your evaluation. There are scores of designs and many more data collection strategies that can be used. The keys to successful evaluation are matching these options to the purposes and questions of your client while keeping within the budget and timeline of the study. Unfortunately, traditional evaluation textbooks do not provide sufficient practical guidance in the area of methodology because the examples they include are usually based upon the assumption that one design will suffice (e.g., a quasi-experimental design comparing an instructional innovation with a "traditional" one). Experienced evaluators can attest that most evaluations demand multiple designs and multiple methods (cf., Baker, Herman, & Gearhart, 1996; Mark & Shotland, 1987).

One of the reasons that you will probably want to include multiple methods in your evaluation is the need to "triangulate" your findings. You can triangulate findings by using more than one method to collect data about an issue in the evaluation. For example, suppose you are interested in student attitudes toward the use of a new instructional CD-ROM in a course. A general questionnaire designed to elicit their opinions of the CD-ROM would be one way of collecting that data, but students are often turned off by questionnaires, and they may provide you with little detailed information about their real reactions to the product. A better strategy would be:

1) begin your data collection by interviewing a few selected students about their reactions to the CD-ROM;
2) design a questionnaire based upon the interview data and distribute it to a larger group of students; and
3) follow-up the questionnaire with a focus group of students to elaborate or clarify the results of the questionnaire.

Methods

No single evaluation design can encompass the six major questions specified for the evaluation of the SAE interactive multimedia CD-ROM. Therefore, a variety of evaluation designs and methods will be utilized to collect the information required to address these questions. The data collection methods include:

a. anecdotal records
b. user questionnaires
c. user interviews
d. user focus groups
e. usability observations
f. online data collection
g. expert review

Figure 4.8. Methods section of an evaluation plan.

A good way to succinctly present how your evaluation methods align with your questions is to use a matrix. Figure 4.9 is a matrix that illustrates the relationship between specific questions and the data collection methods used in an evaluation. On one axis of the matrix you list the questions that are to be addressed by your evaluation. On the other axis of the matrix you list all the data collection methods that are reliable, valid, and feasible for this particular evaluation. (The example in Figure 4.9 is by no means an exhaustive list of all the evaluation data collection methods that could be employed in an evaluation. Other chapters in this book provide examples of additional methods.) An advantage of using a matrix is that you, your colleagues, and your clients can review the articulation or alignment among the evaluation questions and proposed methods of collecting data to address these questions.

The matrix not only provides an overview of the evaluation methods. It also allows you to ensure that each question is addressed by one or more data collection methods. Although it is not always in every evaluation, it is desirable to triangulate most questions with more than one evaluation method. (Examples of the instruments used with each method are usually placed in appendices to the plan.)

METHODS	a. What are the logistical requirements?	b. What are user reactions?	c. What are teacher reactions?	d. What are expert reactions?	e. What corrections must be made?	f. What enhancements can be made?
anecdotal records	X	X	X		X	X
user questionnaires		X	X		X	X
user interviews		X	X		X	X
user focus groups	X				X	X
usability observations	X				X	X
online data collection		X			X	
expert reviews				X	X	X

Figure 4.9. Data collection matrix of an evaluation plan.

Sample

This section specifies exactly which learners, instructors, experts, and other personnel will participate in the evaluation. If necessary, a rationale for sample sizes should be included as well. Involving people in an evaluation should not be done carelessly because you are asking for their valuable time and energy.

The nature of your sampling strategies will vary considerably depending upon the purpose of your evaluation and the status of the program or product being evaluated. For example, early in the stages of development of a new interactive learning system, you will usually use fewer participants for longer and more intensive evaluation sessions. On the other hand, a Web-based product that is ready for beta testing can be shared with large numbers of reviewers around the world who might try it out and complete a brief survey about it after the trial period (Perkins, 2001). Figure 4.10 illustrates the "Sample" section for an evaluation plan.

Sample

The participants in this evaluation will be:

- a panel of content and instructional experts who are yet-to-be-identified;
- 10 teachers and 30 student volunteers from a local middle school; and
- 8 representatives from the Imagination sales and marketing department.

Figure 4.10. Sample section of an evaluation plan.

Instrumentation

This section (Figure 4.11) describes the instruments to be used in the evaluation. Copies of instruments should be included in appendices for review by your clients or others. The descriptions in this section should provide enough information to permit readers to judge the various purposes and uses of different instruments. Some evaluations of interactive learning systems will require the development of new instruments, in which case the plan may only include an outline of how the instruments will be developed.

Whatever types of instruments you use, you'll need to be concerned with issues of reliability and validity. The reliability and validity of instruments must be considered in light of the purposes of the evaluation (Patton, 1997). Reliability deals with the consistency of measurement or data collection. For example, a bathroom scale that provides the same weight if you step on it ten times in a row is probably reliable. Validity is about the degree to which an instrument achieves its aims. For example, if you want an accurate report of your weight, your reliable bathroom scale will need to be calibrated with another scale of recognized accuracy. It could be giving you the same weight ten times in a row, but be off by five pounds! Although any evaluator should know the fundamentals of establishing the reliability and validity of evaluation instruments, it may be necessary to hire measurement specialists to provide expert consultation in this area, especially when new instrumentation is being developed.

Limitations

This section spells out any limitations to the interpretation and generalizability of the evaluation. Frankly, we have found that most people put too much faith in the findings of evaluations, perhaps assuming that if they read a report in print, it must be true. Every evaluation has limitations and/or room for alternative explanations. The limitations section of your plan should describe potential threats to the reliability and validity of the evaluation design and instrumentation. Figure 4.12 provides an example

Instrumentation

Appendix A includes a sample Anecdotal Record Form which all developers involved in the creation of the SAE interactive multimedia CD-ROM will complete. This instrument requires a description of any incident determined to be important to the project and a separate interpretation of the event. A model of a completed Anecdotal Record Form is also included in Appendix A. Anyone who observes an incident or has an experience which should be reported for this evaluation should complete an Anecdotal Record Form as soon as possible after the incident or experience so that an accurate record and interpretation can be made.

Appendix B includes a sample User Questionnaire that the students and teachers participating in this evaluation will complete after they try the prototype SAE CD-ROM for at least one hour.

Appendix C includes a protocol for the User Interviews that will be conducted with selected students and teachers who have used the prototype SAE CD-ROM for at least one hour.

Appendix D includes a protocol for a User Focus Group that will be conducted with selected students and teachers who have used the prototype SAE CD-ROM for at least four hours.

Appendix E includes a description of the protocols to be followed when using the portable usability lab to record student and teacher interactions with the prototype SAE CD-ROM.

Appendix F includes a list of all the data to be collected by the computer while users are trying the prototype SAE CD-ROM. This data includes both navigation paths and response choices.

Appendix G includes brief resumes of fifteen interactive multimedia experts from whom a panel of three will be selected to review the prototype product. A list of scientists and geographers who may be requested to review the content of the SAE and TAE CD-ROM is also included.

Figure 4.11. Instrumentation section of an evaluation plan.

Limitations

Two constraints on this evaluation should be clarified. First, all contents of the CD-ROM must be regarded as changeable during the formative evaluation phase, and indeed they are expected to be modified in response to expert and user reactions. The "moving target" nature of the SAE interactive multimedia CD-ROM should be viewed as an advantage in that its flexibility increases the likelihood that the information yielded by the formative evaluation will be used to make substantive improvements in the structure and operation of the program. The second constraint has to do with the different perspectives of the participants in this evaluation. The sales and marketing participants are concerned primarily with selling this program, while the end user participants will be concerned primarily with its appeal, effectiveness, and value. These distinctive perspectives must be kept in mind whenever the results of the evaluation are considered. Failing to consider the seller vs. user perspective could result in misinterpretation of the findings.

Figure 4.12. Limitations section of an evaluation plan.

– WEB LINK –
For information about Microsoft Project, go to: http://www.microsoft.com/office/project/

Logistics

This section (Figure 4.13) spells out who will be responsible for the various implementation, analysis, and reporting aspects of the evaluation. There are a variety of computer programs and tools that can assist in your efforts to keep an evaluation on schedule and within a budget. (Microsoft Project 2000 is an example of project management software.) Much of the data you collect in an evaluation is time-sensitive. For example, the responses that you get from a student immediately after trying a new product will be different from the responses you get after a delay of only a few hours. Sometimes, you will want to delay data collection, but most often you will want to collect evaluation data while someone actually uses a new program or product, or as soon as possible thereafter.

Logistics

Tom Reeves and John Hedberg will coordinate the implementation of this evaluation plan, including scheduling, data collection, and data transmission, with the course development staff, primarily Gwen Glass, who is the course manager for this project. All data will be processed, analyzed, interpreted, and reported by Tom Reeves and John Hedberg. All reports will be provided to managers and members of the development team at the Imagination Corporation. Further dissemination of the evaluation findings will be determined by the managers. Additional details about the logistics are found in the timeline section of this plan including due dates for deliverables.

Figure 4.13. Logistics section of an evaluation plan.

– WEB LINK –
For Web-based project management software, see: http://www.project-management-software.org/

Timeline

This section presents the schedule for implementation, analysis, and reporting of the evaluation (see Figure 4.14). Project management software is helpful in preparing a timeline for evaluations, although these programs can be expensive and somewhat complex to use. However, if you conduct many evaluations, developing expertise with project management software is a good investment of your money and time.

Timeline

This evaluation plan has been revised based on an earlier draft prepared in July. The final evaluation plan will be reviewed, revised, and approved by August 14. The initial data collection phase of the evaluation itself will commence August 28 at Lincoln Middle School. The first interim report will be delivered by September 15. The final report of this alpha test of the product will be submitted by September 29.

The beta test phase of the evaluation will occur in October, with the intent of a final report being delivered by October 27. Additional interim reports will be produced as requested. The final release of this product must occur in time for this year's Christmas buying season.

Figure 4.14. Timeline section of an evaluation plan.

Budget

This section "costs out" the finances for the evaluation. Evaluation is very much a people-intensive process. In fact, most of the money spent on evaluation usually will be for personnel and consultant costs. If specialized equipment and facilities such as a software usability laboratory are used, additional costs will be incurred. Budgeting for evaluation is always a challenge because most project managers are somewhat reluctant to spend money for evaluation in the first place. When things get tight during a development project, they often look at cutting the evaluation budget first. A simple sample budget appears in Figure 4.15.

We are sometimes asked to recommend a percentage of a product development budget to be devoted to evaluation. This is difficult to do without the details of any given project, but a general estimate of ten to twenty percent of the development budget should be devoted to evaluation activities, ranging from review through effectiveness evaluation. Impact and maintenance evaluations will require additional allocations.

Item	Rate	Amount
Reeves consulting	4 days @ 1,200	4,800
Hedberg consulting	5 days @ 1,200	6,000
Expert review honorariums		3,000
Usability lab rental	2 days @ 1000	2,000
Travel & per diem	2 trips at $750	1,500
Materials, printing, copying		500
Donation to participating school		2,000
Total		19,800

Figure 4.15. Budget section of an evaluation plan.

Managing the evaluation process

Managing evaluations is just as important as planning them. There are several time-tested strategies that can help you meet the management challenge. These include evaluation diaries, status reports, and sign-off forms.

Evaluation diary

An evaluation diary is a collection of the documents that can be used to keep track of the planning, implementing, analyzing, and reporting aspects of an evaluation. A diary is an excellent management tool, especially for large-scale evaluations. What should be kept in an evaluation diary? Figure 4.16 is a list of 10 typical components of an evaluation diary.

You will need to take special security measures with data collected and stored in an evaluation diary, especially in situations when confidentiality is a major issue. Generally, the evaluation diary is not made available to your clients or other members of a development or implementation team. It is a management tool for you and others who are involved directly in the evaluation effort rather than a type of evaluation report.

There are certainly other types of documentation that can be maintained in an evaluation diary or log. The important thing is to begin maintaining careful records from the very beginning of the evaluation. It is extremely difficult and in some case impossible to document your evaluation efforts later in the process. In the age of the "paper-less office," all the documentation for an evaluation can be maintained online. However, in light of computer thefts, crashes, and other mischief, we recommend keeping a hard copy backup of all your evaluation documents. These can be organized into three-ring binders or a set of file folders.

Section	Description
Evaluation Plan	A copy of the most current plan plus various revisions that it went through during negotiations with clients.
Status Reports	Copies of the periodic evaluation status reports (weekly are recommended) provided to clients.
Correspondence	Copies of memos, letters, sign-off forms, and even copies of e-mail if deemed relevant.
Financial Records	Detailed financial records, including printouts of budgeting spreadsheets, receipts, invoices, etc.
Instrumentation	Copies of evaluation instruments that were obtained, developed, and/or revised for the evaluation.
Data	Backup copies of all the data (raw and processed) collected during the evaluation.
Analyses	Printouts of the analyses run on the data, both quantitative and qualitative.
Reports	Copies of all the interim and final reports generated during the evaluation.
Timeline	Timeline and documentation for any changes that may have been made in the schedule.
Notes	Copies of your personal notes from evaluation meetings, observations, etc.

Figure 4.16. Typical components of an evaluation diary.

Status reports

Evaluation status reports are brief reports distributed to evaluation team members, your clients, and sometimes to selected primary or secondary audiences for the evaluation. Figure 4.17 presents an example of an evaluation status report.

Status reports serve two essential purposes: first, updating everyone about the current status of the evaluation, and second, documenting controversial decisions and other important events. How often status reports are issued depends upon the schedule and intensity of an evaluation effort. In larger-scale evaluations, they are often prepared on a weekly basis, whereas on longer-term or smaller-scale evaluations, less frequent reports may suffice. Generally, it is better to err on the side of keeping your clients and other stakeholders over-informed about the status of the evaluation effort than to leave them under-informed.

Evaluation Status Report:
Science of Amazon Exploration CD-ROM

Date: September 12 From: John Hedberg

Accomplishments: (Since August 28)

- Began the CD-ROM evaluation at Lincoln Middle School on schedule.
- 21 students and 4 teachers have completed questionnaires and interviews.
- Focus group is scheduled for Friday, September 15, in the school auditorium.

Pending Items:

1) Complete reviews with the other students and teachers.
2) Analyze questionnaire and interview data.
3) Prepare draft final report due September 29.

Concerns and Recommended Actions:

1) It is proving more difficult to get teachers to review the CD-ROM than expected. We may not have 10 teachers in the final sample, but we will try. The teachers' schedules are very tight. We are trying for at least five teachers.
2) There are major problems in the CD-ROM if certain options are selected. When students try to create their own multimedia reports, the whole system crashes. These bugs must be fixed before further user testing is undertaken. A timeline for fixing these bugs must be established.

Remarks:

1) The programmers from the development team are working hard to fix the bugs in the CD-ROM, but they are also having trouble with the authoring software. The problems may be beyond their control. What contingency plans do we have?

Figure 4.17. Sample evaluation status report.

Sign-off forms

A sign-off form is an invaluable tool for managing the evaluation of interactive learning systems. The sign-off form documents client approval of an evaluation plan, interim report, final report, or any other document considered important within the context of the evaluative effort. For example, most evaluators prepare draft reports at regular intervals. Draft reports should be reviewed carefully by your clients, and their review process should be documented. The sign-off form indicates the client's approval to proceed with the next step of the evaluation and to pay for work completed, if applicable. Figure 4.18 presents a sample sign-off form.

A sign-off form is a powerful instrument that will help you keep your evaluation effort moving and prevent the client from constantly rethinking the evaluation. Of course, sometimes the client will have good reasons for wanting to change the questions addressed or methods used in an evaluation. If you have carefully documented previous negotiations, you will be in a stronger position to request the additional finances, time, or personnel that may be required to fulfill the new requests.

Sign-Off Form

Project: SAE CD-ROM Evaluation

I have reviewed and approved the Interim Report of the evaluation of the SAE CD-ROM being conducted at Lincoln High School by Tom Reeves and John Hedberg.

I hereby give you approval to proceed with preparing the final report of this evaluation. I also give my approval for you to invoice the Imagination Corporation for satisfactory completion of this phase of the evaluation plan.

I understand that further changes to the evaluation (aside from those specified in the plan dated August 14) will likely result in a delay in the final report date and could result in additional charges to the Imagination Corporation.

____________________________ ____________

[signature] [date]

Gwen Glass, Project Manager

Figure 4.18. Sample sign-off form.

Documenting the design and implementation processes

We have not included documentation on our list of the major functions for evaluating interactive learning systems (as outlined in Chapter Three) for several reasons. First, the activities, procedures, and tools of documentation as an evaluation function often overlap with the work of the Management Information System (MIS) personnel within a particular agency or group. Second, regardless of who does it, documentation is not a function that occurs within the context of one particular phase of the instructional design process, but instead cuts across all the major phases involved in the design and implementation of interactive learning systems. Third, the data derived from a comprehensive project documentation system can often be reused within the context of other evaluation functions, and thus planning and establishing documentation activities is often a precursor to other functions.

Why should you document your development and evaluation activities?

One purpose of documentation is to account for resources expended during the development and implementation of interactive learning systems. Information about how resources have been used and when various tasks have been completed is essential in making better decisions. As illustrated in Figure 4.19, you, your project manager, and other people involved in a project will often be called upon to make critical decisions about an interactive learning system as it is being developed or implemented. Each decision can be based upon habits, ignorance, or preferably, the type of information provided by good documentation. Whether data is provided by an in-house MIS or a special set of documentation activities followed by your team, decision making should be informed by data.

Decision	The development project may take longer than planned. Should I ask for more time?
Politics	The team leaders tell me we'll never finish on time, and the team members seem stressed out. I'd better ask the clients for more time so the team members don't quit!
Ignorance	I don't have a clue where we are with the schedule, but the clients will be upset if I ask for more time. I'd better ask the team members to do more!
Documentation	The PERT chart indicates that we have slipped behind a day in our timeline, but we have some slack days built into next week's programming schedule. We'll catch up then.

Figure 4.19. A decision and three approaches to making it.

Documentation is an essential component of any systematic effort to develop interactive learning systems. As noted above, documentation is analogous to a management information system (MIS) in a business. Just as a well-designed MIS provides managers with up-to-date information about sales, profits, losses, schedules, inventory, and other factors needed to make timely business decisions, a well-designed and carefully implemented documentation system can provide team members with the information they need to make decisions involved in managing instructional design and implementation projects.

In fact, the similarity between a good MIS and good documentation may be so strong that you might assume that the latter effort is unnecessary. This sounds good in theory, but it is weak in reality. Many companies lack a strong MIS, and so there is often no other source of the type of information provided by documentation activities. Further, even when a MIS exists, it may not be focused on the typical data needed by managers of interactive learning systems. A corporate MIS may focus on profits, inventory tracking, and personnel issues, whereas the instructional design or implementation project manager may require detailed information about expenditures and schedules. Of course, if a good MIS is available, you should tap it for as much information as you can and avoid duplicating any data collection.

What kinds of decisions can you anticipate?

Suppose one of the instructional designers on a development team asks for a raise. The project manager wants to know if this person has done more than his share of the work as claimed. Checking your documentation records (e.g., the "Development Activity Logs" illustrated in Figure 4.20 on page 90), you discover that this person is consistently putting in 15-20 more hours per week than anyone else, and you report this to the manager. Of course, the manager doesn't automatically make a decision about the pay raise based upon this information alone. The manager must balance the overtime data with her opinion of the quality of this person's design work, but the data you provided does give her an important piece of information needed to make the decision. That's what documentation is all about!

There are many other practical examples of the need for documentation. For instance, as a developer of an interactive learning system, you can expect that the project will lag behind schedule from time to time. You may also experience budget cuts, and you might even have team members who change jobs in the middle of your project. Each of these and numerous other problems that occur on an almost daily basis will require you to make decisions. Should you modify the scope of the product to save time and money? Should you hire more staff or motivate existing team members to be more productive? Should you request a budget increase or a project extension? There will be no shortage of decisions that can be informed by better documentation data!

What questions should be answered before making decisions?

A key to effective documentation is anticipating the questions that managers, clients, team members, or others may ask about the project before making decisions. Some are obvious whereas others are subtle. For example, a manager might ask questions about the morale of a development team. Designing interactive learning systems is essentially a creative process, and people involved in creative work are prone to argue from time to time about the quality and quantity of the work being accomplished. Although tracking the morale of a development team is challenging, it may be something you'll be asked to do.

Fortunately, most of the documentation questions asked by project managers and team members are about issues more concrete than team morale. For example, before making decisions about project resources, people need reliable answers to questions about the schedule, the budget, and other types of resources. Typical questions include: What is the current state of the development schedule? Who has accomplished what tasks? What is the status of the budget? Is there any lag time in the schedule? Making decisions without accurate answers to these and other questions may force you and others to base decisions upon less-reliable foundations such as intuition, habit, rumor, or guesswork.

What kinds of information do you need to answer questions?

The tasks involved in developing interactive learning systems range from project conception and proposal writing to marketing and implementation. Each of these tasks requires some expenditure of resources, whether they be human, temporal, and/or financial resources. Unless you work in Hollywood, there will probably be major limitations on your resources in each of these categories, and it behooves you to have current information about their status. At a minimum, documentation activities should provide you with reliable, valid information within each of these three categories, i.e., people, time, and finances.

What do you need to know about people? You need to know what their jobs are, especially in terms of responsibility and authority for different tasks within a project. You need to know what they have done and what they still have to do. You may even want to know their attitudes toward the project, themselves, their colleagues, and so forth. Is their job satisfaction high or are they looking for another position? You would not want project success to hinge on just one person who simply might not show up tomorrow.

What do you need to know about time? You need to know how much time has been allocated for each phase of a project. You need to know if those tasks that must be accomplished synchronously are being done according to schedule. You need to know where there is slack time in the schedule so that extra time can be put in when other deadlines are missed. In today's fast-paced world of e-learning development, completing a project on schedule is sometimes much more important than keeping within a specific budget (Rosenberg, 2000).

What do you need to know about finances? You need to know the state of the budget, including, in many institutional settings, the amount of money allocated to "overhead." You need to know what has been spent and what costs still loom ahead. You will want to know how the costs of various items or services are changing during the lifetime of a project.

In addition to information about people, time, and money, you may want to collect evidence that can be used to tell the "story" of your project. What really happened? How has it affected the people involved in it? What were the high and low points of the project? While at first glance telling the story of your project may seem frivolous, it could prove to be invaluable, especially with respect to creating what Senge (1990) calls a "learning organization" in your company or institution. The bottom line is that documenting today's successes and failures can help you improve your next project.

How should the information be collected and reported?

A key element of sound documentation is integrating data collection and reporting into the work habits of all team members. A useful instrument for this is a "development activity log." Figure 4.20 presents the critical elements of this log. If each team member accurately records his/her time spent on each of the various tasks involved in the development of an interactive learning system, you will possess the basic information required to know the current status of the project, and you will be able to estimate possible problems, such as schedule delays or budget shortfalls.

DEVELOPMENT ACTIVITY LOG

1.0 Analysis	2.0 Design	3.0 Production	4.0 Evaluation
1.1 Conducting Needs Assessment	2.1 Creating Treatment Specifications	3.1 Authoring IMM	4.1 Documenting Project
1.2 Preparing Audience Assessment	2.2 Specifying Interactions	3.2 Creating Graphics	4.2 Testing IMM
1.3 Specifying Content and Objectives	2.3 Flowcharting	3.3 Preparing Adjunct Materials	4.3 Validating IMM
1.4 Selecting Authoring and Delivery Systems	2.4 Prototyping	3.4 Conducting Pre-production	4.4 Conducting Impact Evaluation
1.5 Planning Project	2.5 Writing Scripts	3.5 Conducting Production	
1.6 Planning Evaluation	2.6 Formatting Screens	3.6 Conducting Postproduction	
	2.7 Conducting Formative Reviews	3.7 Mastering Optical Media	
		3.8 Integrating Optical Media and Code	

Date	Hours	Project Code	Activity Code	Explanation
1/17	4	A27	1.1	Met with seven science teachers at Jackson School to assess needs.
	6	A24	2.7	Conducted usability tests of the environmental prototype.
1/18	8	A27	1.2	Wrote audience assessment for school science project.

Figure 4.20. Sample development activity log instrument.

Ideally, the development activity log should be computer-based so that team members can easily log in their accomplishments on an hourly or daily basis. Paper-based systems can also be used, provided you have clerical resources to enter the data into a spreadsheet or statistical package for timely analysis and reporting.

The primary problem you are likely to experience in making a development activity log part of your documentation evaluation is a human one. Many people are inexperienced with the process of documenting their work. Others lack the commitment to maintain accurate records of what they have accomplished. You, in collaboration with the project managers, will need to motivate their active participation in the documentation process through a variety of means. Of course, there is a precedent for logs in many work places, i. e., time cards, but these usually only entail recording "in" and "out" times. Training will probably be required to help team members perceive the value of a more elaborate documentation log. But it is worth doing! Not only does it provide you with timely, accurate information about the current state of the project, it also yields invaluable information the next time you prepare a proposal or budget for a similar project. How much it costs to develop interactive learning systems has never been stated definitively. Per hour development cost estimates range from as low as $5,000 per hour of instruction to as high as $50,000. If more development teams maintained accurate and complete development activity logs, we would have a much better understanding of what it costs to produce interactive multimedia learning environments.

The "Development Activity Log" illustrated in Figure 4.20 is only an example. Your particular project will probably entail a different set of activities, depending on whether it is focused on development, implementation, or both. Your logging system should contain the level of detail regarding activities that will be useful to you, your project manager, and other team members. Do not collect more data than you can actually use. Columns in the log can be used to record dates, time spent, project codes, activity codes, and other helpful explanation. (If your team members are working on only one project, the column for recording project codes can be eliminated.) Ideally, this type of instrument would be provided to your team members as an electronic tool coordinated with an electronic appointment calendar accessible via desktop computers, laptops, personal digital assistants, and digital phones. Some Web sites include a shared calendar function that can fulfill this role for the project team.

Similar to the Evaluation Diary described earlier in this chapter (see Figure 4.16), another useful tool for documentation evaluation is a "project diary" (Greer, 1991, 1992, 1996, 1997). A project diary can be kept as an electronic resource using word-processing, spreadsheet, and database programs or it can be simply maintained in a three-ring binder.

Recommended components of a project diary are:

- multimedia development project proposal
- contracts and subcontracts

- schedules such as PERT charts or timelines
- budget reports and invoices, receipts, and payment records
- project status reports
- sign-off forms
- anecdotal records

— WEB LINK —
For more information about project diaries and other project management tools, an excellent resources is Michael Greer's Project Management Resources site at: http://www.michaelgreer.com/

Project status reports are brief reports for clients as well as project team members and management that update everyone about the current project status and document controversial decisions and other important events. Project status reports are similar to evaluation status reports (see Figure 4.17 in this chapter) except the former are focused on the project as a whole and the latter are focused on the evaluation effort. Figure 4.21 presents an abbreviated project status report for a typical project.

Home Safety CD-ROM Project

Date: January 27 From: Rick Wheelwright

Accomplishments: (Since January 13)

1. Storyboards for fire safety (Module 3) have been approved by client.
2. New home safety standards have been obtained from the CDC.

Pending Items:

1) Complete storyboards for other modules by February 15.
2) Cast talent for video production.
3) Revise scripts as per expert reviews.

Concerns and Recommended Actions:

1) The home we had planned to use for Module 3 video was destroyed by fire.
2) Let's use the project manager's house.

Remarks:

1) Team morale seems very high after last week's retreat at Mount Snow.

Figure 4.21. Sample project status report.

For every deliverable, include a sign-off form (see Figure 4.18) for your client to formally acknowledge receipt and approval of the deliverable. As described above, a sign-off form documents client approval of a given project milestone, e.g., a draft script or a video sequence. Developing an interactive learning system is analogous to an engineering project in that it yields tangible draft programs at regular intervals that should be reviewed by clients. The sign-off form indicates the client's approval to proceed with the next step of the development cycle and to pay for the completion of this step, if applicable.

Despite the best planning possible, disagreements about design features are inevitable within any significant instructional development project. Documenting client reviews and having carefully recorded sign-offs can be the single most important tool in your documentation toolbox. Our experience is that some development projects get mired in controversy and even legal wrangles when such agreements are not carefully documented.

As noted earlier in this chapter, documentation is not just a matter of compiling facts and figures. If feasible, you should also consider telling the human side of any development project. Development projects have highs and lows, and there are important lessons to be learned all along the way. One way of telling the story of a project is to keep a narrative journal of what happens during the course of a development or implementation project. Keeping such a journal or log is not easy, especially if you don't have time during the day to record the major events, but it is a professional habit that we recommend highly. Some people find it easier to record the story of a project using a small hand-held recorder. Clerical personnel can transcribe the tapes for later reference. You might even recruit an intern from a university or college design program to document "the making of" your interactive product with digital pictures, interviews, and a Web site that can be shared with other members of the project team and beyond.

An anecdotal record form (see Figure 4.22) can also be a useful instrument for recording the human "stories" that are integral to a large-scale, creative development project. An important aspect to note about the anecdotal record form instrument is that it requires you to distinguish carefully between what you observed and your interpretation of that observation. You should try to be as descriptive as possible in the first part of the anecdotal record form without rendering explicit judgments about the meaning of what was observed. This will allow others to make their own interpretation of the meaning of the anecdote before reading your interpretation.

In our experience, this type of instrument is particularly useful when your interactive learning system has been disseminated to different sites, and you want to get the local site managers to provide you with information about how the system is working under realistic conditions. The stories that come in from the field can be among the most enlightening forms of evaluation data you will collect. Anecdotal records collected during a pilot evaluation might reveal that an otherwise innovative and effective e-learning program that the central office training manager was promoting was being underutilized in the field because the Web browser plug-ins it required conflicted with the locked-down desktop that had been established by the managers of the information technology infrastructure at each site. (If this scenario sounds familiar, it is because it is more common than you think!)

ANECDOTAL RECORD FORM

DATE: July 23 PLACE: Production Site 3 ____

PROJECT: Home Safety CD-ROM NAME OF OBSERVER: Lucy Schweitzer

Description of the incident: *The fire scenes for the "Home Fire Safety" module were shot today. During lunch, I sat with the fire marshal who is serving as the content expert during the video production. He told me several horrible stories about recent home fires in this city where many lives had been lost despite the presence of smoke detectors in the homes that were burnt. It turns out that the fire department's research indicates that 43% of the homes with fire and smoke detectors have dead batteries or other malfunctions. He said thousands of people go to sleep in this city every night thinking they are protected when they are not.*

Interpretation: The *fire marshal's stories horrified and shocked me, (I certainly plan to check my smoke detectors tonight!) It might help motivate our team on this project to have the fire marshal speak to the whole team at the next project meeting.*

Figure 4.22. Sample anecdotal record form.

Yet another source of tools for project documentation are sophisticated project management software packages such as Microsoft Project. These programs integrate various project planning and tracking tools (e.g., PERT and GANTT charts) with resource analysis features and timelines. Our experience shows that an initial investment in learning how to use these complex programs can pay-off in the long run as you endeavor to document the ups-and-downs of a major development project or a large scale implementation effort.

Summary

This chapter has introduced you to the process of planning and managing evaluations of interactive learning systems. Obviously, you can't be expected to become expert in these processes instantly. Substantial experience is required to refine your knowledge and skills in these areas. Much of the expertise required for planning and managing evaluations involves negotiation skills. It is beyond the scope of this book to provide you with an introduction to the art of negotiation, but most libraries and bookstores contain numerous volumes on the process of negotiating. It might be worth your while to read one or two of these books or perhaps even attend a workshop on negotiating skills when one is provided in your area. Evaluation inevitably involves clashes of values and goals. Negotiation skills are essential for successful evaluators.

This chapter has also introduced some rudimentary procedures and tools for setting up a documentation system for your development or implementation project. Any information you collect for documentation purposes is also likely to be useful in fulfilling some of the other functions of evaluations. The next chapter is focused on "Review," the first of the six major functions we have identified in our model.

References

Baker, E. L., Herman, J. L., & Gearhart, M. (1996). Does technology work in schools? Why evaluation cannot tell the full story. In C. Fisher, D. C. Dwyer, & K. Yocam (Eds.), *Education and technology: Reflections on computing in classrooms* (pp. 185-202). San Francisco: Jossey-Bass.

Bransford, J. D., Sherwood, R. D., Hasselbring, T. S., Kinzer, C. K., & Williams, S. M. (1990). Anchored instruction: Why we need it and how technology can help. In D. Nix & R. Spiro (Eds.), *Cognition, education, and multimedia: Exploring ideas in high technology* (pp. 115-141). Hillsdale, NJ: Lawrence Erlbaum Associates.

Brown, J. S., Collins, A., & Duguid, P. (1989). Situated cognition and the culture of learning. *Educational Researcher*, *18*(1), 32-41.

Cognition and Technology Group at Vanderbilt. (1992). The Jasper experiment: An exploration of issues in learning and instructional design. *Educational Technology Research and Development*, *40*(1), 65-80.

Greer, M. (1991). Organizing and managing the ID process. In L. J. Briggs, K. L. Gustafson, & M. H. Tillman (Eds.), *Instructional design: Principles and applications* (pp. 315-344). Englewood Cliffs, NJ: Educational Technology Publications.

Greer, M. (1992). *ID project management: Tools and techniques for instructional designers and developers.* Englewood Cliffs, NJ: Educational Technology Publications.

Greer, M. (1996). *Project manager's partner: A step-by-step guide to project management.* Amherst, MA: Human Resources Development Press.

Greer, M. (1997). *Project management for workgroups: Facilitator's guide for the project manager's partner.* Amherst, MA: Human Resources Development Press.

Mark, M. M., & Shotland, R. L. (Ed.). (1987). *Multiple methods in program evaluation.* San Francisco: Jossey-Bass.

Patton, M. Q. (1997). *Utilization-focused evaluation: The new century text* (3rd ed.). Thousand Oaks, CA: Sage.

Perkins, R. (2001). Remote usability evaluation over the Internet. In R. J. Branaghan (Ed.), *Design for people: Essays on usability* (pp. 153-162). Chicago: Usability Professionals' Association.

Rosenberg, M. J. (2000). *E-learning: Strategies for delivering knowledge in the digital age*. New York: McGraw-Hill.

Senge, P. M. (1990). *The fifth discipline: The art & practice of the learning organization*. New York: Doubleday.

CHAPTER
5

Reviewing a Project Concept

Objectives

After reading Chapter Five, you should be able to:

- identify methods for evaluating development project concepts;
- describe key questions to ask at the early stages of a development project;
- utilize procedures for review; and
- select alternative ways of presenting the results of review activities.

Why should you conduct review as an evaluation function?

The overall purpose of review as an evaluation function is to provide information to guide decisions about whether the original conceptualization for an interactive learning system has merit and is feasible given inevitable constraints on time and money. The development of an interactive learning system is not a project that should be taken on without careful consideration of the market for the program, how it will be distributed, what people are willing to pay for it, and how the program will be supported. The history of the development of interactive learning systems, from the earliest days of mainframe computers to today's cutting-edge e-learning systems accessible around the globe via the Web, is marked by relatively few products that have been market successes. For every commercially viable product, such as The Learning Company's *Where in the World Is Carmen Sandiego?*, there are scores, if not hundreds, of failed products.

As illustrated in Figure 5.1, several different types of decisions must be made when the development of a new interactive learning system is first being considered, each of which is tied to one or more specific questions that can be addressed by review activities.

Decisions	Example Questions
Should a design and development project be initiated?	What is the potential market for the system? What are the competing products? How have delivery options evolved?
Should funding for a design and development project be awarded?	What will it cost to produce the program? What are users willing to pay for such a program? What level of profit is required?
Should a project be developed in-house or outsourced?	What are the design and development capabilities in-house? What will outside developers charge to develop the interactive system?
What features should the new program have?	What are the features of competing products? What features are required for the potential users to learn the specific knowledge, skills, and attitudes that the program will address?

Figure 5.1. Typical decisions and questions addressed by review.

Obscure beginnings

Often the source of many interactive learning projects is shrouded in mystery or at least hard to pinpoint. Whether a development project arose from discussions at a corporate team meeting, the report of a critical incident, the reflection of an experienced instructor who happens to mention that students always have problems learning about topic X, or even the whim of an educational administrator just back from a technology conference, the birth of a project concept initiates a process which has many points of review aimed at the basic question, "Is this project worth doing?" At first, the project concept may be very sketchy and the idea largely untested, but it is from such obscure beginnings that successful projects have been developed. Although there is no substitute for creativity, the success of information collection during the early review phase of a nascent project will suggest the best directions for the project and often reduce the time spent on wasteful activities that do not support the project's ultimate goals.

Starting points

> ... Teaching is a rhetorical activity: it is mediated learning, allowing students to acquire knowledge of someone else's way of experiencing the world. (Laurillard, 1993, p. 29)

Diana Laurillard, from the Open University in the UK, has presented a framework for examining academic learning by describing a model that focuses upon how the student comes to know about the world and how it is described. From her extensive experience with mediated learning in distance education, Laurillard has generated a view that emphasizes the role of the instructor (or instructional designer) in creating a view of the world and introducing the language which is used to describe it. This is an important starting point for any interactive learning system, as it focuses on the very task the designer of an interactive learning system desires to achieve. At the end of the project, there will be a particular representation of ideas and phenomena which are the substance of the interactive learning system. The project designer must also make decisions about the different ways the ideas are described, represented, and manipulated. It is this last attribute, manipulation, which is unique to the interactive experience in that users can undertake tasks with interactive materials in distinctly different ways from traditional textbooks or linear media.

As noted above, the idea for a new project may come from many sources. First, the idea may originate with someone who has extensive professional experience. For example, a statistics professor may identify areas that students have perennial problems in grasping, such as understanding the type of measurement scale that is being used. An interactive system that will represent these measurement principles in new ways may be extremely useful in enhancing student learning.

Alternatively, a project such as the development of a software package which allows students to undertake complex tasks (e.g., brainstorming) might begin with a sudden insight into a link between previously disparate elements. An interactive program may be produced to allow people to reorganize the ideas flowing from a brainstorming session into concept maps. This project germination might be driven by a link between a knowledge of software engineering and a programmer being introduced to a new graphical way of visual thinking.

Or, a new project may be simply a logical extension of a set of previously successful products or programs. For example, a publisher could decide to create an interactive Web site based upon a successful textbook series. The extension to the Web may provide a useful way of allowing students alternative ways of manipulating and accessing the information in the books. Indeed, this format could enable different learning strategies than afforded by the printed versions. Of course, the primary motivation for the publisher is the goal of selling more textbooks.

Each of these project ideas is founded upon the belief that the resulting interactive learning system will be useful to its intended audience and could even be a marketable product. So how should these initial project concepts be evaluated? One starting point would be to confirm that such a development would be a novel one or at least competitive with other approaches. Thus, comparing the project or product concept with other similar products is an obvious first step.

A number of years ago, one of us came up with a project concept aimed at developing software to help students generate alternative ways of looking at careers and career choices. In this project, we started the review process by looking at other software that was being sold in the same area. As we examined the software, we looked carefully at the approaches taken by the designers to present ideas and how users were (or were not) allowed to manipulate elements of the programs. After reviewing existing software, we determined that most of the current software focused on a prescriptive approach, i.e., the student took a test and then the software suggested an occupational choice or choices. As a result of this review, we concluded that our software should enable a more exploratory approach to the task of finding a career. We wanted students to discover the impact of actually manipulating the variables involved in career decisions so that they could see how each contributed to the final choice. With this approach, students would be able to respond to a series of preference questions to generate their own unique preference profile. Then, they could modify the profile and see how the changes they made affected the final suggested outcomes. Using these ideas, we wrote a brief project concept statement. The project concept statement was adopted by the project management team on the basis of this inherent difference between the design of our proposed software and the existing products. The generation of this alternative approach to the task of career advice was considered the main purpose in this project, and the element which would make it unique and potentially useful to the target school population.

Providing evidence to evaluate the concept

Three typical starting points for interactive design projects were outlined above: (1) detecting learning problems, (2) combining new ideas, and (3) building new products within an established area. These are just examples, and it should be clear that interactive projects get started in many diverse ways. In any case, each of the starting points described above will require different types of review evidence to assess their likelihood of being turned into successful, complete projects.

Project concepts based upon learning problems

If project conceptualization originates from learning problems that have been detected, then the advice provided by Laurillard (1993) neatly summarizes the starting points for many interactive learning activities. She begins with two known sources of learning difficulties, alternative conceptions and difficulties in generating and interpreting representational forms. She then suggests that developers address a series of questions:

> 1. What technical terms have everyday meanings that could lead to their misinterpretation?
>
> 2. What kinds of naïve conceptions might be prevalent in this topic?
>
> 3. In what ways might the internal logical structure of the main concept be distorted?
>
> 4. Which forms of representation (linguistic, notational, diagrammatic, graphical, symbolic, iconic, numeric) are difficult to handle? (p. 193)

Evidence that can be used in reviewing this type of design concept is the same kind of evidence that is often collected as part of Maintenance Evaluation (see Chapter Ten). In an academic setting, this data may be standard performance data on tests and examinations. Frequently missed items may indicate areas of difficulty for students, or they may be poor test items. Other data may include the number of times a particular learning resource, e.g., a course Web page, is used. A decline in access rates would indicate that either the resource was no longer working, that it was no longer required as part of a course, or that students perceive it as irrelevant to their learning. The number of times students request assistance with a task may also indicate the need for an interactive product that would remedy a learning problem.

Thus, the main questions to ask in this type of situation are:

1) What is the nature of the learning problem?
2) What hard evidence can you show that the problem is authentic?
3) What misunderstandings between expected and actual student learning would explain the nature of the problem?

During the review stage of a project concept, it is unlikely that you will be able to collect complete information about the nature of the learning problem. Such insight may not be available until a thorough needs assessment is done (see Chapter Six). What is required at this phase is a sensitivity to the context and an informed understanding of current developments and trends with respect to learning in the area of focus. For example, in science education today, it is widely recognized that students often fail to construct robust mental models of fundamental scientific principles such as force and acceleration. This gap has led some to propose the development of e-learning courseware that would enable students to challenge their naïve theories of these phenomena and contrast them with real-world data. A complete needs assessment would help to reveal the full nature of students' misconceptions. Decisions and recommendations based upon review data should be made with the understanding that there is always a margin of error.

In education contexts, projects are usually driven by learning problems, whereas in the training world, projects are more likely to be driven by performance problems. Slumping sales or increased job-related accident rates are two examples of performance gaps that may lead managers to conclude that the development of a new interactive training system should be supported. The main questions to ask in this type of situation are:

1) What is the nature of the performance gap?
2) What hard evidence can you find that the performance gap is authentic?
3) What are alternative explanations for the difference between expected and actual performance?

Interviewing employees and their supervisors may reveal that the causes of the performance problems will not be remedied by interactive training. For example, slumping sales may stem from the fact that a competitor has released a better and less expensive product. Or the sales commissions for the sales personnel may have been reduced. Industrial accidents may stem from low morale in the wake of an impending plant closure. The assumption that a performance problem warrants a new training program is one that should be examined closely during the review phase. As Rosenberg (2000) points out, training is the "default" approach to performance problems, but it is not always the best solution. Careful review of an e-learning project concept will avoid the expensive development of training that no one needs.

Project concepts based upon new ideas

If the project represents the combination of new ideas, then exposing the concept to a number of experts in the knowledge domain may be appropriate. For example, suppose you want to develop a new concept mapping tool to assist users with limited confidence to generate new ideas and build alternative representations of them. In evaluating the potential of this project, you could describe a number of different ways of generating and representing ideas so that these ways can be reviewed by a group of creativity experts.

Questions to ask the experts might be:

1) Has anything like the proposed software been developed before?
2) Does the proposed product follow established practices or current theories for how brainstorming should be undertaken?
3) What would you expect people to pay for this type of software?

The experts may tell you that there is software already available that does what you have proposed. On the other hand, they may find the idea so compelling that they want to become involved in its development. One way the data from a project review might be collated is in the form of a matrix in which a comparison of options is made for a series of attributes. Figure 5.2 presents an example of a matrix charting the attributes of existing and proposed products under comparison.

Attribute	**Instance**		
	Product A - Existing	Product B - Existing	Product C - Proposed
Cost	Low	High	Medium
Features	15	23	18
Complexity	Low	Low	Medium
Marketshare	40%	20%	N/A

Figure. 5.2. Matrix to chart comparative attributes.

Project concepts based upon new products in established areas

The third type of project concept stems from the desire to develop an interactive version of a static medium. Suppose you want to develop interactive versions of popular health or diet books. The publishers would know about previous book sales, but they might not be able to tell you anything about the size of the market for interactive options in this area. Catalogs and Web resources should be consulted to determine what products are currently offered in this area. If other interactive learning products exist, they should be reviewed to determine if they use a less than optimal learning strategy. It is also important to keep in mind that with interactive learning systems, there are competing delivery options.

— **WEB LINK** —
A source to find information about interactive training products in the training world is: http://www.trainingsupersite.com/

Imagine that you want to develop a CD-ROM version of a best-selling book called "Eat Your Way to Good Health." If you only reviewed competing CD-ROMs, you would miss interactive products that are available via other delivery modes, such as the Web or DVD.

In this type of situation, we might ask questions such as:

1) What are the competing products?
2) Do they cover the same knowledge domain?
3) Do they employ the same learning strategies?
4) Is this particular delivery technology the most appropriate for the potential audience?

– **WEB LINK** –
A source for information about the e-learning world in general is: http://www.elearningmag.com/

The answers to some of these questions are likely to be found in industry magazines or Web resources that project sales or report on unit sales for different types of interactive products. People with new project concepts will inevitably be tempted to answer questions about the viability of their product ideas superficially or with the "rose-colored" bias of wishing something to be the case. Thirty years ago, we were told that the answer to home use of video would be an "EVR recording system" (a system in which the video program was recorded onto 8mm film by a commercial provider and replayed in the home through a scanner connected to a television set). This EVR system would have met anti-piracy and quality reproduction requirements, but nowadays, no one has even heard of such a technology. Indeed, it was a great solution until someone invented the VCR and the videotape cassette. And even VCRs have had a complicated evolution. Consider the demise of the Sony Beta format videotape recorders in the home market. Even though the system was better technically, it never overcame the marketing and penetrating competition of the VHS recording system.

What is an interactive learning project seeking to do?

Most interactive learning systems are intended to achieve some learning outcomes, and so as part of a review for a new project, you should consider how users will be able to demonstrate that they have achieved the intended learning outcomes. The assessment methodology should match the intended outcomes. This may seem too obvious to mention, but we have observed that many projects are seemingly conceived without a clue about how or whether outcomes might be assessed.

In addition, if the resultant project is supposed to be interactive, then it is extremely important that the review process also enable the interactivity claim to be validated. Interactivity has many meanings within the context of interactive learning systems, ranging from simple "page-turning" to high-fidelity simulations (Sims, 2000). You can address the interactivity issue in the early part of the design process by employing a three-level approach (see Figure 5.3).

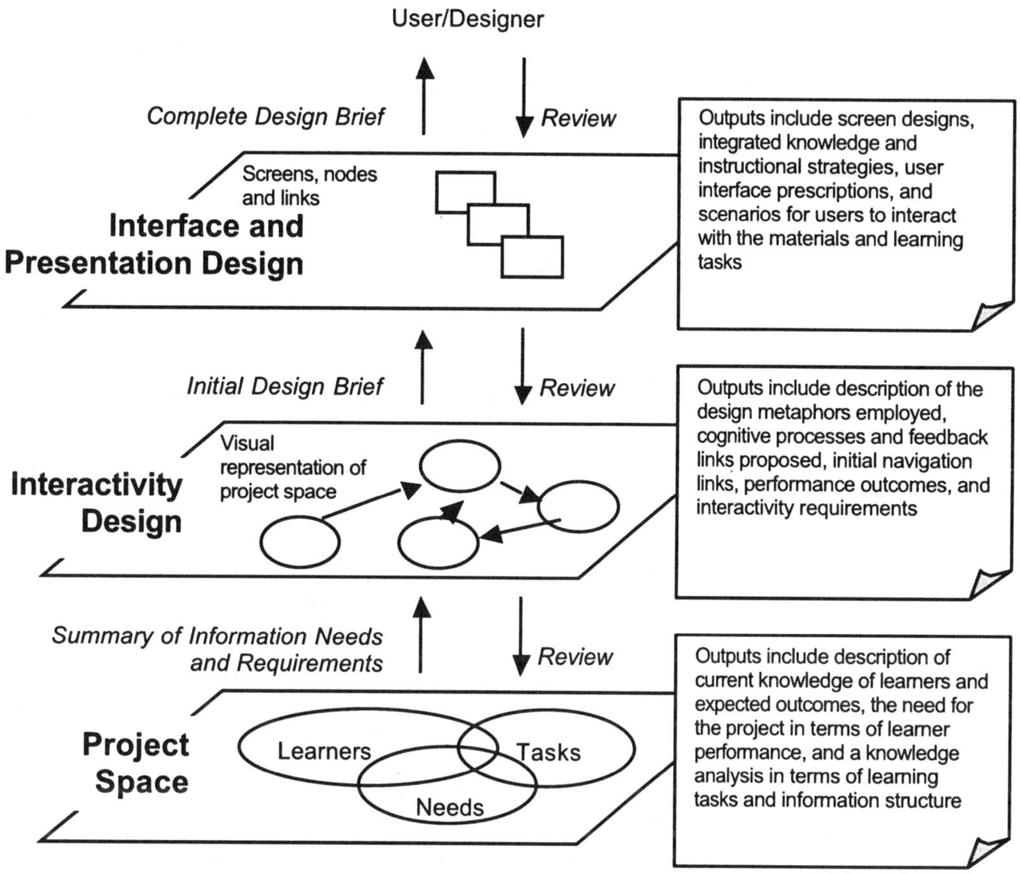

Figure 5.3. An iterative model of the early stages of design for interactive learning systems (adapted from Hedberg *et al.*, 1994).

The model in Figure 5.3 addresses a set of three concerns, which should be addressed in an iterative manner:

1) What knowledge domain is the project trying to address, with what audience, and to what end (Project Space Definition)?
2) What instructional strategy is being used (Interactivity Design)?
3) How is the underlying knowledge domain represented to the user, and how can the user manipulate that domain using the chosen strategy (Interface and Presentation Design)?

The model in Figure 5.3 is presented at this point because it is important to identify the stage of development of the project before you begin your review. If you are called upon to provide advice at the lowest level, the types of data you can obtain will either be historical or based on sketchy prototype designs. As the project design becomes clearer and other layers further up the diagram are described more precisely through design briefs, then your review can be focused more tightly. On the other hand, the later the review starts, the less likely the design will be informed by its results.

At the first level review, you are seeking to answer three questions:

1) What learning task is the project trying to accomplish, and in which knowledge domain?

2) For whom is it intended?

3) Why is it being attempted at all or what drives this project?

Essentially, your answers to these questions will define the project's conceptual space. The review results will support some approaches to the initial design and debunk others. We have suggested a range of information sources above (e.g., consulting experts or reviewing competitive projects), but the actual data sources you use will be unique to the context of the project.

For example, if you were thinking about producing interactive courseware to help middle school students develop robust mental models of scientific phenomena, it would be wise to interview middle school science teachers to determine the degree to which they focus on such higher order learning outcomes in their teaching. The recommendation to "build it and they will come" sounds appealing, but many interactive development projects have floundered on this assumption. Estimating the market for new products is always difficult, and you may need to hire special consultants in this area. Or you may wish to take a business course that focuses on market-risk analysis for new products.

Presenting the results of review activities

It is always possible to present review results and make recommendations in traditional text formats. However, we recommend that you consider, especially in the early review stages, a range of other options for presenting results. Alternative methods might enable the development team and management group to see ideas in a different light or to perceive unexpected relationships between ideas. In this section, we want to encourage you to go beyond checklists or textual descriptions to find alternative ways of presenting ideas, since traditional methods often fail to show how ideas interrelate or which ideas are more important than others within the knowledge domain of the project.

One approach to collecting and representing project ideas to others is through the use of visual mapping techniques. It is possible to collect massive amounts of data through brainstorming or surveys, but unless you represent the data using some of the following visualization techniques, you will only have ideas that are not linked to each other.

Summarizing ideas with a concept map

Concept mapping (Novak, 1981, 1998; Van Patten, Chao, & Reigeluth, 1986) is a useful strategy for sorting out initial concepts. It allows you to combine elements into meaningful statements or propositions. Links then enable you to begin to see the relationships between concepts and build on the conceptual framework. A concept map (see Figure 5.4) is a two-dimensional diagram representing the conceptual structure of subject matter.

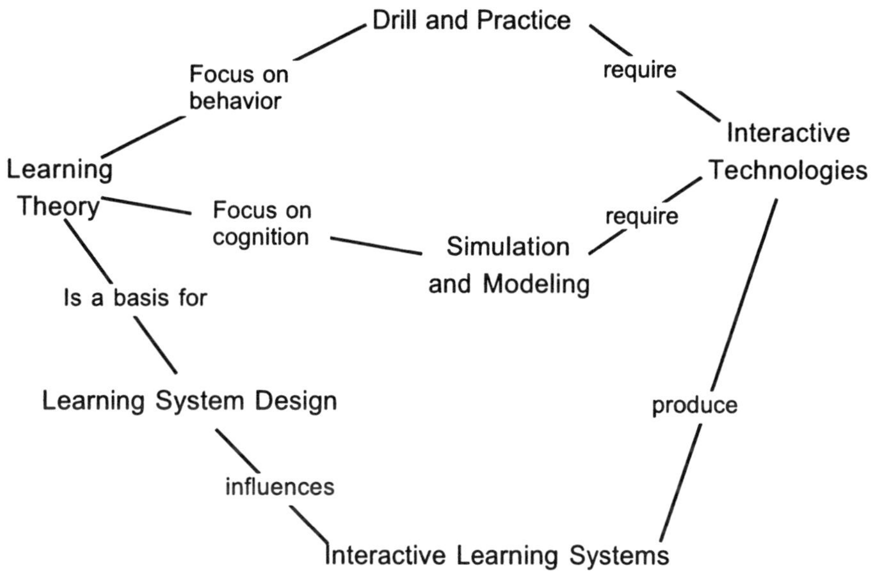

Figure 5.4. Concept map of a knowledge domain.

To construct a concept map:

1) Identify the concepts and principles to be included in the application. A good beginning technique is to write each concept on a small Post-it note that can be posted to a large sheet of paper or a whiteboard for easy manipulation.
2) Arrange the content elements in a hierarchical order from general to detailed, top to bottom (or bottom to top). The most general, most inclusive concepts are placed at the top (or bottom) and the more specific concepts in two or more "levels" below (or above) them.
3) Draw a line between each two related elements to show the linkage, and write on it the proposition that makes the link. In the ex-

ample in Figure 5.4, the concepts "simulation and modeling" and "interactive technologies" are linked by the word "require" to form the proposition "simulation and modeling require interactive technologies."

Joseph Novak (1981) identified three criteria of effective concept maps:

1) Does the map show a good hierarchy? There is rarely a "best" hierarchy, but you should consider whether the concepts and propositions shown represent an acceptable order in terms of moving from a more general, more inclusive concept to a less general, less inclusive one as related to the particular study material.
2) Are the propositions shown valid and "correct"? Are all concepts "connected" into propositions?
3) Are there "cross-linkages" between map segments? Do directional arrows make sense within the context of the knowledge domain?

Consider the concept map in Figure 5.4. It is designed to illustrate how elements of a typical knowledge domain (in this case, interactive learning systems) might be interrelated. Is it adequate? How does it differ from a mere list of concepts related to the topic?

Showing interrelationships by networks

Another form of representing ideas is a network (see Figure 5.5), where you identify the important concepts or ideas and describe the interrelationships among these ideas in the form of a network diagram using nodes and links. The network diagram provides a visual, spatial organization of the information and helps you see an overall picture of the material. A network can be used as an advance organizer for the design of an interactive product. Networks can be examined by experts to determine whether they are incomplete or inaccurate. They can indicate the degree of comprehensiveness of planning as well as possible misconceptions that might be inherent in a project plan.

A network representation can provide a description of the knowledge domain that should inform the development of an interactive learning system. It also can demonstrate how the information might need to be accessed by users. One of the key elements of interactive learning systems is the idea that they can provide many paths into the same information structure. A network can indicate how information should be presented and re-presented as the nature of the question or search by the user changes.

Consider the network illustrated in Figure 5.5. It is a map that shows the various data sources in a CD-ROM entitled *Exploring the Nardoo* (1996). Note, in particular, the resources have been designed to be retrieved either by investigation at the problem level or through a comprehensive index of the materials located elsewhere in the package. Also note the positioning of the help structures, which are located so that they can be accessed at any point. The help focuses on supporting not only the finding of resources for the problem solution, but also on suggesting a process through which the problem might be solved. This synchronization of content, function, and cognitive process becomes very important in interactive learning systems. It is clear in Figure 5.5 that the focus of the project is the embedded problems; the network emphasizes this perspective.

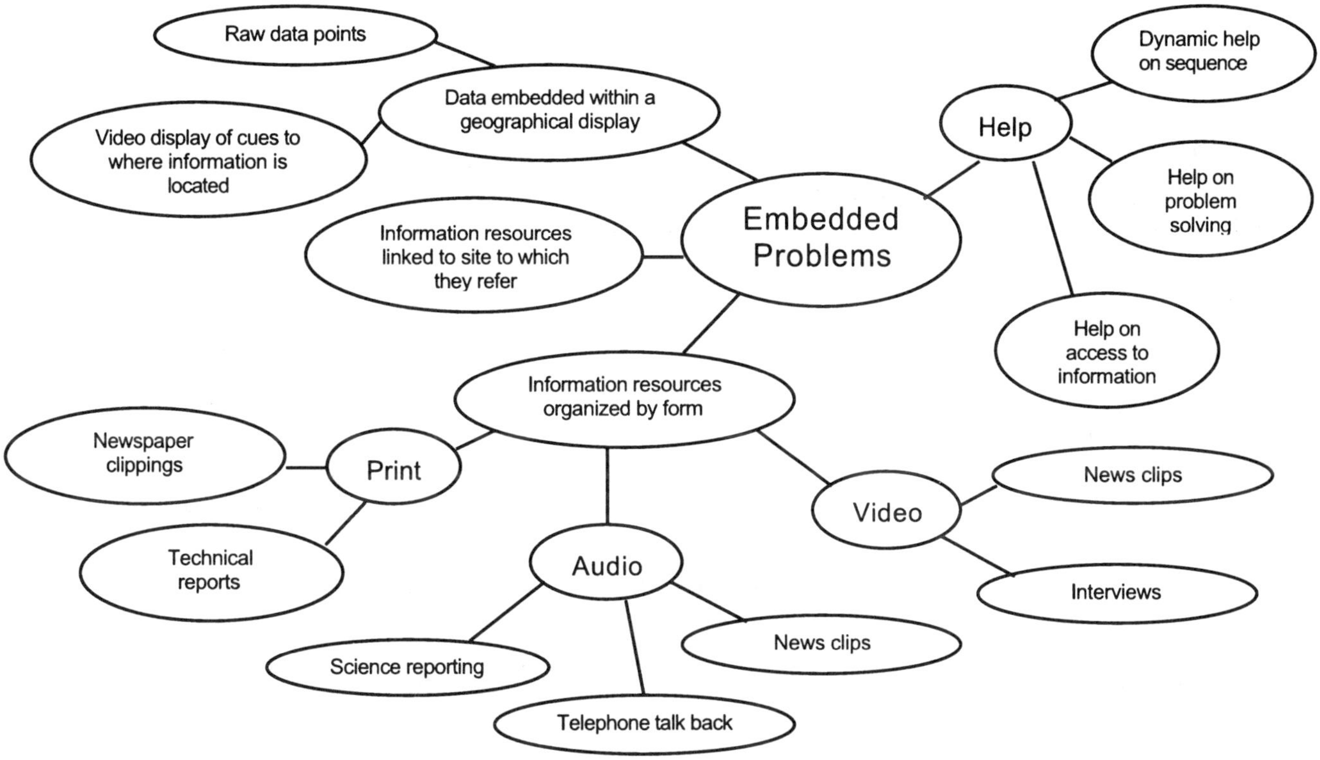

Figure 5.5. Network diagram of elements within a multimedia CD-ROM.

Creating areas of mutual interest by mind maps

Another form of representing initial ideas is a mind map (see Figure 5.6) in which a central organizing idea is broken into smaller ideas and each of the contributing ideas are linked by writing a description along the link lines. Mind maps are somewhat easier to draw for some people than more spatially-related concept maps or network diagrams.

— WEB LINK —
Several companies market software to assist in the production of visualization techniques such as concept maps: www.conceptsystems.com, www.coco.co.uk, or www.mindjet.com

In the example illustrated in Figure 5.6, we have represented the concepts that should be considered when designing an interface for an interactive educational product. This type of mind map also indicates groupings that might be discussed meaningfully together. In our design work, we have found that this type of visualization can inspire early design concepts for navigation and screen design.

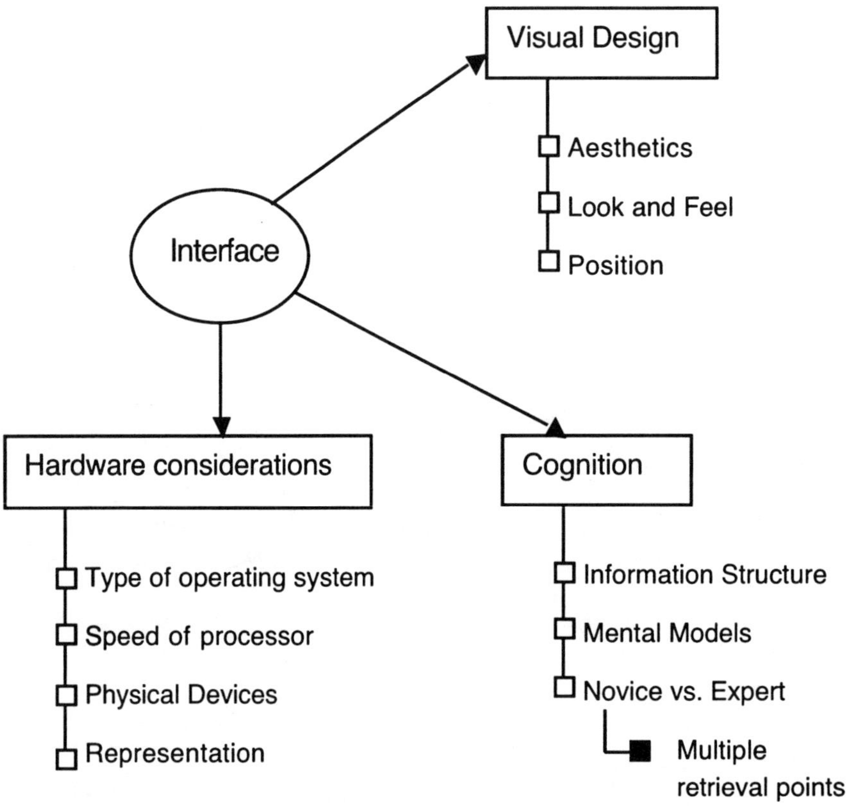

Figure 5.6. Mind map of issues addressed when designing an educational interface.

— WEB LINK —
A popular software tool for developing concept maps and related representations is Inspiration. More information can be found at: www.inspiration.com

Concept maps, network diagrams, and mind maps are not end products in themselves. Instead, they are valuable tools for use in planning a project, and allowing others to review the initial conceptualization of a new interactive learning system. Creating maps and diagrams is not easy or automatic, and most people will require some practice before they become adept at using these and other visualization techniques. However, these types of visualization techniques are used increasingly in business and education (Novak, 1998), and the well-skilled evaluator should develop some expertise with them.

Other important organizing influences

There are three other theoretical and practical issues that are worth considering during the review stage for a new interactive learning system. These are:

1) Expert versus Novice Perspectives
2) Information Processing
3) Usability

Developing expert versus novice perspectives

When conceptualizing the design of a new interactive learning system, attention should be paid to the different cognitive characteristics of experts and novices within particular performance domains. In planning for an interactive product, it is important to elicit information regarding how experts and novices differ in the content component of what they know and in the set of processes they use for performing a sequence of cognitive actions on the content (Chi, Glaser, & Rees, 1982). If an interactive learning system is designed solely from an expert perspective, the system is unlikely to provide sufficient "scaffolding" (Hogan & Pressley, 1997) and cognitive support required to help novices develop more expertise.

The expert knows more domain-specific concepts than the novice, and these concepts appear to be more differentiated and interrelated, with each of the expert's concepts closely connected in long-term memory with many other concepts. Hence encoding, storage, and retrieval are facilitated. In addition, the expert is more likely than the novice to use cognitive strategies such as planning and analysis before processing information. This simplifies the processing procedure as the expert calls to mind appropriate templates for cognitive action from a rich "bank" of stored experiences and memories. In other words, the expert's response can be more "automatic," unconscious, and effortless (Shuell, 1990; Sweller, 1993). The differences in processing between experts and novices require that multiple starting points and access/retrieval strategies be devised into an interface for interactive learning systems.

Information processing

– WEB LINK –
Information about John Anderson's work is at: http://act.psy.cmu.edu/

As a way of evaluating the proposed structures of an interactive learning project, look carefully at how information processing is supposed to occur. Examine the extent to which information processing tasks are integral to the learning outcome. John Anderson of Carnegie Mellon University has proposed an Adaptive Control of Thought (ACT) system (Anderson 1982, 1983, 1990; Lohman, 1989) to support interactive learning. Anderson claims that the acquisition of new knowledge is related to three processes: the expansion of *declarative knowledge,* the development of *procedural knowledge,* and the transaction between the two.

Declarative knowledge is our knowledge about things. This knowledge is hypothesized to be structured as an interrelated *network* of facts that exist as propositions. In other words, we don't know 'Blue Green Algae Bloom' as a static concept, but rather we know about the concept 'Blue Green Algae Bloom' because of its relationship to a number of other concepts such as scientific theories about ecology, how algae blooms can be measured, algorithms for modeling them, and so on. Any one concept is networked with any number of other concepts, and it is this networking that ultimately gives the concept meaning and enables us to remember it. The richness of the networking ensures that particular concepts are more memorable and can be more easily retrieved from long-term memory. In essence, Anderson is proposing a method for representing what cognitive psychologists have termed a *schema.* A schema for the concept 'Blue Green Algae Bloom' illustrating declarative knowledge is presented in Figure 5.7.

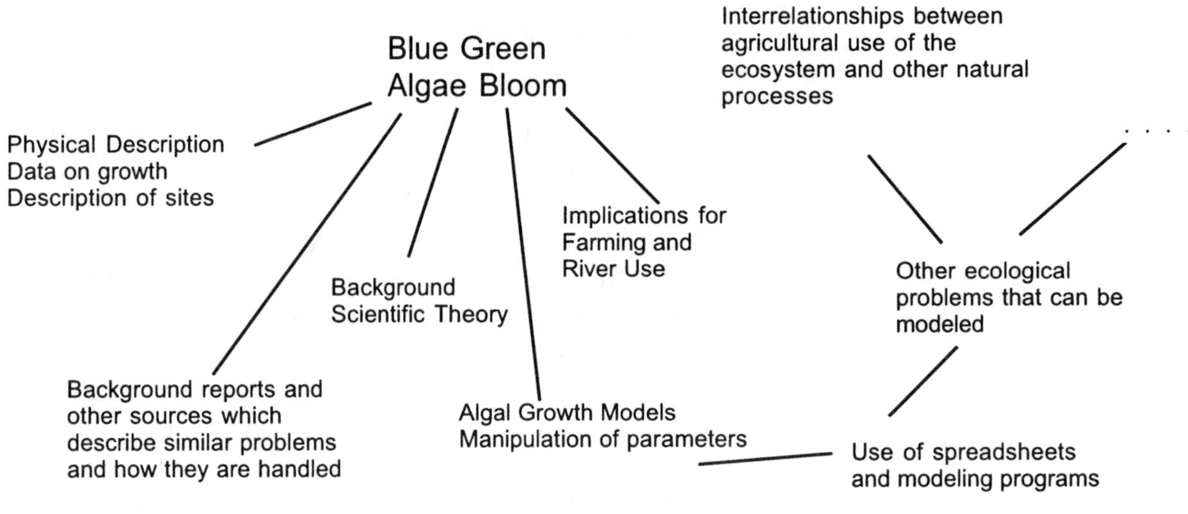

Figure 5.7. Anderson's ACT schema for a Blue-Green Algae Bloom problem.

Procedural knowledge is knowing how to perform various cognitive activities, such as how to calculate the size of an algae bloom using a formula. In this case, there is a transaction between the declarative knowledge and the actions performed upon it (procedural knowledge). In Anderson's conception, when encountering new information, the learner seeks to place it in some relationship with existing propositions and ideas. Different nodes in the network may have different strengths that reflect, among other things, the degree of practice associated with the node. New knowledge links will be stronger or weaker depending upon where and how easily they are placed in the schema and how the new knowledge is used in the course of working through problems or tasks that are presented with an interactive learning system. The declarative knowledge is compiled into higher-order procedures (called productions) that apply the knowledge to solve problems. These productions are in the format "if a certain condition holds, then perform a certain action." When reviewing interactive project design concepts, the more successfully remembered links will be those that are well supported by logical relationships and that require the learner to construct ideas in some logical relationship.

As the user attempts tasks within an interactive learning system, the tasks are either supported or refuted by the package, and thus the learner's understanding of meaning is either confirmed or diminished. Confirmed "productions" are the learning and understandings of the relationships among concepts supported by the package. In any interactive learning system project review, the coherence of a plan for the presentation of declarative and procedural knowledge and its execution will be critical to the effective use of the technology. Clear expectations about the schemata involved and how they will be supported by the project will be an important basis for review.

Usability

The cognitive load demanded by the information processing related to learning should be within the capabilities of the learner. Cognitive load refers to the mental processing capacity for learning that someone has at any given moment. Cognitive load is affected by factors such as intelligence, interest, fatigue, anxiety, distractions, etc. For example, although some learners may be able learn while a television is on or a radio is playing, others will find that their concentration and cognitive load capacity are diminished by such environmental factors.

With respect to interactive learning systems, the capacity to process information is decreased if the user must devote too much mental processing to understanding the interface of the program. This relates to the concept of usability (Nielsen, 1993). According to Shneiderman (1987), the usability of any type of computer program is determined by a combination of five user-oriented characteristics: (1) ease of learning, (2) high speed of user task performance, (3) low user error rate, (4) subjective user satisfaction, and (5) user retention over time. Although usability testing (Nielsen, 1993) is normally employed as a formative evaluation process (see Chapter Seven), it can be conducted during the review stage, provided that simple mock-ups of screens and interactions can be created. The usability of Web-based interactive learning systems is especially challenging (Nielsen, 2000). In fact, usability is a moving target in light of the ever-increasing complexity of interactive products and the evolving technical skills of the general population.

Estimating project scope

Another big area of concern during review is the estimated size and scope of the project. Consider asking the following questions:

1) Is the project a simple application similar to those that you or others have created, or is it so novel that major investments of people, money, and time will be required for its development?
2) What is the most expedient approach to project development considering the intended scope and size?
3) Does the way in which the user will manipulate the concepts and ideas in an interactive learning system need to reflect the way a person would manipulate them in professional practice?

The first two questions are straightforward, but the answers can help avoid an uneconomical approach to project development. If the likely audience is small, ask yourself whether the product is really going to be worth the proposed time and investment of money and people. There are many answers to these questions, but understanding the audience and the context of use is critical to the amount of resources invested. To address the third question, consider the task of training automobile drivers. It is possible to create a series of multiple choice questions to test the knowledge domain which all drivers must know, and many states in the U.S. include such a test as an integral part of the process of issuing drivers' licenses. It is also possible to develop a test with authentic video representations of driving and simulated steering and pedals to test specific driving skills and response time. This second form of interaction is likely to be more valid in that you can measure a wider variety of variables, such as reaction time and complex control sequences in ways that the multiple choice questions would never allow. The latter will be much more costly to develop, and such a high-fidelity simulation approach must be carefully justified during the review process.

Alternatively, an interactive system may be designed to simply present a series of information items. This is not necessarily bad in itself, but such presentations do not always motivate learners to use them. Such a system may be enhanced if the user can do things via the technology which takes the experience beyond that of turning pages of a "book." A critical factor will be defining the tasks that users will be challenged to complete while engaged in the program. For example, an interactive learning system can provide multiple ways of searching for information, but searching is a means to an end rather than an end in itself. Searching should serve some task. Ideally, the task will be as authentic as possible and closely linked to the learner's interests.

Incorporating any given feature, such as searching, into an interactive learning system, will demand careful review of that feature's importance and the cost and effort required to produce it. Consider whether a program will allow users to search by media format or by a keyword that collects information irrespective of its form of media format. Students seeking information about the Titanic may wish to retrieve information about the ship's design, the latest film made about the tragedy, or pictures of film stars who might have appeared in the many films about that "night to remember." However, the more elaborate the search strategies that are enabled within the program, the more complicated and the more expensive the design and production process will be. Careful review should help you to determine the relative importance of such features.

In preparing a written review document, you will need to place the project idea in its appropriate context. Consider the outline illustrated in Figure 5.8 as the basis for your report.

Overview of the Project	Assessment of the idea
Technical Feasibility	Technical platform/hardware issues Product design
Project Management	Project plan Budget
Market Assessment	Specific markets Market size Pricing Competitors
Potential Marketing Organizations	Publishers and their specialties Software developers and distributors Commercial arrangements
Sources of Data	Experts Users Supervisors Web
Summary statements	Bottom line recommendations Go/No Go

Figure. 5.8. Outline for written review report.

Summary

As the first phase in the evaluation process, reviewing the project concept essentially involves trying to describe the ideas underlying a project and how the developers plan to execute the ideas. Review is not often included as a formal evaluation phase in existing evaluation models. It is more likely that you will be asked to "scope" out a project, which is essentially the same as conducting a review. The paramount question is: "Is this project worth doing by the means the designer or project originator is suggesting?"

Your overall goal in conducting a review is to decide whether the project should make it to the next phase of the instructional development and evaluation process, i.e., a full "Needs Assessment," which is the subject of the next chapter.

References

Anderson, J. R. (1982). The acquisition of cognitive skill. *Psychological Review, 89*, 369-406.

Anderson, J. R. (1983). *The architecture of cognition*. Cambridge, MA: Harvard University Press.

Anderson, J. R. (1990). *Cognitive psychology and its implications* (3rd ed.). New York: Freeman.

Chi, M. T. H., Glaser, R., & Rees, E. (1982). Expertise in problem-solving. In R. Sternberg (Ed.), *Advances in psychology of human intelligence* (Vol. 1). Hillsdale, NJ: Lawrence Erlbaum Associates.

Exploring the Nardoo. (1996) Canberra, Australia: Interactive Multimedia, Project Manager: Barry Harper, Instructional Design: Barry Harper, John Hedberg, Rob Wright, Grant Farr, and Christine Brown (CD-ROM based interactive multimedia package produced in collaboration with NSW Dept of Land and Water Conservation).

Hedberg, J. G., Harper, B. M., Brown, C., & Corderoy, R., (1994). Exploring user interfaces to improve learner outcomes. In K. Beatie, C McNaught, & S. Wills (Eds.), *Interactive multimedia in university education: Designing for change in teaching and learning* (pp. 15-29). Amsterdam: North Holland, Elsevier.

Hogan, K., & Pressley, M. (Eds.). (1997). *Scaffolding student learning: Instructional approaches and issues*. Cambridge, MA: Brookline Books.

Laurillard, D. (1993). *Rethinking university teaching: A framework for the effective use of educational technology*. London: Routledge.

Laurillard, D. (2002). *Rethinking university teaching: A conversational framework for the effective use of learning technologies* (2nd ed.). London: RoutledgeFalmer.

Lohman, D. F. (1989). Human intelligence: An introduction to advances in theory and research. *Review of Educational Research, 59*, 333-373.

Nielsen, J. (1993). *Usability engineering.* Boston: Academic Press.

Nielsen, J. (2000). *Designing Web usability: The practice of simplicity.* Indianapolis, IN: New Riders Publishing.

Novak, J. D. (1981). Effective science instruction: The achievement of shared meaning. *The Australian Science Teachers' Journal, 27*, 5-13.

Novak, J. D. (1998). *Learning, creating, and using knowledge: Concept maps as facilitative tools in schools and corporations.* Hillsdale, NJ: Lawrence Erlbaum Associates.

Rosenberg, M. J. (2000). *E-learning: Strategies for delivering knowledge in the digital age.* New York: McGraw-Hill.

Shneiderman, B. (1987). *Designing the user interface: Strategies for effective human-computer interaction.* Reading, MA: Addison-Wesley.

Shuell, T. J. (1990). Phases of meaningful learning. *Review of Educational Research, 60*, 531-547.

Sims, R. (2000). An interactive conundrum: Constructs of interactivity and learning theory. *Australian Journal of Educational Technology, 16*(1), 45-57.

Sweller, J. (1993). Some cognitive processes and their consequences for the organization and presentation of information. *Australian Journal of Psychology, 45*, 1-8.

Van Patten, J., Chao C-I., & Reigeluth, C. M. (1986). A review of strategies for sequencing and synthesizing instruction. *Review of Educational Research, 56*, 437-471.

CHAPTER 6

Conducting a Needs Assessment

Objectives

After reading Chapter Six, you should be able to:

- identify methods for collecting data which will provide insights into the need for an instructional product development project;
- describe the key issues which will be addressed in a needs assessment;
- identify the assumptions in common checklist approaches used in needs assessments; and
- identify effective ways of presenting the results of a needs assessment.

Why should you conduct a needs assessment?

The overall purpose of needs assessment is to provide information to guide decisions about aligning an interactive learning system with important needs of specific audiences. In the words of Allison Rossett (1995), one of the foremost experts on the subject, needs assessment seeks to:

> ...gather information to assist professionals in making data-driven and responsive recommendations about how to solve the problem or introduce the new technology. (p. 183)

As illustrated in Figure 6.1, different types of decisions must be made when you attempt to determine the needs to be addressed by an interactive learning system. Each need is tied to one or more specific questions that can be addressed by needs assessment activities. The failure to conduct an adequate needs assessment is one of the main reasons that so many instructional products fail to find a substantial market (Dick & Carey, 2001). "Build it and they will come" is a myth to which many fall prey.

Decisions	Example Questions
How can the objectives of this product be defined?	What needs should the product address? Which needs are critical? Which needs are optional?
How should an interactive product be marketed?	Who are the most likely users of this product? What are the characteristics of the potential users? Should the product be marketed to organizations, individuals, or both?
How should the product development be funded?	Does the product have a likelihood of making a profit? Does the product address needs so important that foundations or other agencies will fund its development?
How should the product be evaluated?	How can attainment of the objectives be measured? What assessment methods are already available? How can implementation of the product be monitored?

Figure 6.1. Typical decisions and questions in a needs assessment.

What is needed?

Assessing the need for an interactive learning system is both simple and complex. Experts such as Roger Kaufman (Kaufman, 2000; Kaufman & English, 1979) and Allison Rossett (1987, 1998) have given us general principles and practices that are useful in guiding the development of instrumentation for needs assessment. They have also provided assistance in clarifying the potential stakeholders who should be involved in the needs analysis process. We recommend that you consult these classic works on needs assessment and use the ideas in them as part of any formal approach to this task.

Formal needs assessments for large scale projects can take months, but developers of most interactive learning systems rarely have that kind of time. Therefore, we'll focus on "quick and dirty" approaches to needs assessment. The key questions in needs assessment are:

1) What unique or important goals and objectives are going to be addressed by the proposed product?

2) For whom is the product aimed and does the product concept match the target audience or market?

The sources of data include the usual suspects, such as reviewing existing records and conducting surveys, interviews, or focus groups. There are other standard procedures, such as using a checklist, that are often employed during a needs assessment. In this chapter, we suggest the types of questions you should ask about a proposed interactive learning system under conditions when it is necessary to have a prototype available for testing within a month. Traditional ISD models recommend spending much more time on needs assessment. Seemingly this is a good idea, but it is one that has led to the criticism of ISD as being too slow and even unrealistic (Gordon & Zemke, 2000; Piskurich, 2000). In our experience, needs assessment for interactive learning systems usually must be somewhat more expeditious than traditional ISD models suggest (Milano & Ullius, 1998; Sink, 2002).

Needs assessment is conducted to determine if a project is to be undertaken, what it should contain, and how it should "work." The results of a needs assessment should include a list of well-defined objectives as well as a high-level design document (Kruse & Keil, 2000). With an interactive learning system, the needs assessment will often be integrated with a continuous process of successive approximations of the eventual product. The rapid prototyping approach (Hamblen & Furman, 1999) to developing interactive learning systems, used in many contexts today, allows the development of a series of approximations which can be reviewed by the client or potential users. In this book, we would like to guide you toward a series of smaller scale needs assessments which continuously refine the product requirements and how those requirements are matched to user characteristics. In Chapter Seven (formative evaluation), aspects of user testing are more completely discussed.

Traditional approaches to needs assessment

The following summary, adapted from Rossett (1995), is a useful guide to a common approach to needs assessment:

Step One: Determine purposes based on initiators.

Projects often arise to solve identified skill deficiencies, the requirements for new skills with changes in methods or technologies, or through mandated requirements by legal bodies. The process thus requires you to distinguish between what is actually happening and what should be happening, and then to identify how to get to the latter state.

Step Two: Identify sources.

Clarifying what is and what should be requires consulting the best sources of reliable information. Where is the important information kept? Who are the stakeholders and what are the key sources to gain more complete insight into the problem? The issue of identifying the most relevant or important information is very context dependent. However, the person or agency who contracted with you for the design task in the first place is probably very aware of what should or might be included in a new interactive learning system. This is a logical place to start.

A key strategy is to obtain rankings of information from each person with whom you speak during a needs assessment, but at the same time, to remain aware of the competing pressures and demands on each stakeholder as well as his or her own interests and biases. Managers and workers have different perspectives on the needs addressed by training, and teachers and students often disagree on the relevance of various parts of a curriculum. All things being equal, the key needs should be identified and reinforced from different perspectives. Rossett (1987) has suggested six types of questions that should be asked as you sift through sources of information:

1. Ask questions which provide a general picture of the situation.
2. Ask questions which provide fine details on aspects of the problem.
3. Ask for evidence that the responses are not just hearsay, but that there are some data or observations to back it up.
4. Ask for feelings about the idea, proposed training, or likely success of any possible solutions.
5. Ask for suggestions about why the problem exists, or how it might best be solved.
6. Ask about the respondents' expertise or experience for use in judging the value of their responses to your questions. (p. 79)

Step Three: Select tools.

The most frequently used methods are interviews, observations, inspection of existing records, focus groups, and questionnaires. We recommend using a questionnaire as a last resort, as it requires time to prepare, it may not be welcome, and the response rate will almost certainly be lower than that of any other method. Frankly, most people hate getting questionnaires, and yet so many evaluators leap to this method without thinking. The proliferation of questionnaires being sent via e-mail today is especially burdensome. Think of the last time you received a questionnaire. Did you give it the attention the sender sought?

Step Four: Conduct the needs assessment in stages.

You cannot do everything for a needs assessment in one day, so create a plan which will enable you to build on the data as you go. Talking with key people and gradually building a picture of the critical issues are important aspects of the process. Don't be overly concerned with asking everyone the same set of questions. Needs assessment is not formal research! Instead, apply your wisdom and insight to identify the key issues which the proposed development project must address. However, do be sure that you confirm the major issues with each key stakeholder.

Step Five: Use findings for decision making.

If you are going to inform decision making about the project, you will not only need to ensure that the information is useful to the decision makers, but also that any recommendations you make are viable. This might seem self-evident, but some creative ideas may not be appropriate to the specific context in which you are working and therefore cannot be used. Your creative side may want to recommend giving every worker or student a new laptop and installing a wireless network, but the reality is that most interactive learning systems have to work on an installed base of older computers. If you make recommendations that take into account these feasibility issues, your report is more likely to be accepted, and you are more likely to be considered for other evaluation projects.

Traditional needs assessment approaches focus on what should be happening or being achieved (Optimals) and what is actually happening or being achieved (Actuals). The discrepancy is seen as the "need" for something to be done. Of course, in developing interactive learning systems, traditional analyses should often be applied, but we suggest that, in addition, it is important to address the subtleties. Often the rationale for interactive products is less than clear. For example, the impetus might be to develop a product that will be a best seller (Everyone will buy a CD-ROM about baby seals!) or to keep up with competitors (They have a Web site so we have to have one too!), rather than responding to real needs or to the difficulties of a group of learners. If you think you already have the idea for the next great interactive learning system, and therefore no needs assessment is necessary, we encourage you to go to a large office supply store to peruse the discount bins full of interactive products that were going to make a killing and ended up getting killed in the market. Needs assessment helps you and your clients be more realistic than perhaps you or they want to be.

Getting a good design approach to the content

One of the greatest problems we have noted in reviewing many innovative ideas is that the translation from concept into a working system is often limited and poorly conceived. As an initial starting point, consider the goal of teaching children about friendship. Suppose you were asked to design an interactive multimedia product for five-to-eight year-olds which seeks to address the following lessons:

- friends are important, and they can be fun to play with;
- being fair and sharing equally helps support a friendship; and
- having a good time depends on respecting other people's values.

> Stop! Before reading on, reflect on these outcomes and list the ideas that immediately come to mind. Capture these ideas on a piece of plain white paper, brainstorming ideas for design. Try it before reading the next paragraph.

Where could you start?

Obviously, if we started to develop a list of possible learning tasks and then showed the list to teachers who teach children of these ages, they might be able to rank the tasks and suggest missing elements. But you should have already realized that these objectives are not the type that can be addressed easily using a simple tutorial strategy. They cry out for some inventive environment in which a child might become immersed so that he or she would discover the relationships and concepts we are trying to develop. In this case, the process is more difficult than simply linking a set of learning tasks. So we might need to collect information which will give us an idea about the type of situations children of this age group find interesting, and the range of possible strategies which they will spontaneously generate to address the situations in which they find themselves. You'll probably want to interview practicing educators and parents, and you may even recruit a professional child psychologist to identify any relevant research. After collating the ideas, you'll need to rank and order them. Using these ideas, some quick prototypes might be produced and tested with a few students of the target age groups.

The generation of concepts and ideas in this type of situation might involve unusual instrumentation. For example, in one training needs assessment, one of us generated an instrument on which the respondents were asked to:

1) Use one piece of paper to jot down ideas as they come to you while you visualize a typical trainee and the problems you have seen in the workplace over the past year.

2) Group these concepts on another piece of paper, this time with a circle in the middle. Place what you consider to be the key concepts in the circle, and then around the outside, list the remainder.

3) Draw linking arrows between the topics until all the relationships are shown.

4) Place a sequential number against each topic to indicate what might be a preferred sequence.

This may seem like a lot of work and might appear a little complex, but at the end of the process, we had a list of key topics (organized as core and desirable or elective) along with a suggested linkage and sequence. A more traditional needs assessment might have involved the development of a large-scale survey that could have taken weeks, but yielded results no better than the ones we obtained through this much faster approach. The process can be extended to ask the respondents to review a previously prepared series of possible learning tasks, and then to add new tasks to their lists if they felt anything had been omitted. Using a technique of this type can produce ways of working with the data that traditional questionnaires don't permit.

Assessing the need for an interactive learning system

Assessing the need for interactive learning systems which are Web-based is an interesting challenge that more and more of us are facing these days. There are a number of issues that should be addressed in any initial briefing. Consider questions such as:

1) How will students access the informational aspects of the learning system?
2) How do you envision they will interact with the instructor and/or other students?
3) How will assessment work? Will tests be online? Or will the students submit their work for assessment through other means?

4) How will nurturing and feedback to the students occur? How will the progress of each student be monitored? How will problems that occur be addressed expeditiously and effectively?

Subsidiary questions might involve specifics pertaining to the discipline the students are studying:

1) What support systems will need to be integrated into the learning tasks?
2) Do students need some audio or visual support to help them understand specific concepts or principles?
3) Do students need some templates to help them organize their work or understand the expectations being placed upon them?
4) Are there specific student characteristics (e.g., language abilities) that the interactive learning system must accommodate?

The last question relates to a unique advantage of an online learning system. In working with students using a Web chat space, we found that the students who had difficulty in understanding English in the classroom were able to contribute to class discussions in the chat space. This technology enabled them to read and type their response without having to vocalize the words, and consequently they contributed to discussions, whereas they would have remained silent in a face-to-face class.

Above all, in this type of situation, you have to answer the question: Is there a requirement that, as part of the learning process, the learner must interact with content (e.g., manipulate online resources) in order to learn the underlying concepts or ideas or to develop specific skills? This is a simple question; however, the answer is difficult to obtain. Much instructional software has been condemned as "page turning." This book-based put-down reflects the inability of software designers to move beyond older forms of interaction or to take advantage of the unique features of interactive learning systems.

The "page turning" problem is persistent. Already in the short life of Web-based instructional materials, there is a well-justified concern for the relative lack of meaningful interaction with the resources available (Kearsley, 2000; Khan, 1997, 2001). Although many developers agree with Sugrue's (2000) statement that "the Web has become a universal metaenvironment for learning" (p. 133), what passes for education and training on the Web is predominantly made up of passive resources (e.g., text to read) or interactive drill-and-practice programs that could have been delivered 35 years ago with mainframe computers. Fortunately, the state-of-the-art of design has evolved in recent years to take advantage of the human preference for story or narrative.

Interactive narrative structures

— **WEB LINK** —
More information about the creation of *Myst* can be found at:
http://www.cyan.com/

One of the key elements of interactive learning is the structure and sequence of the narrative that is produced. One learner will experience a very different story than another. As a way of estimating the types of experiences possible, think about the type of story being told. Consider the models that interactive games software provide. An intriguing example is the classic exploration story of *Myst* (1993), where users are presented with a series of puzzles in a landscape of visual complexity and beauty. This particular piece of interactive software creates its own expectations and instruction in the story, which are pieced together as the user examines the artifacts and devices in the landscape.

An interesting subtlety of *Myst* is that the player is presented with a visual display in which, using the rules of mechanics, wheels are turned, and cogs move winches. Gradually, the player learns to manipulate the environment. With continuing exploration, the player can piece together the story as each element and interaction confirms or refutes the tacit assumptions made by the player. In this example, the player constructs the story as he or she progresses through the program. The use of feedback elements such as a cursor changing to indicate type of movement, or the graphic shifting to indicate an acceptable command, create an interpretation of this world and how it "works."

As new learning software is developed, the use of interactive narrative forms of interactions can make products more intriguing and can even foster a suspension of disbelief. This, in turn, will result in learners being actively engaged and even immersed in the tasks that the product presents. Therefore, one goal of a needs assessment is to identify an appropriate form of interactive treatment.

Whether a product is Web-based or an interactive CD-ROM or DVD, information will be presented and the user will interact with it in many different ways. However, in estimating the likely chances of success of a design and whether it will achieve a result which is more than digital "page-turning," the methods proposed for creating a compelling narrative should be assessed. In general, each option will present a situation in which the user will be required to make a choice. If you wish to take some lessons from the games developers in assessing your design concepts and how they might be implemented, we recommend considering the following five structures.

Hierarchy of choices

The most typical narrative format is the *hierarchy of choices*, from which there is a branch every time there is a decision point in the program.

Depending upon the structure, this may result very quickly in a huge multiplication of scenes or screens. Obviously, when developing an interactive structure, you must be concerned with costs and with the time required to create the interactive environment. Costs can become excessive if many difficult-to-produce screens are only seen by a small portion of the users. The hierarchy of choices format is most popular with information compendium designers. It does enable the user to access all the elements available from the top point down. However, if the hierarchy does not allow any lateral moves, it becomes a tedious drilling down to the final result. If this design is appropriate, screen elements can be reused to reduce the sheer number of individual screens that must be produced, but this will require having graphic artists and programmers experienced in multimedia production on your team.

Linear structure with tiger doors

Another design is the *linear structure with tiger doors* in which, if the correct choice is not made, something horrible happens to you. If you choose the other door, something even more horrible happens. (Alternatively, something good could happen with one door, and something even better with the other.) While it might be dressed up by clever graphics, this sequence is very similar to a tutorial with multiple choice decision points. Here, learner motivation can often be maintained by the accumulation of scores for correct choices. If you get more questions correct, you get more "lives" or gain points.

Linear sequence with doors

In the *linear sequence with doors* design, puzzles (tasks) are hidden behind each door that the user must solve (or complete) to continue on to new tasks. If you design an interactive experience which provides further elaboration or more tutorial work to support the path chosen, you are using this structure. While the choices are not seen as disastrous, as in the tiger door design, the validity of the experience is dependent upon the relatedness of the puzzles and tasks which flow from the choice. In some "edutainment" software, the choices and tasks are so random and/or irrelevant to the content that they add little to the learning outcomes. Anything you can do to increase the perceived relevance of the choices to the user will enhance this type of learning system design.

Parallel story structure

In the *parallel story structure* design, things happen in multiple spaces, and the participant switches from one into the other. This type of structure is fine for interactive television where the simulated world is working on many planes and the decision is simply choosing to "jump" between the different spaces in the world. All of the options are simply in reserve until called upon. Information spaces can use this approach if the resources located in different areas all contribute to the ongoing stories, although they may be parts of different stories at other times. Of course, the likelihood of misunderstanding increases if learners cannot discern to which story the information refers.

World of possibilities

— **WEB LINK** —
Information about Dr. Joe Henderson's award-winning medical simulations is at: http://iml.dartmouth.edu/

Yet another design is the *Virtual World* in which "real" things can be done, some of which lead to different outcomes. The story line is driven by the activities completed and choices made and not by any necessary sequence of events. This format is less appropriate if the precise learning outcome for a session with the product is difficult to define. However, if you are seeking to develop a package that creates immersion in a simulated world (e.g., a hospital ward or an airplane cockpit) and presents realistic challenges, then this form of narrative structure can be useful. Some of the best examples of interactive immersion learning programs have been created as medical simulations by Dr. Joe Henderson and his design team at the Interactive Media Lab at Dartmouth Medical School.

Each of these narrative structures is complex and requires significant time to produce the visual and authoring elements of the interactive learning experience. If we compare this list with the traditional structures from computer-based learning, you will notice some similarities but also some new deviations. Twenty years ago, when CAI developers talked about drill and practice programs, tutorials, simulations, and games, design conceptions and the learning narrative were driven by the limits of the available technology and how difficult it was to create the interactive experience. Today, all of these strategies are possible and more (Laurel, 1993), as learners can be presented with challenges appropriate to their level of understanding and their ability to solve problems.

Reporting needs assessments

We have presented some of the standard questions asked during this part of the design and development process. We have suggested that although the development of interactive learning systems may require a traditional approach to assessing needs, there are many other issues that should be included in the resulting documentation generated at this stage of a project. The two most important elements of any needs assessment report are the list of objectives the product will address and a high-level description of the design. Figure 6.2 provides a list of questions that should be answered in your needs assessment report.

As suggested by Lee and Owens (2001), a traditional needs analysis that lasts many months is a luxury few companies can afford in the fast-paced world of e-learning today. Too much investment in needs assessment can lead to analysis paralysis. On the other hand, too little needs assessment increases the risk of developing an interactive learning system for problems and audiences that really don't exist. Finding the proper balance is an ongoing challenge (Rossett, 1998).

What problem is the project seeking to solve?	What is the problem? Why is it happening? What data are there to indicate a problem exists?
What is the market niche the project is seeking to fill?	What is the discrepancy between Actuals and Optimals? How is the project planning to redress the differences?
What are the specific objectives of the proposed project?	What are the key learning objectives? How can attainment of the objectives be assessed?
What is the recommended design for the product in light of the objectives and characteristics of the target audience?	What type of product should be designed, e.g., tutorial or simulation? How can the user's interests be captured and maintained by the program? What is the feasibility of the proposed design given budgets and temporal constraints?
Is the design appropriate and consistent with the project scope?	What variations need to be made? Will the users understand the narrative? Will the users be able to manipulate the elements to achieve the outcomes? Can the solution be designed within the project resources? Will it be acceptable to key stakeholders?

Figure 6.2. Outline for a needs assessment report.

Assessing a project using a checklist

Although it is not possible to provide a complete checklist for needs assessment for any proposed interactive learning system, we have prepared a sample checklist that you can modify to assess a particular interactive program (see Figure 6.3). It may be comforting to employ a checklist in the belief that it will provide for the complete identification of all the issues which need to be considered when you evaluate a product or system. But complete reliance upon a checklist is not advised. They may also blind you to seeing only what is on the list and may even block you from perceiving other possibilities. With that in mind, review the checklist in Figure 6.3, which was designed to gauge the utility of educational software. Although the checks themselves provide valuable information, the comments that the rater adds may be more important, especially if they clarify issues that were not included in the checklist items. It would be a mistake to blindly apply this or any other checklist. We recommend that you read it over carefully, and using a separate piece of paper, note any potential issues that each item in the checklist might bring to light.

Checklist for Evaluating an E-Learning Program or Courseware

YOUR NAME ____________________ DATE ____________________

NAME OF PROGRAM EVALUATED ____________________________

TYPE OF COMPUTER USED ________________________________

TYPE OF PROGRAM (Tutorial, simulation, or drill and practice) ____

Area to be evaluated — Rating Scale

CONTENT	Good	Ade-quate	Poor	N/A	Com-ments
Objectives are clearly defined					
Prerequisite skills are clearly defined					
Content is presented clearly and logically					
Content is transferable and generalizable					
Vocabulary level is appropriate for the subject level and learner					
INSTRUCTIONAL DESIGN					
Learner controls the rate and sequence of instruction					
• can return to the previous screen					
• can return to the previous chapter					
• can choose sections					
• can exit at any point					
Program can be used independently of teacher					
Program minimizes typing					
Program accepts misspellings					
New material is presented in context and is related to previous material					
Summaries and reviews are provided					

Figure 6.3. Checklist example.

(Continued)

Area to be evaluated	Rating Scale				
INSTRUCTIONAL DESIGN	Good	Ade-quate	Poor	N/A	Com-ments
Program can be adjusted by teacher for local needs					
Graphics used are motivational					
Displays are clear & understandable					
Color is used appropriately					
Sound can be turned off if distracting					
Feedback					
• is useful					
• is not confusing					
• does not leave the learner unsure of what to do next					
Instruction is active rather than passive (it is not just a page-turner)					
Learner expectancies are established (learners know what is expected)					
The program has a consistent display rate (screens load quickly)					
RECORD-KEEPING MANAGEMENT					
Program keeps accurate records of learner response					
Program keeps ongoing learner records					
Program includes diagnostic or evaluative testing					
Program generates further assignments					
Program graphically illustrates learner progress					
Program provides statistical information on learner progress					
Program allows printout and screen display of records					

Figure 6.3. Checklist example (continued).

Anatomy of a checklist

The checklist in Figure 6.3 is obviously aimed at providing a structure for an expert review. No section is presented that will allow the reviewer to include data derived for target users. Of course, different users will provide very different results. For example, instructional designers and teachers often have different perspectives on what students need for learning. Many people, "blown away" by colorful, dynamic screen images, fail to perceive the instructional value, or lack thereof, of what is presented. When working with young children, we have found that they judge a colorful set of screens as more interesting than something that might be seen by experts as showing more taste and coherence. Novices may select bright, garish colors and not be fazed by the gaudiness of a program that would make an experienced graphic artist gag.

In Figure 6.4, we comment on each aspect of the checklist to illustrate what might be potential problems with its use. Any instrument similar to this one should be seen as a "work-in-progress" that can be reviewed and revised over time. Indeed, it may be desirable to develop a bank of checklist items from which different checklists can be developed for specific purposes.

CONTENT	**Commentary on the item**
Objectives are clearly defined	Many of the items in this checklist do not mesh easily with the checklist rating scales. In terms of learning software, when would non-specification of objectives really be not applicable?
Prerequisite skills are clearly defined	Often requisite skills are not specified, especially if the marketer of the product is trying to reach a wide audience. What are you going to recommend if the rating here is less than good?
Content is presented clearly and logically	Really the underlying question is: Can you understand the apparent structure of the knowledge domain and how it is represented to the user? Often in a random sequence structure, the logic of the sequence is determined by the user, and it is difficult to say that it is not appropriate from just a review.
Content is transferable and generalizable	This item assumes that all content is transferable and can be used in other situations. Clearly, some knowledge domains are highly specific.
Vocabulary level is appropriate for the subject level and learner	This item is fine, but a better question is probably to ask for a comment rather than a rating!

Figure 6.4. Checklist commentary. (Continued)

	Commentary on the item
INSTRUCTIONAL DESIGN	
Learner controls the rate and sequence of instruction	This is a two-edged sword, as sometimes this is in direct conflict with the objectives of the software.
• can return to the previous screen	What is the previous screen? Often in interactive packages the previous and next arrows do not make sense, as they might in a traditional linear sequenced program.
• can return to the previous chapter	This seems to assume that the whole structure is somewhat sequential and rather like working through a book.
• can select desired sections	Often learner control is seen as a positive value within software. Limiting control to menu selection is not challenging learners to control their own learning sequence.
• can exit at any point	Learners can escape from most programs, which probably says more about the intrinsic motivation than being an attribute of a good instructional package.
Program can be used independently of teacher	Again there are two values. Probably the underlying issue is: Can a teacher give some tasks to students and can they work without a teacher being present, or conversely, can a teacher modify or augment the package so that students can learn using it on tasks determined by the teacher?
Program minimizes typing	What about a package that teaches typing? Probably this question is more related to the development of the technology, and really it seeks to focus on the appropriate match between the task and how the users are expected to manipulate or contribute their response. It is easy to click and drag to compile elements together, and this should be possible rather than requiring learners to use codes and arrows keys to move objects.
Program accepts misspellings	Again, this is only a problem when clever forms of interaction are not chosen. Often correct spelling is required as part of the learning outcome.
New material is presented in context and is related to previous material	Interactive multimedia packages often use metaphor to provide a structure for introducing new concepts. Devices such as these will be more often the case than requiring the program to refer back or even simply provide some background help files.
Summaries and reviews are provided	Often these should be undertaken as part of the learning experience of the learner. Asking the learner to collect and annotate the learning experience will more often result in higher quality learning than by providing the same summary for every student.
Program can be adjusted by teacher for local needs	This is a difficult question as it depends upon the structure of the package and how it is intended to be used.
Graphics used are motivational	Graphics should be intrinsic to the learning task. If they are and are well employed, this question will or should be irrelevant.
Displays are clear and understandable	This should have been answered in the user testing of the product or system. If this has to be commented upon at this point in the product's life cycle, then it will probably mean the QA process is severely lacking.

(Continued)

Figure 6.4. Checklist commentary (continued).

	Commentary on the item
Color used is appropriate and motivational	Again, this is a relic of a former age when it was claimed that color might be distracting. Nowadays, color might be used cleverly to encode ideas or simply to make the product more attractive. What is more important is to ask, does the graphic style match the content and the target audience?
Sound can be turned off if distracting	Probably the more important issue is: Can the sound be heard and is it crucial to understanding the learning outcome? Often in a classroom, the sound can be difficult to hear if many computers are in use. This question needs to be viewed in terms of how the sound is being used. Often it is critical to the product. For example, the game Myst uses sounds to create the atmosphere for the island and the different spaces around it.
Feedback	Often we forget that intrinsic feedback is there all the time. If the cursor changes as you move over different parts of the screen, this will provide clues to what might be the options available.
• is useful	Depends on the state of the progress through the program.
• is not confusing	Interface guidelines should be taken into account.
• does not leave the learner unsure of what to do next	The general design of the interface should answer this question; it should not be left to one piece of feedback!
Instruction is active rather than passive (is not just a page turner)	This might occur in many ways, but the main point is that the activity requires a cognitive effort, not simply a chance selection.
Learner expectancies are established (learners know what is expected of them)	Many products create very limited expectations, and certainly do not challenge the user to try new ideas and new strategies.
The program has a consistent display rate (screens do not take too long to load)	This is largely the combination of hardware configuration and software engineering. It will always be a problem if you are trying to load the latest software on less than the newest technology.
RECORD-KEEPING AND MANAGEMENT	
Program keeps accurate records of learner response	This assumes a correct answer is possible, but often software does not provide the answer; rather it provides the resources which have to be manipulated into a final product. The latter is often best assessed by a real live person who can judge how the thinking and strategy has been employed.
Program keeps ongoing learner records	Often software involves signing in and keeping records on each person. This may be desirable in a classroom where multiple students must access the same resources on the same machine. Today, many interactive learning programs are integrated with a Learning Management System (LMS) that handles these functions.
Program includes diagnostic/ evaluative testing	This should only be a consideration when the skills are specifically required for the product; otherwise, you are asking for a lot of support in a world that will probably not provide it.
Program generates further assignments	Good, challenging software will get the user to go beyond the information given.

(Continued)

Figure 6.4. Checklist commentary (continued).

	Commentary on the item
Program graphically illustrates learner progress	Being graphical doesn't mean that it is useful. What might be useful is an audit trail included as part of product testing, but simply providing a graphical representation might be more expected from a spreadsheet program.
Program provides statistical information on learner progress	Unless you are installing a major system of computer managed learning, you are unlikely to find this one. But maybe the top 10 scores are one approach.
Program allows print-out and screen display of records	This really is part of an older style CMI (computer managed instruction) system. Most interactive learning packages will require the users to work with other learners and check their understandings with these other learners or their instructor.

Figure 6.4. Checklist commentary (continued).

Overall comments

Consistency must characterize the design and development of an interactive learning product so that it is at the correct degree of difficulty for the people who will use it and addresses the required learning outcomes. Just because an interactive program claims it enables users to learn something does not mean that it is effective. A few years ago, some of our graduate students undertook an evaluation of two software packages which claimed to teach reading. One had cute click-on animations on each screen which kept students amused for hours, and the other used one simple cartoon, but focused on help with the text in terms of color-coded phrasing and speaking sections. While the cute program had similar goals, students spent little time with the text because interacting with the animated characters was more interesting. The cute product sold well – perhaps because its flashy look and feel also appealed to parents who, although they were unfamiliar with instructional design principles, were the actual purchasers. However, the less flashy product, when used well with students, actually helped the students to read and understand language better than the animated program. Judging a program by its presentation is as unwise as judging a book by its cover. Flashy programs may not always produce the best learning outcomes!

Summary

In this chapter, we have sought to provide guidance for the needs assessment function, and to illustrate ways of judging why a proposed product may or may not work. As do Lee and Owens (2001) and Sink (2002), we have emphasized rapid approaches rather than the more formal approaches used in classic instructional systems design models.

If you are seeking to solve a particular problem, then the resulting analysis of all the data collected during a needs assessment will be a project plan complete with objectives and design specifications. A good needs assessment report can be handed off to a design team with confidence that the resultant product will have a good chance of being successful. Alternatively, the report may be used in the preparation of a request for proposals (RFP) if the development of the product is to be contracted to an outside vendor.

Contrary to popular belief, a needs assessment report can be impressionistic and informal rather than scientific and formal. Ideally, it will be heavily illustrated with concept maps and other forms of visualizations as well as sketches of design ideas. Of course, the needs assessment report should not be looked upon as an end in itself. The bottom line of the value of needs assessment is that it should provide the data needed to support the next level of design decisions so that the project moves forward to prototyping and formative evaluation activities (Kaufman, Rojas, & Mayer, 1993).

References

Dick, W., & Carey, L. (2001). *The systematic design of instruction* (5th ed.). New York: HarperCollins.

Gordon, J., & Zemke, R. (2000, April). The attack on ISD. *Training, 37*(4), 42-53.

Hamblen, J. O., & Furman, M. D. (2001). *Rapid prototyping of digital systems: A tutorial approach* (2nd ed.). Amsterdam, NL: Kluwer Academic Publishers.

Kaufman, R. A. (2000) *Mega planning: Practical tools for organizational success*. Thousand Oaks, CA: Sage.

Kaufman, R. A., & English, F. W. (1979). *Needs assessment: Concept and application*. Englewood Cliffs, NJ: Educational Technology Publications.

Kaufman, R. A., Rojas, A. M., & Mayer, H. (1993). *Needs assessment: A user's guide*. Englewood Cliffs, NJ: Educational Technology Publications.

Kearsley, G. (2000). *Online education: Learning and teaching in cyberspace*. Belmont, CA: Wadsworth/Thomson Learning.

Khan, B. H. (Ed.). (1997). *Web-based instruction*. Englewood Cliffs, NJ: Educational Technology Publications.

Khan, B. H. (Ed.). (2001). *Web-based training*. Englewood Cliffs, NJ: Educational Technology Publications.

Kruse, K., & Keil, J. (2000). *Technology-based training: The art and science of design, development, and delivery*. San Francisco, CA: Jossey-Bass/Pfeiffer.

Laurel, B. (1993). *Computers as theater.* Reading, MA: Addison-Wesley.

Lee, W. W., & Owens, D. (2001). Rapid analysis model: Reducing analysis time without sacrificing quality. *Performance Improvement, 40*(1), 13-18.

Milano, M., & Ullius, D. (1998). *Designing powerful training: The sequential-iterative model.* San Francisco: Jossey-Bass.

Myst. (1993). Novato, CA: Broderbund and Cyan, Rand Miller and Robyn Miller (Designers).

Piskurich, G. M. (2000). *Rapid instructional design: Learning ID fast and right.* San Francisco: Jossey-Bass.

Rossett, A. (1987). *Training needs assessment.* Englewood Cliffs, NJ: Educational Technology Publications.

Rossett, A. (1995). Needs assessment. In G. Anglin (Ed.), *Instructional technology: Past, present, and future* (2nd ed.) (pp. 183-196). Englewood, CO: Libraries Unlimited..

Rossett, A. (1998). *First things fast: A handbook for performance analysis.* San Francisco: Jossey-Bass/Pfeiffer.

Sink, D. L. (2002). ISD: Faster, better, easier. *Performance Improvement, 41*(7), 16-22.

Sugrue, B. (2000). Cognitive approaches to Web-based instruction. In S. P. Lajoie (Ed.), *Computers as cognitive tools: No more walls* (pp. 133-162). Mahwah, NJ: Lawrence Erlbaum Associates.

CHAPTER 7

Formative Evaluation

Objectives

After reading Chapter Seven, you should be able to:

- identify decisions involved in formative evaluation of interactive learning systems;
- specify questions that should be answered before making these decisions about improving interactive learning systems;
- identify the information needed to answer these questions; and
- decide how to collect and report the required information so that an interactive learning system can be improved in a timely manner.

Why should you conduct formative evaluation?

The overall purpose of formative evaluation is to provide information to guide decisions about "debugging" or enhancing an interactive learning system at various stages of its development. As illustrated in Figure 7.1, different types of decisions must be made when you attempt to improve an interactive learning system, each of which is tied to one or more specific questions that can be addressed by formative evaluation activities, such as observations and beta tests.

As described in Chapter Three, formative evaluation is the essential "life-blood" of the instructional systems design (ISD) process. According to Flagg (1990), formative evaluation is "the systematic collection of information for the purpose of informing decisions to design and improve the product" (pp. 1-2). Virtually everything about an interactive learning system can be enhanced at some stage of its development. Sometimes all that is needed for improvement is a flash of creative insight, but more often than not you will need specific information to guide your program improvement decisions. This information can be collected in many different ways from a variety of different people, ranging from subject matter experts to members of the target user population for the interactive learning product.

Decisions	Example Questions
Should the interface be redesigned?	Is navigation clear to users? Are the meanings of icons clear? Do users get lost in navigating through the program?
Should the number and length of video segments be decreased?	Do users select to view video segments? Do users use video replay options? Do users rate video highly?
Should more practice opportunities be added?	Do users pass module quizzes? Do users achieve mastery on unit tests? Do users rate practice highly?
Should the program scope be expanded?	Are the materials coordinated with curricular guidelines? Do content experts rate the program as comprehensive?

Figure 7.1. Typical decisions and questions in a formative evaluation.

Resistance to formative evaluation

Although practices analogous to formative evaluation are common in many fields, for example advertising, there is sometimes resistance to rigorous formative evaluation among both designers and sponsors of interactive learning systems. This may partially derive from an unfortunate tendency within the software industry to develop a new program without substantial formative testing, invest heavily in packaging and marketing the program, and then to use the feedback from the early adopters of the software to fix or improve the program before Version 2 is released. A vice-president of a very large international computer corporation once admonished one of us for promoting formative evaluation of a computer-based education package, exclaiming, "Why should we *pay* for user testing when the first ten thousand people who buy our software will tell us how to improve it for free!"

While it is hard to argue with the "economics" of this corporate attitude, we believe that there is an ethical imperative to evaluate interactive learning systems while they are being developed. After all, interactive learning systems are intended to change people, to modify their knowledge, skills, and attitudes, and to influence them to behave differently. The risk of misguiding learners is too great, and therefore we view formative evaluation as a morally responsible activity.

– **WEB LINK** –
More information about Barbara Flagg's book can be found at: www.erlbaum.com

In her valuable book, *Formative Evaluation for Educational Technologies*, Flagg (1990) identified six reasons why people resist formative evaluation:

- Time – In the rush to meet project deadlines, reducing or eliminating formative evaluation activities is perceived as an easy way to save time.
- Money – Most development budgets fail to provide sufficient funding for rigorous formative evaluation. (The authors of this book recommend at least a 10% allocation to formative evaluation) .
- Human Nature – Many developers are reluctant to subject their programs to potential criticism, especially from users they may view as uninformed or from experts they may view as threatening.
- Unrealistic Expectations – Although formative evaluation can provide information to guide decision-making, it cannot substitute for the expertise and creativity of a qualified developer. In short, you cannot just toss together a rough prototype of an interactive learning system, and expect formative evaluation to turn it into a winner.
- Measurement Difficulties – Although some aspects of formative evaluation are relatively easy to determine (e.g., investigating whether users think various parts of an interactive learning system are appealing), there is a lack of reliable, valid, and feasible methods of evaluating certain kinds of outcomes of interactive learning that a particular program may address, e.g., problem-solving.
- Knowledge – Formative evaluation expertise is not yet widely available within the interactive learning systems development industry or within academe. Most developers lack the skills to conduct systematic formative evaluation in an efficient and effective manner.

Investments in formative evaluation should result in an overall reduction in development and implementation costs over the lifespan of interactive product systems, and hence resistance to formative evaluation should decline as formative procedures become more routine. Even within the software industry, there is an increased emphasis on usability testing and other formative practices (Nielsen, 2000; Preece, 1994), and we predict that this trend will continue.

When should you conduct formative evaluation?

It can be said that conducting formative evaluation should be like voting in mayoral elections in certain large cities, that is, you should evaluate "early and often." Duby (1988) presents a sound rationale for early formative evaluation of instructional products such as educational television. The sooner formative evaluation is conducted during a development project, the more likely that substantive improvements will be made and costly errors avoided. Avoiding expensive mistakes is especially critical with some of the technical elements of interactive learning systems, such as video, which remains a particularly costly component of most products. Producing video per se is expensive enough, but when you add in the costs of compressing video for digital movies on a DVD or transmission via the WWW, you begin to spend "real" money!

A former student relayed a story that illustrates the importance of early formative evaluation. She was involved in the production of a CD-ROM multimedia program about basketball featuring a famous college coach. A crew was sent to the coach's university to videotape him giving tips about playing the game. It was a sunny day and the crew decided to tape him on an outside court so that the light would be good. The coach was videotaped against a background of trees with the wind rustling the leaves. The video looked great, but when they took it into the digitizing software, the compression algorithms were so overtaxed in compressing the constant movement of the foliage that the coach's face and lip movements were distorted. By the time this was discovered, it was too late and too expensive to re-tape the coach against a neutral background. A little formative evaluation of the video compression process up front would have saved the producers a lot of grief.

What kinds of decisions can you anticipate?

Figure 3.1 in Chapter Three presents a typical ISD process for interactive learning systems in terms of the stages, steps required in each stage, the team-members involved in each stage of the process, and a list of the interim products resulting from each stage. Each of the draft documents and interim products represents an opportunity for making important decisions about enhancing the effectiveness and efficiency of the final interactive learning system. Should you increase the difficulty of the program's objectives? Should test item formats be revised? Should the fonts used in different parts of a program be changed? Should more or less humor be incorporated into video scripts? These and other decisions will be faced by you and other members of the development team.

The impetus to make decisions about improving an interactive learning system will come from many directions. You may see a program developed by a competitor that inspires a new interface idea. Your clients may cut your budget, thereby requiring you to cut down on the more expensive elements of a program such as 3-D animation. The colors that looked great on your high-end development machine with millions of colors may look awful on the consumer level machines with reduced color graphic capabilities. These and many other factors will be signals that there is room (and often a need) for improvements in your prototype interactive learning system.

Of course, under the best circumstances, formative evaluation is not something that is initiated when there is a crisis such as a budget cut. Instead, it is a professional practice integral to the overall instructional development process. What's more, a formative evaluation perspective is no less important for those involved in implementing interactive learning systems. The bottom line is that all of us are human and our first efforts to create or do anything are bound to be somewhat flawed. Formative evaluation is the key to detecting and reducing these flaws and eventually attaining the high quality we all desire.

What questions should be answered before making decisions?

Each possible decision will inspire many different types of questions about improving your interactive learning system. Do learners understand what their options are at any given moment? Does the program maintain the learners' attention? Do they accomplish the objectives of the program? Is it feasible to implement the program as designed? It is too late to wait until you have completed an interactive learning system to ask these questions. Instead, they must be addressed throughout the development of the interactive product. As noted above, the earlier these questions can be asked and enhancements made based upon the responses, the more efficient your overall development effort will be.

There are no universal criteria established for formative evaluation of interactive learning systems, but some of the most commonly considered factors are functionality (Does the product work as designed?), usability (Can the intended learners actually use the program?), appeal (Do they like it?), and effectiveness (Did they learn anything?). Different criteria entail many different types of questions. For example, usability implies criteria that can be broken down into small issues such as the quality of the user interface. User interface can be further divided into factors such as navigation, mapping, aesthetics, and control. Finally, a factor like navigation can be examined via several different questions: How do users navigate through the interactive learning system? How does their navigation relate to the underlying pedagogy of the program? What parts of the program are underutilized? Where would users like to go, but don't seem to know how? Answering these and other questions provides the development team with the information they need to enhance the navigational aspects of the program and ultimately improve its usability.

How should formative evaluation be conducted?

The key to sound formative evaluation is to collect data systematically at critical stages of the interactive learning system's development and to utilize the findings of each formative evaluation strategy as much as your personnel, time, and financial resources allow. Numerous articles and books have been written about formative evaluation (Beyer, 1995; Flagg, 1990; Kinzie, 1991; Maslowski & Visscher, 1999; Tessmer, 1994), and there are comprehensive volumes covering individual aspects of formative evaluation (Branaghan, 2001; Hix & Hartson, 1993). As described below, we recommend the following formative evaluation activities as essential within the context of most development projects:

- expert review,
- user review,
- usability testing, and
- alpha, beta, and field tests of prototype program.

Two main classes of usability evaluation methods can be differentiated (Ziegler & Burmester, 1995). One class focuses on users of a particular product and aims to determine usability by studying users while they interact with a product. This approach is referred to as *user review* (or sometimes user testing). The other method is designed to identify specific human factors issues of a product and is referred to as *usability testing*. No matter how much analysis has been done in designing a product, experience has shown that there will be problems that only appear when the design is tested with users, i.e., people as much like those who will eventually interact with the interactive learning systems as genuine learners. The learner's experience of an instructional product's usability is an important indicator of its quality.

Another level of formative evaluation involves consideration of user acceptance. In user acceptance testing, it is recommended that users test not just the product, but all parts of the package that the users will receive, such as training, written procedures, forms, manuals, computer-based training, and online help (McManus & Hammond, 1991, p. 101). This integrated approach ensures that there is no mismatch between the different components and highlights the users' perspective of the whole product rather than a number of the parts. For this testing, a prediction is needed of the organizational and task changes that will occur as a result of the introduction of the new product. For example, if employees are expected to complete interactive training programs on their own computers at home rather than in the workplace, then usability testing should be conducted in homes rather than in corporate usability labs (Mitropoulos-Rundus & Muszak, 2001). Once the new product has been implemented, it is important to follow up with effectiveness evaluation in order to understand the actual learning process, usability issues, and use of the product by novices and experts in realistic work or education contexts.

Expert review

Expert review may be the most frequently used formative evaluation strategy. It is important to remember that there are several different kinds of "experts," and that each type of expert can add unique kinds of information to the review and enhancement process. Content or subject matter experts can help you improve the scope, sequence, and accuracy of an interactive program's content. Instructional experts can assist by critiquing the potential effectiveness of the pedagogical dimensions of an interactive program. Graphic designers can suggest how to enhance the aesthetics of a program's look and feel. Teaching and training experts can help you anticipate the logistical requirements for successful implementation of an interactive learning system in schools or businesses.

– **WEB LINK** –
For the tools presented in this chapter, go to: http://it.coe.uga.edu/~treeves/ilse

With respect to formative evaluation, an expert is anyone with specialized knowledge that is relevant to the design of your interactive learning system. Experts can provide different perspectives on the critical aspects of your program, e.g., its accuracy, completeness, user-friendliness, motivational strategies, aesthetics, instructional validity, effectiveness, efficiency, and feasibility. You should utilize both internal and external experts to the degree that your resources allow.

It is often useful to structure an expert's review so that you are assured of getting the types and depth of information you desire. Figure 7.2 presents an expert review form to guide instructional design experts with experience in interactive multimedia when they critique a prototype interactive instructional program.

Reviewer: Dr. Ima Knowitall **Due Date:** June 10

Please circle your rating and write comments on each aspect of the interactive multimedia (IMM) package.

1 represents the lowest and most negative impression on the scale, 3 represents an adequate impression, and 5 represents the highest and most positive impression. Choose N/A if the item is not appropriate or not applicable to this package. Use additional sheets to write comments.

NA=Not applicable 1=Strongly disagree 2=Disagree 3=Neither agree/nor disagree 4=Agree 5=Strongly agree

AREA 1 – INSTRUCTIONAL DESIGN REVIEW

1. This IMM program provides learners with a clear knowledge of the program objectives.	N/A	1	2	3	4	5
2. The instructional interactions in this IMM program are appropriate for the objectives.	N/A	1	2	3	4	5
3. The instructional design of this IMM program is based on sound learning theory and principles.	N/A	1	2	3	4	5
4. The feedback in this IMM program is clear.	N/A	1	2	3	4	5
5. The pace of this IMM program is appropriate.	N/A	1	2	3	4	5
6. The difficulty level of this IMM program is appropriate.	N/A	1	2	3	4	5

Comments:

AREA 2 – COSMETIC DESIGN REVIEW

7. The screen design of this IMM program follows sound principles.	N/A	1	2	3	4	5
8. Color is appropriately used in this IMM program.	N/A	1	2	3	4	5
9. The screen displays are easy to understand.	N/A	1	2	3	4	5

Comments:

AREA 3 – PROGRAM FUNCTIONALITY REVIEW

10. This IMM program operated flawlessly.	N/A	1	2	3	4	5

Comments:

Figure 7.2. Sample expert review form for a multimedia program.

If you must limit expert review, content experts are probably the most important expert sources of formative information for education and training products. Why? Because if you do not get the content right, the eventual users will be misled. One of the problems with many interactive learning systems is that these programs lack subject matter integrity because of a lack of expert review. This is a major challenge because so much material can be incorporated into a single interactive product. The integrity issue is especially challenging when interactive learning is delivered via the World Wide Web. Many Web sites include links to other sites, and guaranteeing the accuracy and currency of all the related links is beyond the powers of most developers. At the very least, the content of the first two or three levels of links should be examined. Unless the accuracy and validity of information and its organization are carefully reviewed, the level of integrity necessary for educational materials may be lacking.

In addition to instructional design and content experts, we have found that people with special expertise in human-computer interface (HCI) design and the aesthetics of interactive learning systems can provide useful expert reviews. For example, if your team doesn't include an art director who is responsible for the look and feel of the product, it is wise to ask graphic artists to critique your prototype. Of course, you would not decide to make major changes in the design elements of an interactive learning system based on the opinions of just one expert because aesthetic appeal is much more subjective than some of the other criteria to be reviewed. On the other hand, if several graphic artists retch at the sight of your interface, you may have a problem worth fixing!

Experienced designers of interactive multimedia are often the best experts for reviewing user interface issues, but there are people who specialize in HCI issues per se. Figure 7.3 presents a user interface instrument that can be used to guide reviews provided by expert instructional designers and very experienced users of interactive learning systems (Reeves & Harmon, 1994).

Contracting with the "right" experts for review services is a crucial step in setting up a formative evaluation. If subject matter experts (commonly called SMEs) are already part of your team, one of their primary responsibilities will be checking the accuracy and currency of your content. However, even when working with qualified SMEs, it is a good idea to have the content reviewed by other content experts. In 1984, one of us learned this lesson the hard way when we collaborated with a team of nurses on the design of an interactive videodisc program about shock treatment. The video components were taped at a hospital in Philadelphia where nurses still wore traditional nursing hats. Little did we know that these were practically the last nurses on earth still wearing this type of cap! When we showed the program at a medical education conference, many of the nurses in the audience criticized the video for being out of date, even though it had been recorded only weeks beforehand. If we had hired nurses from other hospitals to review the videotaping early on, we would have detected this problem and included nurses with more up-to-date apparel. As it was, the "face validity" of this program was seriously damaged in the eyes of many members of the target audience.

— WEB LINK —
A full explanation of the criteria in the user interface rating form can be found at: http://it.coe.uga.edu/~treeves/ilse/

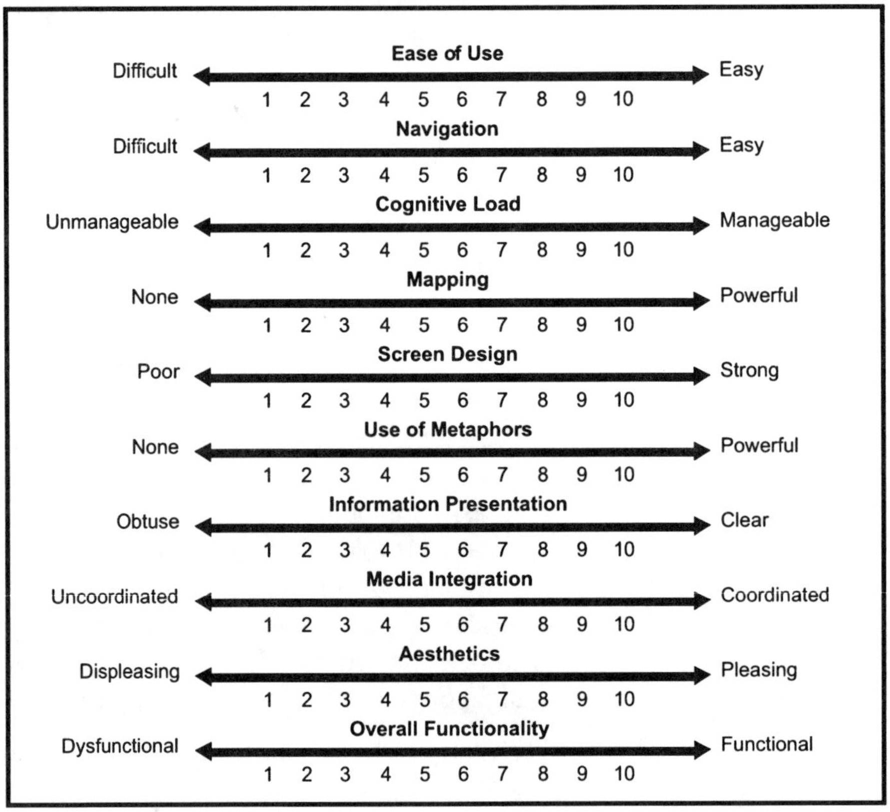

Figure 7.3. Sample user interface review form for ILS.

The costs for SMEs to review interactive multimedia programs can vary widely depending on the field. Some instructional design, graphics, and HCI experts will charge hundreds of dollars per hour to review interactive prototypes, but we have found that using graduate students and university faculty can be a much less expensive source of expert review. Of course, your clients may insist on using the recognized "gurus" in any given area, and they are often worth every cent they are paid because of their insight and creativity. Using the Web for interactive learning delivery is becoming prevalent (Kahn, 1997, 2001), but procedures for expert review of instructional Web sites are not as well defined as they need to be (Reeves & Carter, 2001).

User review

The perspectives of "experts" are valuable, but the opinions of the target audience for your interactive learning system are of equal importance.

User review is based on the analysis of user behavior during the use of the product to be evaluated. Therefore, user review requires an understanding of the actual user profiles, their tasks, and the contexts in which the tasks are performed. As one important objective is to ensure that user differences are accommodated, it is important that user review be done with a sample of people whose background knowledge and expectations approximate those of the final intended users. During user review, users should be allowed to work in realistic conditions, without interruption from an observer, in order to accurately replicate the intended context of use (Bevan, 1995).

Suppose you are designing an interactive learning system for use in schools. In that case, the most valuable information for making decisions about improving the program can be derived from systematic observations of learners while they use the program. Observations can be conducted in the development lab or on-site at a school. Learner opinions, actions, responses, and suggestions will provide you with practical guidance in making decisions about improving your product. Of course, you would also want the teachers who must implement the system to review it, especially with respect to seeking their ideas about how they could integrate it into their existing practices. Widening the review process to include parents, administrators, and school media specialists is also advised in this context. Few interactive learning systems have been successfully integrated into schools (Cuban, 2001), a problem that might have been reduced by more inclusive formative evaluation.

Observations of learners engaging with your interactive learning system at various stages of its development can be a valuable, if somewhat humbling, experience. You may be surprised at how frequently what seemed to be the most user-friendly aspects of your program befuddle would-be learners. Alternatively, what you view as motivating may bore the intended audience. Fortunately, you will often find that your creative design ideas are validated by learners. A sample protocol from the Apple Interface Laboratory is given in Figure 7.4.

During your observations, you will see users doing things you never expected. When you see participants making mistakes, your first instinct may be to blame the mistakes on the participant's inexperience or lack of intelligence. This is the wrong position to take. The purpose of observing users is to see what parts of your product might be difficult or ineffective. Therefore, if you see a participant struggling or making mistakes, attribute the difficulties to faulty design, *not* to the participant. If you are an evaluator, you may be more tolerant of bad news from users than the instructional designers on your team, but they will learn to be more accepting as they see that formative evaluation enhances their products.

User Observation (Based upon Apple HCI Group Protocol)

The following instructions guide you through a simple user observation. With this protocol, you will see where people have difficulty using your product, and you will be able to use that information to improve it.

1 – Introduce yourself	Make the session and task as welcoming as possible. Remember, this test is not designed as a controlled experiment, so keep the environment friendly.
2 – Describe the general purpose of the observation	Set the participant at ease by stressing that you're trying to find problems in the product. For example, you could say: *You're helping us by trying out this product. We're looking for places where the product may be difficult to use. If you have trouble with some tasks, it's the product's fault, not yours. Don't feel bad; that's exactly what we're looking for. If we can locate the trouble spots, then we can go back and improve the product. Remember, we're testing the product, not you.*
3 – Tell the participant that it's OK to quit at any time	Make sure you inform participants that they can quit at any time if they find themselves becoming uncomfortable. Participants shouldn't feel like they're locked into completing tasks. Say something like this: *Although I don't know of any reason for this to happen, if you should become uncomfortable in any way, you are free to quit at any time.*
4 – Talk about the equipment	Explain the purpose of each piece of equipment and how it will be used in the test (hardware, software, video camera, microphones, etc.).
5 – Explain how to "think aloud"	Ask participants to think aloud during the observation, saying what comes to mind as they work. You'll find that listening to users as they work provides you with useful information that you can get in no other way. Unfortunately, most people feel awkward or self-conscious about thinking aloud. Explain why you want participants to think aloud, and demonstrate how to do it. You could say: *We have found that we get lots of information from these informal tests if we ask people to think aloud as they work through the exercises. It may be a bit awkward at first, but it's really very easy once you get used to it. All you have to do is speak your thoughts as you work. If you forget to think aloud, I'll remind you to keep talking. Would you like me to demonstrate?*
6 – Describe why you will not be able to help.	It is very important that you allow participants to work with your product without any interference or extra help. If a participant begins having difficulty and you immediately provide help, you may lose the most valuable information you can gain from user observation: where users have trouble, and how they figure out what to do. Of course, there may be situations where you must step in and provide assistance, but you should decide what those situations will be before you begin testing. You may decide that you will allow someone to flounder for at least 3 minutes before providing assistance. Or you may identify distinct problems you will provide help on. As a rule of thumb, try not to give your test participants any more information than the true users of your product will have. Here are some things you can say to the participant: *As you're working through the exercises, I won't be able to provide help or answer questions. This is because we want to create the most realistic situation possible. Even though I won't be able to answer your questions, please ask them anyway. It's very important that I capture all your questions and comments on tape. When you've finished all the exercises, I'll answer any questions you still have.*

(Continued)

Figure 7.4. Sample User Observation Protocol.

7 – Describe the tasks and introduce the product	Explain what the participant should do first, second, third, etc. Give the participant written instructions for the tasks. **Important:** If you need to demonstrate your product before the user observation begins, be sure you don't demonstrate something you're trying to test. (For example, if you want to know whether users can figure out how to use certain tools, don't show them how to use the tools before the test.)
8 – Ask if there are questions	Before you start, make sure the respondent knows your expectations, then begin the observation.
9 – Conclude the observation	When the test is over: • Explain what you were trying to find out during the test. • Answer any remaining questions the participant may have. • Discuss any interesting behaviors you would like the participant to explain.
10 – Use the results	To get the most out of your test results, review all your data carefully and thoroughly (your notes, the videotape or cassette tape, the tasks, etc). Look for places where participants had trouble, and see if you can determine how your product could be changed to alleviate the problems. Look for patterns in the participants' behavior that might tell you whether the product is understood correctly. It's a good idea to keep a record of what you found out during the test. That way, you'll have documentation to support your design decisions and you'll be able to see trends in users' behavior. After you've examined the results and summarized the important findings, fix the problems you found and test the product again. By testing your product more than once, you'll see how your changes affect users' performance.

Figure 7.4. Sample User Observation Protocol (continued).

Observing learners can be a time-intensive and exhausting process. It can range from a very simple one-on-one observation protocol to a complex arrangement wherein several observers, video cameras, and computers are used to record learners' reactions. Whatever type of procedure is followed, it is important that you record information carefully and that you later deal with each issue that arises during the observations.

Figure 7.5 presents a simple formative evaluation review form with three columns, one for indicating what section of an interactive program is being reviewed, one for recording observations, and the last for recording the actions taken in response to the issues raised by the observations. The last column is very important because it provides the evidence that the evaluation data collected has actually had an impact on design decisions.

Formative Review Log

Program: Learn or else! **Reviewer:** Smyth
Date: May 15

Screen	Comments, Questions, Suggestions	Action Taken
C-17	The forward and back navigation arrows are so small that users seems to have trouble placing the mouse cursor on them.	Enlarge the navigation arrows by 50% and repeat observations.
C-23	The users think that the "Question Mark icon will take them to help, but it takes them to a list of frequently asked questions instead.	Use the "Question Mark icon for help, and find a different icon for the frequently asked questions.

Figure 7.5. Formative evaluation review log for e-learning program.

Usability testing

Usability is an important issue in the design of any software, including interactive learning systems. According to Shneiderman (1987), usability is a combination of the following user-oriented characteristics:

- ease of learning,
- high speed of user task performance,
- low user error rate,
- subjective user satisfaction, and
- user retention over time.

There are several books that provide excellent guidance to evaluating user interface issues, a process known as usability testing (Hix & Hartson, 1993; Nielsen, 1993). Usability testing is especially critical in the design, dissemination, and implementation of interactive multimedia for education, training, performance support, and information access (cf., Blattner & Dannenberg, 1992; Laurel, 1990; Polson, 1988, Preece, 1994; Shneiderman, 1987). Too many formative evaluation studies are only focused on whether users like a program or not, but usability is a much deeper subject.

There are instances when you might evaluate usability without users. Time with users is often limited; it is not a free resource. In addition, users can find it difficult to visualize how a product could behave differently and they therefore tend to evaluate according to what already exists, rather than to what is possible. Some usability criteria will only be reliably identified or articulated by trained human factors evaluators using protocols such as heuristic evaluation or usability inspection (Nielsen, 1993). At least three evaluators with a mix of experience and expertise are required for heuristic evaluation or usability inspection because fewer will not identify all the usability problems (Nielsen & Mack, 1994).

Usability in product development. Designing for usability requires early specification of usability goals (Nielsen, 2000). Usability is built into a new product from the analysis phase of a project by identifying and analyzing the critical features of and interactions between users, their tasks, and the product. Specific contexts in which usability is to be measured should also be identified. These usability goals can then be used to interpret the findings from the user analysis and to identify the goals and constraints that will direct the design and set criteria against which a design can be tested once it is built.

As part of the design phase, prototypes are commonly developed and tested. The outcome of this early evaluation results in iterations of the design. It is important to begin usability evaluation at the earliest phases of design because, if left until just before a product is released, there will be little chance to make any significant design changes. Testing formally for compliance with usability specifications takes place in the testing phase. This is usually at the alpha, beta, or final gold master versions of the product. An alpha version is used in the earliest tests, conducted when the product is still at the prototype stage. Alpha testing is generally done with in-house personnel. Beta versions are released to selected samples of users for testing. The product is more refined at this point, nearing completion, but still needing to be debugged. The gold master version of a product is supposed to be flawless, although anyone who has bought version 1.0 of a new piece of software realizes that this is rarely the case. The persistence of problems (bugs) is why testing even gold versions of a product is important.

There are a number of benefits for usability evaluation if it is iterative and considered in all phases of the development life cycle. Iterative design helps with the management of product development and so reduces the risk of projects going off track. Early testing can detect unclear or unreasonable usability goals. Usability objectives can help to facilitate communication and decision-making between human factors evaluators and product designers. Also, usability testing allows developers to obtain and appreciate a user perspective of their product.

Speed of using software is often the focus for usability studies. It was reported in *Information Week* (Leibs, 1994) that studies conducted at Carnegie Mellon University's Software Engineering Institute estimated that a savings of $2.5 million could be realized by a large company if they developed "an interface that could trim eight-tenths of a second off the time a user needs to perform a repetitive computer-based task, such as order entry or customer service" (p. 28). Although the economics of this particular example may seem inflated, there is no question that big business is increasingly concerned about the computer interfaces that "knowledge workers" must use and the degree to which these user interfaces support effective, efficient performance. Time is money. A second saved may be a penny saved, and when enough pennies are saved, significant economic benefits can result.

Time saved in business and industrial training is also highly prized because corporations generally want to get their employees back on the job as quickly as possible. In fact, increasing the efficiency of training, rather than improving effectiveness, is sometimes used as the primary criteria for summative evaluations of interactive learning systems (Reeves, 1988).

But what about education? Is time important in schools? At first glance, time might appear to be a relatively unimportant resource. To be sure, time is a factor in planning and managing most schools, but it is usually thought of in terms of 180 school days, six and a half hour days, 50 minutes class periods, and so forth. (The days, hours, schedule, etc., devoted to schooling vary considerably from country to country.) But when it comes down to what teachers and students do with their time on an hour by hour, minute to minute basis, there appears to be little concern for accountability.

Hence, speed may not appear to be important in examining educational software, but we will argue that it is an issue. The ease and speed with which a learner is able to engage in meaningful cognitive interactions with an interactive learning system is an indicator of how soon he or she will be able to devote his or her cognitive powers to the content and learning dimensions of the program rather than to figuring out how to navigate through and control the system. After all, human information processing power is limited, and interactive learning systems should be designed so that meaningful engagement with a program is enabled without unnecessary stress. Therefore, the usability of educational software is just as relevant as it is for other types of software.

Formally assessing usability. At the Learning and Performance Support Laboratory at The University of Georgia, we acquired a portable multimedia usability lab (the one depicted in Figure 7.6) to help in formative evaluation, especially usability studies. This lab is transportable to any site where an interactive learning system or any other type of software is being used for education, training, information, or performance support purposes.

A portable lab includes a remote-controlled video camera that can be focused on the user's face, the user's computer, keyboard and mouse, or any other aspect of the user environment considered important in the evaluation. The system simultaneously records whatever appears on the user's screen. Evaluators sit at a control panel that allows them to observe the user directly or on any of the video screens displaying selected aspects of the context. Evaluators can control what is recorded, e.g., most of the user's screen along with a small insert image of the user's facial expressions or body language.

– WEB LINK –
For more information about the portable lab pictured here, go to: http://www.usabilitysystems.com

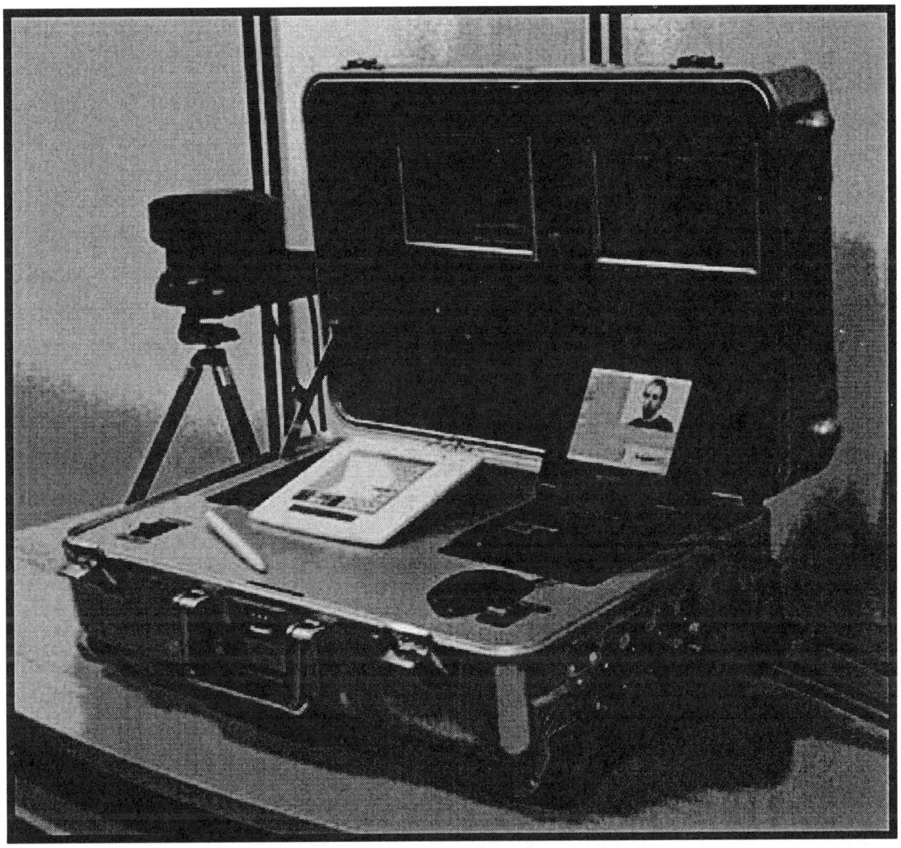

Figure 7.6. Portable usability lab.

Commercial software developers have employed usability labs for formative evaluation of software applications for many years (Branaghan, 2001; Gomoll, 1990). Fixed usability labs generally consist of two rooms separated by a one-way glass window (see Figure 7.7). In one room, a computer user sits at a desk and interacts with the application being evaluated, e.g., a new spreadsheet program. Several video cameras mounted in the room are focused on various aspects in the room. In the other room, evaluators and designers sit at control panels where they can simultaneously observe the user in the room through the one-way glass or any of the video screens displaying selected aspects. The user may be instructed to "think aloud" as he/she uses the program, e.g., talk about why certain choices are made or describe any confusion about the program's interface. Alternatively, the evaluators may question the user via headsets or speakers about why he/she has done certain actions. Users are informed that they will be observed, and they have the right to discontinue a test at any time for any reason. Typically, these sessions are videotaped for later analysis and documentation. Some fixed usability labs feature a third room where clients can observe the usability testing as it is being conducted.

Figure 7.7. Fixed usability laboratory.

A portable software usability lab is patterned after these commercial labs, but rather than forcing users to come to a lab and test software in an artificial environment, the portable lab allows the users to stay in their own environment. We believe that this increases the validity of many evaluation studies. Regardless of what type of lab is used (fixed or portable), usability testing enables evaluators to collect both quantitative and qualitative data related to issues such as user interface, mental models, navigation, documentation utility, effectiveness, and efficiency.

You can do some simple usability testing with only a single video camera, especially if you cannot afford to rent a formal laboratory or buy a portable usability lab. We have used a single video camera to record two users working their way through a prototype package. This has some unique advantages. The fact that there are two people with one system means that they have to talk about their interpretations of screen images and negotiate their actions. Reviewing the video record of these two-person interactions can be very informative. It also circumvents the difficulty of getting users to participate fully in a think-aloud protocol.

Usability protocols

A variety of evaluation protocols are possible to assess usability (Hix & Hartson, 1993; Hughes & Burke, 2001; Nielsen, 1993, 2000). Nielsen

(1993) identified the following methods for gathering usability data: observation, think aloud, questionnaires, interviews, focus groups, logging actual use, and user feedback. Evaluators select the appropriate methods to collect data to address different usability issues and questions. Each of these methods has different strengths and weaknesses, and combining different methods is often necessary to improve overall usability testing.

As noted in the User Review section, you might want to ask questions to users during observations, but asking questions during an observation can change what the user would naturally do. An alternative is a delayed think-aloud approach whereby you record the user with the portable usability lab, and later play the tape back to the user. During the playback, you can ask the user to state what he/she was thinking while interacting with the program or ask specific questions. The tape assists the user in recalling the recorded session. In addition the same tape can be shown to human factors experts for their advice and interpretations. Alternatively, a focus group of designers can review videotapes of users in their actual working conditions to stimulate new ideas about the program.

Formative evaluations sometimes involve the use of experts to judge the performance of learners on various types of tasks. Reliability is an important issue whenever human judges are used. Having videotaped data scored by multiple experts can provide reliability information about the data collection process. Collecting data about benchmark tasks is another use of the portable usability lab. A benchmark task is a common activity the learner performs with the system. These benchmarks are selected by the developer to measure quantitatively the interface design (Hix & Hartson, 1993). The usability system can record the learner's performance on benchmarks for later analysis.

Working with one of the authors of this book, Conyer (1995) provided an excellent summary of a range of literature on the topic of usability testing. She described six alternative methods that can be employed to determine the usability of an e-learning product: 1) heuristic evaluation, 2) pluralistic walkthroughs, 3) formal usability inspection, 4) empirical methods, 5) cognitive walkthroughs, and 6) formal design analysis.

Heuristic evaluation. Originally conceived by Nielsen (1993), this method employs a set of principles (termed heuristics) which have been defined prior to the evaluation. Although usually done with experts, heuristic evaluation can also be done with a sample of intended users. Evaluators (experts or users) independently examine the product and judge its compliance with the set of heuristic principles. Conyer (1995) elaborated:

> Each evaluator works through the interface at least twice, the first time to get a feel for the flow of the interaction and the second time to focus on the specific interface elements within the context of the larger whole. Observers can offer help to evaluators when they are clearly having difficulty and after they have commented on the usability problem they are experiencing (p.40).

The evaluators' comments can be recorded either by themselves or by an observer. Then they are interpreted and summarized for an overall evaluation. Conyer (1995) then recommended that:

> a debriefing session is then held with all evaluators, observers, and representatives of the design team to brainstorm possible ideas to address the major usability problems, as well as to discuss the positive elements of the interface design. A priority list is then drawn up of all usability problems with reference to the heuristics that were not followed in the design, and with a time and cost estimate to correct each problem. Priority is determined according to the frequency and impact of the problem, and if the problem can be overcome in another way, e.g., with training (p.41).

– WEB LINK –
A set of heuristics designed specifically for e-learning can be found at: http://it.coe.uga.edu/~treeves/ilse/

The heuristic evaluation method has advantages and disadvantages. It is less time-consuming than other approaches and it does reveal many important weaknesses in a product. The debriefing session is especially important in determining how the problems identified can be fixed or ameliorated. This method is relatively easy and economical to undertake and can be prepared quickly to provide efficient feedback to a team of designers. However, recruiting experts can be difficult because most experts are busy people. If end-users are involved, getting a representative cross section of the target audience is yet another challenge. According to Nielsen (1993), a further weakness of heuristic evaluation is that it generally does not find as many problems as formal usability testing. The actual heuristics used in this method depend on the nature of the product. Nielsen has defined a set of ten general heuristics that can be applied to any type of software product.

Pluralistic walkthroughs. This method can be used with paper prototypes as well as with fully functioning versions of an interactive learning system. The pluralistic aspect comes from the mix of users, designers, and experts involved in the walkthroughs. Conyer (1995) explained:

> The goal of this method is to systematically review the usability of an interface and its flow from a task-based, user-centered perspective while at the same time considering the design constraints. In the context of task-based scenarios, end-users, product developers, and human factors experts evaluate a product from the perspective of the end-user. The evaluators sequen-

> tially write down each action they would take when pursuing a designated task. A group discussion then follows, with end-users presenting their information first. Subject matter experts are available at all stages for domain-specific questions. (pp. 41-42)

The walkthrough method is task-based, and thus it is more narrowly focused than other methods. Therefore, it identifies more specific problems than general problems. For example, the walkthrough method might be used to examine whether users correctly understand how to log-in and log-off using a course management system.

Formal usability inspection. This approach can be used to examine both cognitive processing and behavioral tasks involved in the usability of a program. However, end-users are generally not involved in this type of evaluation, and it is not conducted in the context in which the e-learning product would normally be used. Instead, members of a design team and external experts participate in this type of inspection, as described by Conyer (1995):

> Usability issues are reviewed within the context of specific user profiles and defined goal-oriented scenarios by applying a task performance model and heuristics. This method captures how evaluators *perceive* the information, *plan* to use the information, *decide* how to proceed, and *perform* the selected action. A six-step process is normally used, namely (1) *Planning;* (2) *Kick-off Meeting*, when the team comes together for the first time; (3) *Preparation*, when the evaluators review the program independently; (4) *Review*, to discuss the aggregated usability issues; (5) *Rework*, when solutions are found and implemented; and (6) *Follow-up*, to determine the effectiveness of the evaluation process. There are clearly defined participant responsibilities, namely: *Moderator*, who manages the process; *Design Owner*, who is responsible for representing and then upgrading the product being inspected; *Evaluators*, who find and report usability problems (such as designers, documentation specialists, and human factors evaluators); and *Scribe*, who records all identified problems and decisions. (pp. 42-43)

The focus of formal usability inspections is more general than in walkthrough methods. Ideally, this type of formal review is conducted as soon as a reasonably complete beta version of the interactive learning system is available. The inclusion of design team members in this process can be especially useful, provided they can keep an open mind with respect to problems that might be identified. However, there should be other participants who are not part of the design team. Just as an author of a book needs an external proofreader to spot errors in a text, design teams need external experts to see the inevitable flaws in a user interface design.

Empirical methods. This approach is effective for establishing cause and effect, or for addressing a specific question or problem through focused testing. However, it can be very time consuming and it does require an evaluator trained in empirical methods. In practice, empirical methods should not be undertaken until a formal prototype is working and is robust enough to test. Conyer (1995) summarized empirical methods as follows:

> Data can be collected in an experimental test to prove or disprove a hypothesis, e.g., the number of correct responses and errors made by a user under controlled conditions. A hypothesis is posed based on a set of objective measures for the evaluation. A plan for how the measures are to be collected is then determined. Subjects are found for the test, data is collected and analyzed to determine if the proposed hypothesis has been proven. (p. 43)

Empirical methods should be reserved for resolving significant disagreements among design team members because of the time and expense involved. Suppose some team members want to use realistic icons and "roll-overs" as a major feature of the e-learning interface where as more conservative member of the team want to employ simple icons with text labels. An empirical test could be set up to compare the effectiveness of the two interface designs, using representative samples of the target population. It would be especially important to examine such a major design issue in light of requirements for accessibility for disabled learners for whom features such as roll-overs may present unnecessary barriers.

Cognitive walkthroughs. This approach is an effective method for revealing problems that affect users' overall performance, and it can capture cognitive processes of both novice and expert users. This method is especially useful in revealing whether an e-learning product presents a "cognitive overload" problem. Human mental processing has limits, and if the interface of a program demands too much of a learner's mental capacity, then there may not be enough left over to engage in meaningful learning. Conyer (1995) provided an overview of this method:

> Cognitive walkthroughs are used to evaluate the ease of learning to use a product, particularly by exploration. The method is a formalized way of imagining people's thoughts and actions when they use a product interface for the first time (Lewis & Rieman, 1994). Cognitive walkthroughs focus most clearly on problems that users will have when they first use an interface without training. The method uses an explicitly detailed procedure to simulate a user's problem-solving process at each step, checking to see if the user's goals and memory for actions can be assumed to lead to the next correct action (Nielsen & Mack, 1994). There are three phases in the procedure, namely (1) *Preparatory*, when the analysts agree on the input conditions for the

> walkthrough, such as type of users, tasks and action sequence for each task; (2) *Walkthroughs,* which can be an individual or group process; and (3) *Analysis.*" (p. 44)

In designing a protocol for this method, designers are forced to consider the user's background knowledge, the user's goal structure, and the cognitive complexity required for a user to use the product. However, the method continually interferes with the interaction, and people not trained in cognitive psychology may find it difficult to decompose tasks into a collection of sub-tasks. Other constraints are the lack of comparable measures of task time and the primary focus on one attribute of usability, namely ease of learning.

Formal design analysis. This method provides assistance in identifying problems early in the design process. It is less expensive, as it can be performed by a single person. In addition, the approach enables the comparison of different design options. Conyer (1995) explained:

> Formal design analysis techniques aim at improving the design process. An example is the "Goals, Operators, Methods and Selection Rules" (GOMS) model developed by Card (Eberts, 1994).... Formal design analysis is based on the premise that understanding of the requirements of the task to be performed is the key to understanding behavior. Tasks to be performed by an expert user are decomposed into *goals* (a series of cognitive and motor components), *operators* (actions that a user executes), *methods* (sequences of steps), and *selection rules* (needed if more than one method is available to accomplish a goal). Algorithms are then applied and each design is rated with a single number. Alternative design possibilities are then compared based on the numerical result. (p. 45)

Unfortunately, the formal design analysis method misses many key components of behavior that must be considered in interface design, such as learning the task, error behavior, and transfer of learning to other products. This method is somewhat difficult to learn, and few instructional designers are trained to do it. Another weakness in the method is the assumption that all cognitive operations are of equal difficulty.

So which methods do we recommend? This depends on your purpose. As illustrated in Figure 7.8, Conyer (1995) suggested different methods and data collection tools that can be considered for different evaluation purposes.

If the purpose of the usability evaluation is to evaluate____	then consider the ____ methodology	using the ____recording method.
the ability of the user to carry out a task using a product in a particular context	Formal Usability Inspection	Verbal Reports Concurrent Think-Aloud Video Analysis Software Support
how easily users can carry out a task	Pluralistic Walkthrough Formal Usability Inspection Cognitive Walkthrough Formal Design Analysis	Verbal Reports Concurrent Think-Aloud Questionnaire Video Analysis Auto-Logging Programs and Audit Trails
how quickly users can carry out a task	Empirical Studies Formal Design Analysis	Video Analysis Auto-Logging Programs and Audit Trails
the overall quality and acceptance of a product	Heuristic Evaluation	Verbal Reports Questionnaire Software Support
problems with using a product	Pluralistic Walkthrough Formal Usability Testing Cognitive Walkthrough Heuristic Evaluation	Verbal Reports Concurrent Think-Aloud Video Analysis Questionnaire Auto-Logging Programs and Audit Trails Software Support
how easy it is for a novice to learn to use a product	Cognitive Walkthrough Formal Design Analysis	Concurrent Think-Aloud Video Analysis

Figure 7.8. Usability testing methods (Conyer, 1995).

Recording methods

When employing usability evaluation methods, there are a variety of recording methods that can be used to capture data. Conyer (1995) summarized the options as:

Verbal Reports

Users provide a verbal report soon after completing their evaluation. This information can then be informally reviewed or formally classified into categories for evaluation (Karat, 1988).

Concurrent Think-Aloud Method

> Evaluators verbalize their thoughts while interacting with a product. The purpose of this method is to show what the users are doing and why they are doing it *while* they are doing it, in order to avoid later rationalizations.
>
> **Questionnaires**
>
> Questionnaires can be composed of items that address information and attitudes. It is important to keep questions specific rather than general and to ask questions about actual product experience rather than hypothetical questions about possible product changes.
>
> **Video Analysis**
>
> One or more videos can be used to capture data about user interactions. For example, in a software usability evaluation, three different video cameras could be used to capture the user's keyboard actions, the screen activity and the user's verbal and non-verbal responses. Video analysis is then used as a tool in the process of interpreting what usability problems occur and why. Even more powerful is to use the video to create a multimedia document which includes annotations of the usability problems.
>
> **Auto-logging Programs and Audit Trails**
>
> Auto-logging programs can be used to track user actions with respect to duration and frequency of use, e.g., number of keystrokes, requests for help, duration, and path or errors [through a piece of software]. (pp. 46- 47)

These methods have pros and cons. Thinking aloud is not something that people are used to doing, and evaluation participants rarely give quality think-aloud reports without prompting. Often, we record two participants while they talk to each other about their assumptions and the choices they are making in a program. This approach is more natural and produces more useful data. Video analysis takes considerable time, but the payoff can be huge. Tools have been developed to link multimedia video recordings to data analysis techniques, such as QSR *Nvivo,* which enables the classification of qualitative reports (Richards, 1999). With respect to audit trails, the volume of data that can be produced and the statistical analysis of such data can be daunting. Frequently, it is necessary to combine this type of evaluation with video analysis to obtain a complete picture of what the user was doing.

In addition to these planned usability methods, you may observe users with a portable usability system over time in their natural environment doing what they decide to do on their own. This is more like naturalistic evaluation than the types of usability evaluation methods delineated by Conyer (1995) and Nielsen (1993). Whereas the formal methods are usually more focused and efficient, natural observation is time-consuming and less directed. However, the generalizability of findings from the naturalistic approach may be greater. Both can be valuable approaches.

Many times in designing an interface, you may have multiple options for designing an interaction with the computer. "Rapid prototyping" usually requires the creation of multiple designs for small components of your interactive learning system (Hamblen & Furman, 1999; Hix & Hartson, 1993; Tripp & Bichelmeyer, 1990). By comparing tasks performed with each option for interaction, you can feel more confident about which design to use. Alternative metaphors for program designs, various types of icons, and different treatments (e.g., humor or drama) can be examined via usability studies.

Finding appropriate users who will allow you to videotape them interacting with a prototype learning system is sometimes difficult. Some authorities suggest only using a few participants that match your target users (Hix & Hartson, 1993). It is not uncommon to reach a point of diminishing returns on the feedback you receive after four to six learners have completed the usability protocol. As noted above, you may wish to supplement these by using one or two experts in human computer interface (HCI) design to review your interactive learning system.

The importance of the "usability" approach to formative evaluation is considerable. Currently, instructional designers have an inadequate base of knowledge about how users react to and learn with interactive learning systems and other types of computer programs, such as electronic performance support systems (EPSS) (Gery, 1991). The data revealed through usability testing provides an improved basis for guiding the design and implementation of interactive learning systems. We believe that the enhancement of our understanding of interactive multimedia user interfaces can improve the dissemination, implementation, and effects of using interactive learning systems at all levels of education and training. Initial marketing of educational multimedia has succeeded primarily on the basis of selling the "bells and whistles" of technology, but now school boards, superintendents, parents, and taxpayers are beginning to demand research-based evidence that multimedia enhances learning (Cuban, 2001). This demand for accountability is even greater in the corporate world (Rosenberg, 2000). Fundamental understanding of how the interfaces for interactive learning systems are understood by students and trainees is an essential part of that evidence. Usability testing can provide you with precisely that kind of evidence.

Alpha, beta, and field testing

Alpha, beta, and field tests are terms borrowed from the software engineering process followed by commercial software development companies. This structure of evaluation events is useful in organizing small group and field trials of an interactive learning system. Suppose that you are developing an interactive learning system with relatively expensive media elements, such as high-quality computer graphics, digital video, and animation. Before spending project resources to produce these materials, you should conduct an alpha test using storyboards or screen mock-ups with a small sample of typical users (Martin, 2000). If instructors will play a significant role in the eventual implementation of the interactive learning system, they should also be involved in the alpha test.

The materials used in an alpha test may be storyboards, but today they are more likely to be a number of prototype screens presented on either the intended delivery system or some easy to program alternative. An Apple Macintosh computer and a software construction program such as Macromedia Dreamweaver or even Microsoft PowerPoint can provide excellent rapid prototyping environments for interactive learning systems regardless of how they will be delivered. Some elements of the eventual program may be represented by paper scripts, story boards, sketches, and other draft documents, but even during an alpha test you should create and evaluate as much of the "look and feel" of the final product as possible.

Critical aspects to be evaluated during the alpha test include the program's interactivity, comprehension, and appeal. You will want to look for evidence that learners know what to do at critical junctions of the program. You will assess their attention levels and level of active responding. You will look for signs that they are enjoying the experience of using the program. If you rely on learners' responses to direct questions about these factors, you must encourage them to be frank, realizing that their human inclination will be to give you answers that please you rather than their real reactions.

Alpha tests are conducted as soon as a reasonable prototype version of the program can be assembled. By contrast, beta tests are conducted with more-or-less complete versions of an interactive learning system in settings as much like the context of final implementation as possible. While internal staff are usually the primary data collectors during an alpha test, you should consider using external evaluators for the beta test if resources permit. As an interactive learning system nears completion, internal staff are naturally less receptive to modifications. External evaluators can provide a fresh perspective on the formative process, seeing things that internal staff may not be able to perceive because of their intensive familiarity with a program, and their commitment to the present version.

Conducting a beta test at multiple sites is also highly recommended. This can be accomplished by offering beta versions of a program to typical users at no cost with the expectation that they will report their reactions and any bugs they find back to you. Multiple sites are important because the idiosyncrasies of an individual test site may unduly influence the findings of a beta test. Although it is a great idea for development team members to visit some of the beta sites to see the program being used in an authentic context, they obviously won't be able to be at all sites at the same time. In many cases, they will have to rely upon secondhand reports gathered from questionnaires, telephone interviews, or focus groups.

Questionnaires, interviews, and focus groups are three of the most frequently used strategies for collecting formative evaluation data. Each of these strategies is a form of survey. Figure 7.9 presents the important steps involved whenever you undertake to use a survey method to collect data. If time, money, and personnel resources allow, consider collecting formative evaluation data with more than one method during alpha, beta, and field tests. For example, a questionnaire might be used to collect information about user reactions to screen designs. Later, interviews or focus groups might be used to collect more detailed information about which aspects of screens can be improved and how. Alternatively, if you are planning to distribute a survey to many people, you might want to use interviews or focus groups first to identify the issues that should be included on the questionnaire.

Step 1	Organize a team to assemble and review the instrument.
Step 2	Determine the purposes of the survey (e.g., collecting user satisfaction data).
Step 3	Identify a representative sample from whom to collect the data.
Step 4	Generate a list of draft questions.
Step 5	Construct a draft instrument (questionnaire, interview protocol, or focus group protocol).
Step 6	Test the instrument with a small sub-sample of your representative sample.
Step 7	Revise the instrument and retest if necessary.
Step 8	Administer the instrument.
Step 9	Process and analyze the data.
Step 10	Report and use the results.

Figure 7.9. Ten steps to using survey methods.

A field test can be conducted with an interactive learning system that has been improved through alpha and beta tests, especially if there is still time or money available for additional enhancements, perhaps in terms of packaging or implementation strategies. Generally, field tests are conducted without the direct involvement of the development staff. Instead, the emphasis is on evaluating the interactive learning system under conditions virtually identical to more widespread implementation.

Using external evaluators to oversee the process increases the credibility of field tests. Most likely, you will find that field tests and product implementation overlap because the pressure to market and/or disseminate interactive programs will be considerable. In fact, don't be surprised if your team is pressured to release programs that have not been completely validated! This is a common (and we would argue unethical) practice in the commercial software arena where programs are expected to be "debugged" by the clients who buy version 1.0 of a program. Admittedly, field tests are expensive, but the product recalls or lawsuits that could result from a poorly tested system should warrant their application, especially when large scale products, such as integrated learning systems, are involved.

How should the information be reported?

Formative evaluation results are often reported to other team members and/or clients in a less formal manner than other types of evaluation reports. The emphasis in reporting data should be on its timeliness and specificity so that necessary and desirable modifications in the interactive learning system can be made as efficiently as possible. Just as motion picture film crews gather together with the producers, director, and actors at the end of each shooting day to review the "rushes," you may want to establish a regular meeting time to review the results of formative evaluation with the members of the development team, especially the instructional designers. Of course, it is advisable to keep a detailed log of the program revision process so that the decision-making rationale can be reexamined at later dates if necessary.

The key to reporting formative evaluation data is to establish good rapport with the other members of the development team. The ideal is that the development team members will eagerly seek out the findings of your formative evaluation efforts, but the reality is that developers may sometimes feel resentful or stressed about the need to make further changes in a program into which they have poured their hearts and souls. Programmers, graphic artists, videographers, and anyone else directly involved in the production aspects of a project may be especially wary of formative feedback when they are working under difficult deadlines. The sensitivity and communications skills demanded of the evaluator should not be underestimated.

Summary

Formative evaluation consists of a wide variety of strategies designed to help you improve the usability, effectiveness, and appeal of an interactive learning system. Generally, the earlier you begin the formative evaluation process, the better off you will be. You should also plan to continue formative evaluation as long as it is economically feasible. Frankly, it is difficult to know when to stop formative evaluation. Anything as complex as an interactive learning system can be constantly "tweaked" to make it better and better, but at some point the costs of collecting more formative evaluation data will exceed its benefits. In other words, at some point, you have to let things go.

Finally, remember to cultivate a spirit of creativity throughout the formative evaluation process. Most people have good ideas, but they will only share these ideas if they know that they are genuinely valued. If you give people credit for their recommendations, they are very likely to work all that much harder to improve the quality of an interactive learning system. Although most people agree that quality is everyone's business, the "formative" attitude must be constantly nurtured and reinforced.

A major goal of formative evaluation is to "optimize" your interactive program before it is subjected to any type of summative evaluation, such as effectiveness or impact evaluation. In the next chapter, we present strategies for evaluating the effectiveness of interactive learning environments.

References

Bevan, N. (1995). Human-computer interaction standards. In Y. Anzai, K. Ogawa, & H. Mori (Eds.), *Symbiosis of human artifacts* (pp. 349-354). Amsterdam: Elsevier Science.

Beyer, B. K. (1995). *How to conduct a formative evaluation.* Alexandria, VA: Association for Supervision and Curriculum Development

Blattner, M. M., & Dannenberg, R. B. (Eds.). (1992). *Multimedia interface design.* New York: Addison-Wesley.

Branaghan, R. J. (Ed.). (2001). *Essays on usability: Design by people for people.* Chicago: Usability Professionals' Association.

Conyer, M. (1995). User and usability testing — how should it be undertaken? *Australian Journal of Educational Technology, 11*(2), 38-51.

Cuban, L. (2001). *Oversold and underused: Computers in the classroom.* Cambridge, MA: Harvard University Press.

Duby, A. (1988). Early formative evaluation of educational television. *Journal of Educational Television, 14*(1), 43-51.

Eberts, R. E. (1994). *User interface design.* Englewood Cliffs, NJ: Prentice-Hall.

Flagg, B. N. (1990). *Formative evaluation for educational technologies.* Hillsdale, NJ: Lawrence Erlbaum Associates.

Gery, G. (1991). *Electronic performance support systems.* Boston, MA: Weingarten.

Gomoll, K. (1990). Some techniques for observing users. In B. Laurel (Ed.), *The art of human-computer interface design* (pp. 85-90). New York: Addison-Wesley.

Hamblen, J. O., & Furman, M. D. (1999). *Rapid prototyping of digital systems.* The Netherlands: Kluwer Academic Publishers.

Hix, D., & Hartson, H. R. (1993). *Developing user interfaces: Ensuring usability through product & process.* New York: John Wiley & Sons.

Hughes, M., & Burke, L. (2001). Usability testing of Web-based training. In B. Khan (Ed.), *Web-based training* (pp. 531-536) Englewood Cliffs, NJ: Educational Technology Publications.

Karat, J. (1988). Software evaluation methodologies. In M. Helander (Ed.), *Handbook of human-computer interaction* (pp. 891-903). Amsterdam: Elsevier Science.

Khan, B. (Ed.). (1997). *Web-based instruction.* Englewood Cliffs, NJ: Educational Technology Publications.

Khan, B. H. (Ed.). (2001). *Web-based training.* Englewood Cliffs, NJ: Educational Technology Publications.

Kinzie, M. B. (1991). Design of an interactive information program: Formative evaluation and experimental research. *Educational Technology Research and Development, 39*(4), 17-26.

Laurel, B. (Ed.). (1990). *The art of human-computer interface design.* New York: Addison-Wesley.

Leibs, S. (1994, August 15). Why can't PCs be more fun? *Information Week*, 26-34.

Lewis, C., & Rieman, J. (1994). *Task-centered interface design.* Shareware.

Maslowski, R., & Visscher, A. J. (1999). Formative evaluation in educational computing research and development. *Journal of Research on Computing in Education, 32*(2), 239-255.

Martin, L. C. (2000). Storyboarding multimedia interactions. *Performance Improvement, 39*(5), 31-37.

McManus, B., & Hammond, J. (1991). How to make usability work in the real world. In J. H. Hammond, R. R. Hall, & I. Kaplan (Eds.), *OZCHI91: Australian CHISIG Conference Proceedings* (pp. 97-102). Sydney: Ergonomics Society of Australia.

Mitropoulos-Rundus, D., & Muszak, J. (2001). Consumer "in-home" usability testing. In R. J. Branaghan (Ed.), *Essays on usability: Design by people for people* (pp. 131-151). Chicago: Usability Professionals' Association.

Nielsen, J. (1993). *Usability engineering.* Boston: Academic Press.

Nielsen, J. (2000). *Designing Web usability.* Indianapolis, IN: New Riders.

Nielsen, J., & Mack, R.L. (Eds.). (1994). *Usability inspection methods.* New York: John Wiley & Sons.

Polson, P. G. (1988). The consequences of consistent and inconsistent user interfaces. In R. Guindon (Ed.), *Cognitive science and its applications for human-computer interaction* (pp. 59-108). Hillsdale, NJ: Lawrence Erlbaum Associates.

Preece, J. (1994). *Human-computer interaction.* New York: Addison-Wesley.

Reeves, T. C. (1988). Effective dimensions of interactive videodisc for training. In T. Bernold & J. Finkelstein (Eds.), *Computer-assisted approaches to training: Foundations of industry's future* (pp. 119-132). Amsterdam: Elsevier Science.

Reeves, T. C., & Carter, B. J. (2001). Usability testing and return-on-investment studies: Key evaluation strategies for Web-based training. In B. Khan (Ed.), *Web-based training* (pp. 547-557) Englewood Cliffs, NJ: Educational Technology Publications.

Reeves, T. C., & Harmon, S. W. (1994). Systematic evaluation procedures for interactive multimedia for education and training. In S. Reisman (Ed.), *Multimedia computing: Preparing for the 21st century* (pp. 472-505). Harrisburg, PA: Idea Group Publishing.

Reiterer, H., & Opperman, R. (1995). Standards and software-ergonomic evaluation. In Y. Anzai, K. Ogawa, & H. Mori (Eds.), ' *Symbiosis of human artifact* (pp. 361-366). Amsterdam: Elsevier Science.

Richards, L. (1999). *Using NVivo in qualitative research.* Thousand Oaks, CA: Sage.

Rosenberg, M. J. (2000). *E-learning: Strategies for delivering knowledge in the digital age.* New York: McGraw-Hill.

Shneiderman, B. (1987). *Designing the user interface: Strategies for effective human-computer interaction.* Reading, MA: Addison-Wesley.

Tessmer, M. (1994). Formative evaluation alternatives. *Performance Improvement Quarterly*, *7*(1), 3-18.

Tripp, S. D., & Bichelmeyer, B. (1990). Rapid prototyping: An alternative instructional design strategy. *Educational Technology Research and Development, 38*(1), 31-44.

Ziegler, J., & Burmester, M. (1995). Structured human interface validation technique. In Y. Anzai, K. Ogawa, & H. Mori (Eds.), *Symbiosis of human artifact* (pp. 899-906). Amsterdam: Elsevier Science.

CHAPTER 8

Effectiveness Evaluation

Objectives

After reading Chapter Eight, you should be able to:

- identify decisions involved in evaluating the effectiveness of interactive learning systems;
- specify questions that should be answered before making these decisions;
- identify the information needed to answer questions about the effectiveness of interactive learning systems; and
- decide how to collect and report information so that the effectiveness of an interactive learning system can be demonstrated.

Why should you conduct effectiveness evaluation?

The overall purpose of effectiveness evaluation is to determine whether an interactive learning system accomplishes its objectives within the immediate or short-term context of its implementation. As illustrated in Figure 8.1, different types of decisions must be made concerning the dissemination, adoption, and/or implementation of interactive learning systems, each of which is related to one or more specific questions that can be addressed through the strategies used in effectiveness evaluations.

Think back on an education or training program you recently completed. Perhaps you had to be trained on how to handle hazardous chemical spills in your work place. Or you may have been trained in using a complicated new telephone system your company recently installed. Alternatively, you may have recently completed a graduate degree in Instructional Technology. Regardless of the instructional methods used in the education or training program, e.g., teacher-led, interactive multimedia, lecture, video, etc., hopefully there was some degree of difference between the knowledge, skills, and attitudes (KSAs) you possessed before the instruction and the KSAs you had after the instruction (Kirkpatrick, 1998). Determining that difference is the focus of effectiveness evaluation. Evaluating whether you actually apply those KSAs in the work place or in your life is the focus of another facet of our evaluation model, i.e., impact evaluation, which is presented in Chapter Nine.

Decisions	Example Questions
How should the interactive system be marketed?	Do learners achieve the objectives of the program?
Should this program be adopted?	What are implementation requirements? What are the outcomes of the different implementations of this program?
How should instructors be trained to implement this interactive learning system?	To what degree do instructors implement the program as designed? What creative adaptations of this program have instructors made?
What price should be charged for this program?	How do the results achieved with this program compare to alternatives?

Figure 8.1. Typical decisions and questions in an effectiveness evaluation.

When should you conduct effectiveness evaluation?

If what you are concerned about ultimately is changing the performance of people in the work place or helping students become lifelong learners, making an effort to measure learning in the immediate context of education or training may seem like a waste of time. After all, why not focus on impact evaluation, i.e., evaluating the long term effects of your interactive learning system? There are several problems with this notion. To begin, suppose you look for impact and find none. Should you then conclude that your interactive learning system was ineffective? Not necessarily! It could be that people learned new knowledge, skills, and attitudes with your e-learning program, but the larger environment did not allow them to put the new KSAs into practice. This occurs more often than you think. Employees are given training to learn new skills, but when they return to their jobs, they find that their managers or peers force them to keep doing things "the old way" or "our way."

Suppose instead that you conduct an impact evaluation that actually reveals a great deal of evidence supporting the impact of your interactive learning system, e.g., sales went up, accidents decreased, or customer satisfaction ratings soared. But should all (or any) of the credit for these improvements be attributed to the training if you don't have evidence of immediate effectiveness? Others factors in the larger environment may provide better explanations for the increased sales (a new advertising campaign), reduced accidents (elimination of hazards in the work place), or higher customer satisfaction (lower prices). Unless you present evidence that your program was effective in the short-term context of the training per se, you will not be able to build a convincing case for impact.

Finally, as will be explained in the next chapter, evaluating impact is extremely difficult, even impossible, in many situations. After all, how long is long enough to detect your impact on the lifelong learning habits of your students? Gathering short-term effectiveness data may be the best you can do with respect to evaluating the outcomes of your interactive learning system.

What kinds of decisions can you anticipate?

Evidence of the effectiveness of interactive learning systems is often desirable (if not required) for marketing. Whether you are developing training or education programs for internal clients or commercial markets, you will need to make decisions about how to market your interactive program. Although an idealized marketing strategy involves providing hard evidence that the program accomplishes what it is intended to accomplish, interactive learning systems are more often marketed on the basis of other criteria, such as novelty (This detergent is new and improved!), endorsements (Ninety-two percent of dentists surveyed approve of our gum.), or veiled threat (Don't go anywhere without it.).

How will you decide to market your interactive learning system? Should you provide evidence of the knowledge, skills, and attitudes resulting from the program? Should you use learner or instructor endorsements? Should you stress the "bells and whistles" of the new multimedia delivery system used to deliver the instruction or the powerful pedagogical dimensions the program enables you to implement? (Hopefully, unlike many "charlatans" in the software industry, you'll decide to emphasize the pedagogy over "bells and whistles"!)

In addition to marketing decisions, effectiveness data are useful in making decisions about program adoption, adaptation, and implementation. For example, you may find that your interactive learning system works as designed with experienced corporate employees, but new hires need a simpler version or a modified implementation of the program. Or you may find that an interactive learning system that worked well at beta sites during your formative evaluation fails miserably at customer sites where no one has taken responsibility for insuring that the program is installed properly. Effectiveness evaluations provide valuable data in making decisions about training, help, and other forms of user support.

Evidence of effectiveness is also likely to influence decisions about future development efforts, including deciding whether or how to modify your development process, whom to hire or fire for your development team, how to prepare a budget for the next project proposal, and what delivery and authoring systems to adopt. The business of developing interactive learning systems is so volatile that no company, university, or government agency can rest on the laurels of past accomplishments for very long. Using effectiveness information to guide "business decisions" is essential.

What questions should be answered before making decisions?

Before making your marketing, training, implementation, and/or support decisions, you will want reliable, valid answers to questions about the appeal, effectiveness, and efficiency of your interactive learning system. What are learner reactions to the program? What are instructor reactions? What knowledge, skills, and attitudes do learners derive from your program? Does your e-learning system accomplish its objectives in less time than competing programs? Or does your program allow more people to be trained or educated within a given amount of time?

Unfortunately, there is a tendency within business circles to boil the issue of effectiveness down to one simple question: "Is the interactive learning system more effective than the training program previously used (or some competing training program)?" This simplified approach to evaluation questions may be due to the widespread influence of Kirkpatrick's four levels of training evaluation model, which was first introduced in the 1950s and continues to be promoted today (cf. Kirkpatrick, 1998). Although Kirkpatrick's model represents an important contribution to the development of evaluation theory and methodology, it is not sufficient to deal with the complexities of training and education today.

Kirkpatrick (1998) includes four levels of evaluation as described in Figure 8.2. "Level 2 – Learning" of Kirkpatrick's model corresponds most closely to what we mean by effectiveness evaluation, but the actual strategies he recommends for evaluating learning are too simplistic. Kirkpatrick presents the following guidelines for evaluating learning:

> 1. Use a control group if practical.
> 2. Evaluate knowledge, skills, and/or attitudes before and after the program.
> 3. Use a paper-and-pencil test to measure knowledge and attitudes.
> 4. Use a performance test to measure skills.
> 5. Get a 100 percent response.
> 6. Use the results of the evaluation to take appropriate action. (p. 40)

Level	Label	Question
1	Reaction	What levels of satisfaction do trainees express about the training program?
2	Learning	How were the knowledge, skills, and attitudes of the trainees changed by the training?
3	Behavior	How does the behavior of trainees change in the workplace?
4	Results	What is the impact of training on results such as production, sales, profits, accidents, etc.?

Figure 8.2. Kirkpatrick's four levels of training evaluation.

Why do we consider Kirkpatrick's approach to be overly simplistic? First, there are few instances when control groups are feasible within education or training contexts, and even when a control group can be included, there are numerous problems with such comparisons, as will be described later in this chapter. Second, the recommendation to use paper-and-pencil tests is unrealistic in light of the lack of reliable and valid instruments to measure most of the KSAs learners are intended to develop as a result of using interactive learning systems. Third, with the possible exception of a military base, where are evaluators likely to get 100% representation in an evaluation? In our experience, effectiveness evaluations almost always entail major compromises between ideal and real conditions for sampling and data collection. Fourth, although the advice to use the results for action is sound, Kirkpatrick neglects to acknowledge the reality that most evaluations are only one source of influence on decision making, and that a great deal of negotiating and dealing with local politics are necessary before any actions result from effectiveness evaluations (Patton, 1997).

In our opinion, effectiveness is a difficult beast to pin down, and instead of relying on simplistic designs and tests, you should plan your evaluation activities and procedures in ways that will yield as much evidence as possible to build a case that your interactive learning system is effective. As noted in Chapter One, this approach to evaluation has more in common with the work of an attorney trying to build a case for a client's innocence than it does to the experimental scientist measuring the behaviors of rats in a laboratory.

What kinds of information do you need to answer questions?

Effectiveness data take many forms. The most widely used type of effectiveness data is based on testing, although all too often the tests used have questionable reliability and validity. Effectiveness data can also be derived from questionnaires, interviews, focus groups, observations, ratings, simulations, and other methods. At a minimum, you will want to consider gathering information about the effectiveness of an interactive learning system in the following categories:

- knowledge
- skills
- attitudes
- appeal
- implementation

Knowledge takes many forms. Much knowledge is conceptual in nature. For example, a computer company may offer training to increase the "mind share" that their computers hold in the minds of salespersons who sell their systems as well as competing machines. Knowledge may take the form of specific rules, e.g., a bank teller knowing the protocol for signaling a robbery in progress. Often, knowledge is quite diffuse, involving a complex network of associations among concepts and rules, e.g., principles of perception and cognition learned in an introductory psychology class. The meaning of knowledge is changing in Western society as a result of the so-called "cognitive revolution" in learning theory, and what we thought of as knowledge in the past (facts and figures) is changing to a conceptualization of knowledge as the capacity to learn (Simon, 1987). These changes have enormous implications for how we conduct effectiveness evaluations.

Skills are also quite diverse. They can be as discrete as knowing how to forward a telephone call to another office or as general as the ability to make an effective diagnosis of patient illness. In training, as opposed to education, skills generally are regarded as being more important than knowledge. Of course, educators have long stressed the "basic skills" of reading, writing, and mathematics, but they are also beginning to realize the critical importance of "learning to learn" skills. Contemporary cognitive scientists have come up with various taxonomies of learning. One we find especially useful was developed by Kyllonen and Shute (1989) at the U.S. Air Force Armstrong Laboratory in San Antonio, Texas. Their taxonomy represents the spectrum of internal states with which cognitive psychologists are concerned, beginning with simple propositions (e.g., stating that Japan sells more electronic products than any other nation), proceeding through schema, rules, general rules, skills, general skills, automatic skills, and finally, mental models (e.g., estimating the potential of a trade war between Japan and the United States based on an analysis of balance-of-trade trends). The latter type of knowledge seems particularly important because mental models are the basis for generalizable problem-solving abilities (Halford, 1993).

Attitudes are perhaps the instructional outcomes most difficult to measure. Attitudes include such factors as motivation, morale, values, and prejudices. These are frequently measured with self-report instruments, but the differences between self-reported attitudes and actual attitudes are often considerable. Sometimes people are purposefully deceitful in reporting attitudes, but more often they just don't know how they feel or are unable to express their attitudes.

Appeal of interactive learning systems for education and training is related to understanding effectiveness because you generally hope that learners perceive using these systems as desirable, even enjoyable, experiences. If learners enjoy using an interactive learning system for education and training, the enjoyment generally creates internal states that support learning, such as alertness, motivation, and stimulation.

Implementation of an interactive learning system refers to the program as it actually occurred as opposed to the way it was planned. Learners as well as teachers have "bad days." Power failures, fire drills, and other unplanned disturbances disrupt the best-laid implementation plans for interactive learning. An instructor, programmer, or someone else might decide to add "something new" to the interactive learning system at the last moment with the result that it crashes when learners access it. (We both have had this happen!) Deviations from the interactive learning system as designed can be either positive or negative, but it is essential to evaluate the kind and degree of divergence as much as possible. Otherwise, you won't know if the outcomes you measure resulted from the system as designed or some alternative version of it.

How should effectiveness information be collected?

You are strongly advised to prepare a careful evaluation plan before you undertake an effectiveness evaluation (or any other facet of evaluation). As described in Chapter Four, an evaluation plan is a document that spells out in considerable detail the whys and hows of an evaluation effort. Planning and negotiating an evaluation will often represent the major part of the effort you will invest in evaluating an interactive learning system. In fact, once you have a well-designed plan in hand, accompanied by a set of reliable and valid evaluation instruments, it is often possible to turn much of the actual implementation of the plan over to other people. Figure 4.1 in Chapter Four presents a list of the major components of an evaluation plan.

One advantage of an evaluation plan is that it is a public document that your clients can review and approve. You are advised to have your evaluation plan thoroughly reviewed by clients and have them indicate their approval using a sign-off form (see Figure 4.18 in Chapter Four). Another useful tool in planning an effectiveness evaluation is a data collection matrix, as illustrated in Figure 4.9 in Chapter Four. Down one side of the matrix, you should list your evaluation methods, and across the other side, you should list your specific evaluation questions. Then you can consider the acceptability, feasibility, reliability, and validity of each data collection method in reference to each question.

Acceptability is one of the criteria you must consider in selecting data collection methods. Some methods may not be acceptable in certain training contexts, e.g., if union rules do not permit employees to be tested. Feasibility is another of the criteria you must consider. Although you might consider participant observation as a powerful indicator of effectiveness, you may lack the resources to use this method in a specific evaluation context. Reliability is the criterion concerned with the consistency of a measure. For example, whenever you use multiple experts to review the effectiveness of a program, you have to be concerned with their inter-rater reliability. Finally, validity is the criterion that addresses the issue of whether you are measuring what you really intended to measure. You are probably familiar with training situations in which a test was administered that seemed to be assessing KSAs that had very little to do with what you actually learned in the training. The test itself may have been a well-constructed one, but it was invalid for that purpose.

Determining the reliability and validity of outcome measures is an often ignored aspect of effectiveness evaluation. Few evaluators have sufficient psychometric expertise to conduct reliability and validity studies. In addition, clients are inclined to accept test results as somehow sacrosanct, viewing a test score as something valuable in and of itself. We regard establishing the reliability and validity of evaluation instruments as a professional responsibility. There are books that can help (Gronlund, Linn, & Davis, 1999; Loewenthal, 2000; Morris, Fitz-Gibbon, & Lindheim, 1987; Wiggins, 1998), but testing consultants are often required.

Implementation logs

Implementation logs are useful in effectiveness evaluation because unless you know how the interactive learning system was actually implemented, you will have little basis for interpreting the outcomes you measure. Implementation logs are used to assess the fidelity of the implementation. Sometimes, there may be major differences between an interactive learning system as designed and the program as implemented. For example, consider an interactive program that assumes that pairs of learners will complete the program. Occasionally, that same program might be used by a larger group than was intended or even by an instructor with a whole class. Although these divergent uses may be unavoidable, it is necessary to have some record of the actual use. Figure 8.3 provides an example of a completed implementation log.

The log in Figure 8.3 indicates precisely what should occur during the training day. It also has space for noting any discrepancies between the planned implementation and what actually took place. The form is designed to encourage the evaluator to think about how problems that occurred might be avoided in the future. Finally, it has space for noting creative changes to the program that might be recommended. Deviations from the planned implementation are not always negative, and you will want to record ideas for improving your strategies.

Whereas implementation logs are usually maintained by an instructor or evaluator, trainees may also keep logs during their use of an interactive learning system. A version of the formative review log presented in Figure 7.4 in Chapter Seven may be used for this type of data collection. You should estimate the degree to which keeping such a log may interfere with the learning process, and if the interference seems too great, consider other methods of data collection. Some interactive learning systems are designed with online logs that learners can use to record their feedback to the developers and administrators of a program as they use it. Or it may be appropriate to save learners' work automatically and then collect work samples for analysis at other times.

IMPLEMENTATION LOG

DATE: *October 2-3* PLACE: *Chicago* TIME: *9:00 - 5:00*

TRAINER: *Larry Jones* NUMBER OF TRAINEES: *15*

Time	Recommended Activities	Actual Activities	Comments
09:00-09:15	Introductions of participants and review of agenda. (Leader-led)	*No changes.*	
09:15-09:30	Overview of new course. (Leader-led)	*No changes.*	
09:30-12:00	Trainees begin Module 1. (multimedia systems)	*One system failed to function because someone removed system files.*	*I need to check systems personally before course begins.*
12:00-01:00	Lunch Break.	*Two trainees chose to skip lunch and keep working.*	
01:00-05:00	Trainees continue working through the modules.	*No changes.*	*Frequently had to refer trainees to help.*

1. What activities would you like to modify the next time you conduct this course?
I will personally check each of the multimedia systems to insure that the modules function as designed.

2. How can the training materials used in this course be enhanced?
Trainees pointed out several errors in the data communications module. See attached list.

Figure 8.3. Sample implementation log.

Questionnaires

Questionnaires are one of the most frequently used methods of collecting effectiveness data. As noted above, the acceptability and feasibility of measurement instruments are major concerns in selecting any type of data collection method. Collecting data about learner reactions to instruction, which is Level 1 in Kirkpatrick's (1998) classic evaluation model, is widely acceptable and usually quite feasible in any context. This explains the popularity of the post-instruction questionnaire that you and virtually every other learner complete at some point. These instruments have been variously called "evaluation forms," "happiness indexes," and "smilometers." It is tempting to assemble evaluation questionnaires hastily, but you should invest considerable planning and revision time in these instruments. Figure 8.4 presents a sample questionnaire used in the evaluation of interactive multimedia in a university course. Several different types of closed and open-ended questions are posed in this instrument.

ECOLOGY 100 — Stream Lab Data Analysis Program

We need your feedback to help us develop better interactive tools for the Ecology 100 course. Your responses are anonymous. Thank you for your time.

Today's Date? ____________ Your T.A.'s Name? ________________

Your Age? ____ Years Class? __FR __SO __JR __SR __ Other _______

Gender? __M __F Major? ______________________________

1. Please circle your responses to the following statements using the scale below.

1 = Strongly Disagree 2 = Disagree 3 = Neither Agree or Disagree 4 = Agree 5 = Strongly Agree

a.	The "Stream Lab" field work was a valuable learning activity.	1	2	3	4	5
b.	Using the "Stream Lab" multimedia program was a valuable learning activity.	1	2	3	4	5
c.	The "Watershed" animation helped me to understand what a watershed is.	1	2	3	4	5
d.	The "Effects of Land Use" simulation helped me to understand how differences in land use affect stream quality.	1	2	3	4	5
e.	The "State Botanical Gardens Walk" helped me to understand the land uses in the State Botanical Gardens.	1	2	3	4	5
f.	The "Tanyard Branch Walk" helped me to understand the land uses surrounding Tanyard Branch.	1	2	3	4	5
g.	The "Bioassessment Pamphlet" helped me to understand why we sampled macroinvertebrates in the stream.	1	2	3	4	5
h.	The data analysis portion of the "Macroinvertebrate Bioassessment" was an effective learning tool.	1	2	3	4	5
i.	The overall multimedia treatment or design of this "Stream Lab "is appealing and easy to use.	1	2	3	4	5

2. What is the best thing about the "Stream" program? (Use back if needed.)

3. How would you improve the "Stream" program? (Use back if needed.)

4. Please write any other comments about this course on the back of this sheet.

Figure 8.4. Sample student evaluation questionnaire.

Developing questionnaires is the subject of many workshops and books (Converse & Presser, 1986; Fink & Kosecoff, 1998; Fowler, 1995), and you are advised to avail yourself of the opportunity to develop advanced survey skills if questionnaires are going to be a major tool that you will use in effectiveness evaluations. Alternatively, you can hire a survey consultant to develop your instruments. Questionnaires should be reviewed carefully by other members of the development team as well as by any external clients to make sure that all of the salient issues are addressed. It is also important to pilot a questionnaire with individuals who are as much like the eventual respondents as possible. Even the most carefully crafted questionnaires will have items that are confusing for some and misunderstood by others. Eliminating as many of these problems as possible involves several rounds of testing the instrument with typical respondents.

Interviews

Interviews are powerful tools for collecting data about the effectiveness of interactive learning systems. Interviews provide participants in an evaluation more opportunities to speak in their own voice instead of merely responding to the categories of questions that others have defined for them. It is important to plan your interview protocol carefully. This will often involve several trial interviews and subsequent revisions of the questions. Figure 8.5 presents a typical post-training interview protocol.

Most interview protocols allow adjustments in questioning strategies to fit the nature of individual interviewees. You should always be prepared to ask questions in areas that may not have been anticipated by the designers of the interview protocol.

Recording interview data presents challenges. Audio or video recorders may be used, but these devices may intimidate interviewees so much that their responses are skewed. Practice taking brief notes during an interview, and subsequently recording a more detailed transcription of the interview immediately after its conclusion. If possible, it is advisable to do a "mind dump" (writing everything you can recall) concerning one interview before starting to conduct another. Otherwise, you are liable to confuse the responses from one person with those from someone else.

It is sometimes difficult to strike a balance between reporting a highly subjective interpretation of the results of interviews and a verbatim report of all the interviewees' responses. Most decision makers will reject the former as being too biased and will reject the latter for being too long. The following tips may help:

- Have several different people read interview transcripts and then use group brainstorming techniques to tease out the major findings.

- Look for exemplary quotes which capture in well-spoken words the feelings and beliefs of a significant portion of the interviewees.
- Provide appendices of complete transcripts of the interviews so that readers can spot-check your interpretations.

Another useful strategy is to have interviewees themselves review your reports, adding clarification as needed.

INTERVIEW PROTOCOL

A subset of the personnel completing the Learner Questionnaire will be interviewed either in person at the work site or via telephone. The following interview protocol is likely to be modified during use. All interviews will be audio-recorded and transcribed for analysis.

1) What previous experience have you had with interactive multimedia programs?
   - What kinds of computer games have you played?
   - What kinds of multimedia training have you experienced?
   - What other kinds of multimedia have you used?
2) How does the experience of using this program compare with your earlier experiences?
   - How does it compare with computer games?
   - How does it compare with other multimedia training programs?
   - How does it compare with other kinds of multimedia you have used?
3) Describe your experiences with using the World Wide Web (WWW).
   - How have you used the WWW to find information?
   - How have you used the WWW to purchase things?
   - How have you used the WWW for entertainment?
   - How have you used the WWW to learn?
4) What would you say to other workers with jobs like yours about this program?
5) What would you say to the company managers about this type of training?
6) What hardware and software would you need to use this type of program at home?
   - What kind of personal computer would you need?
   - What kind of software would you need?
   - What kind of Internet access would you need?
7) What areas of training and education would be suitable for this multimedia approach?
8) What is your preferred way of using this program, alone or with someone else?
   - What are the advantages and disadvantages of working with someone else?
   - What are the advantages and disadvantages of working alone?
9) Should this type of multimedia training program be used more widely within this company? Why or why not?
10) What other feedback can you provide concerning this program?

Figure 8.5. Sample interview protocol.

Observations

Observations are useful as measures of the implementation of interactive learning systems and as relatively unobtrusive measures of effectiveness. Observations require carefully designed protocols to provide useful data (see Figure 7.4 in Chapter Four). Observations are somewhat time consuming and labor intensive compared to other data collection methods, but the rich nature of the data obtained often justifies the extra work required to observe a program in use. Depending on the complexity of the interactive program, you may want to videotape your observations or simply keep notes as you observe. Participant observation is an especially powerful variant of observational methods. Having development team members actually participate in a training session using the interactive learning system they developed can be an extremely enlightening experience for all, especially the team members.

Automated user tracking

Computers are usually essential components of the delivery system for interactive learning systems, and because this is so, you automatically have access to a reliable and tireless electronic observer. The computer can record every key stroke, mouse click, screen touch, or other interaction with the interactive program while providing precise times down to the microsecond for each action. This results in what can be called an "audit trail" of the learner's progress through an interactive learning system (Schwier & Misanchuk, 1993). Of course, you will soon be drowning in an empirical swamp of data unless you carefully plan ahead for the data you want and how you are going to analyze it.

Consider a typical e-learning program that includes a number of discrete modules, with each module containing several different types of instructional options, e.g., tutorials, quizzes, practice exercises, and mastery tests. You can record trainee paths through the modules, their choices among the instructional options, and their quiz and test scores. Most learning management systems (LMS) include audit trail functions (Hall, 2001). You could even make your online data collection proactive by displaying questions on the screen that inquire about the trainee's reactions to various aspects of the interactive program at pre-specified intervals or points.

The analysis of audit trail data within complex multimedia or hypermedia programs is especially challenging (Salter, 1995). When learners can go wherever they want in any sequence, the possibility of detecting interpretable paths without the input of the learners becomes almost impossible. This problem is even more complex when the World Wide Web is used for the delivery of interactive learning. It is technically quite easy to track wherever a user goes on the Web, and in fact, commonly used browsers automatically keep track of path data. However, the interpretation of such data involves a great deal of inference. Even more problematic is the issue of the ethics of tracing where someone goes on the Web. In most cases, you are not advised to collect audit trail data unless complete anonymity can be guaranteed, and even then, learners must be informed that such data are being tracked.

Tests

– **WEB LINK** –
Valuable free information on testing can be found at the ERIC Center on Assessment and Evaluation: http://ericae.net/

Although testing is widely accepted as an effectiveness evaluation strategy, you should be wary of tests unless you have evidence of their reliability and validity. Paper-and-pencil tests using multiple choice test items are pervasive as evaluation methods, but the reliability and validity of these instruments are often suspect. There are many different types of test questions (e.g., short answer, true-false, simple multiple choice, complex multiple choice, and essay), and each has advantages and disadvantages in terms of acceptability, feasibility, reliability, validity, and security. You are advised to consult a test construction manual before attempting to assemble a test for effectiveness evaluation (Haladyna, 1999; Morris, Fitz-Gibbon, & Lindheim, 1987; Westgaard, 1999).

Angelo and Cross (1993) provide an excellent introduction to alternative assessment strategies. Viable alternatives to traditional paper-and-pencil tests are performance tests or mini-simulations of the ultimate performance that your interactive learning system is designed to teach. Suppose your interactive learning system trains healthcare workers how to dispose of syringes and other sharp medical instruments without risk of cutting themselves or others. A paper-and-pencil test item might ask them to recite rules for handling this situation, but a simulation or performance test can be set up that actually requires the trainees to demonstrate the knowledge, skills, and/or attitudes being trained. Of course, it is often more difficult and expensive to use performance tests, but the validity of this method is usually high.

Expert review

Expert review can be used for effectiveness evaluation as well as formative evaluation. The immediate supervisors of trainees may provide you with an insightful perspective on the effectiveness of your interactive program if they are given the opportunity to observe or actually participate in the training. Depending on the type of technology you are using, you may also want to utilize instructional experts to review your product's effectiveness. Content experts are more frequently used for formative evaluation, but they can also provide you with important information about the perceived effectiveness of interactive learning systems.

A few final caveats must be issued regarding effectiveness evaluation. First, you should not rely on only one or two measures of the effectiveness of your interactive learning system. Instead, attempt to "triangulate" effectiveness by measuring it with as wide a variety of approaches as your resources allow. Second, it is as important to evaluate implementation of a program as it is to assess effectiveness because, without knowing how it was actually used, you can't judge outcomes fairly. Third, rarely trust test data in isolation. Reliable, valid tests are exceedingly difficult to construct, and their security is frequently compromised in education and training contexts.

How should effectiveness studies be designed?

Don't be surprised if your managers or clients want you to set up a comparative evaluation wherein the effects of the new interactive learning system will be compared with the effects of a competing instructional approach. This type of "horse race" evaluation is frequently conducted, but these kinds of studies usually reveal "no significant differences" in effectiveness between the alternatives. This unfortunate outcome can often be traced to weaknesses in the comparative evaluation design itself and/or a lack of understanding of the dimensions that are common to both programs (Reeves, 1993a, b).

If you must do a comparative evaluation, you are advised to expand the criteria for comparison beyond traditional effectiveness measures to include such dimensions as the experiential value, costs, safety, flexibility, and efficiency of the competing programs (Reeves, 1988). Despite the hype surrounding multimedia and the World Wide Web, interactive learning systems are not always more effective than traditional methods of education and training. However, the implementation of interactive learning systems can often be justified by other criteria. Consider experiential value. There is considerable evidence that experiential learning is more motivating, and if an interactive learning system can be designed to provide more realistic and challenging scenarios than traditional lectures or linear media, learners may be more motivated to learn. The award-winning medical simulations designed by Dr. Joe Henderson (1991) at Dartmouth Medical School are excellent examples of programs with high experiential value.

Another important criterion on which to base a comparative evaluation between interactive learning systems and alternative methods is costs. Although many uninformed people automatically assume that technology-based instruction will always be more expensive than teacher-centered instruction, this isn't necessarily the case. Gustafson, Reeves, and Laffey (1990) describe the results of *Macintosh Fundamentals*, an interactive videodisc-based training system developed for Apple Computer, Inc. (This program was described in more detail in Chapter Three.) Although the program cost a million dollars to develop in the late 1980s, 10,000 people completed an average of over nine hours of training via the system during its first year of use alone. The cost per hour of this training compared quite favorably to the cost of any instructor-led approach.

Safety is another important factor in education and training. There are numerous examples of interactive learning systems in science education where hazardous laboratory experiments have been simulated with high fidelity. Also, in an age of rampant litigation, teachers are much less likely to be able to take their students outside the school for field research, especially in dangerous habitats such as lakes and rivers. Fortunately, ground-breaking innovative CD-ROMs like *Investigating Lake Iluka* and *Exploring the Nardoo* enable high school students to carry out research in simulated environments (Hedberg *et al.*, 1994; Wright, Harper, & Hedberg, 1999). In some situations, including military and industrial training, an evaluation based on safety alone may justify the adoption of interactive learning systems even if effectiveness is not greater and costs are higher. Airlines have recognized this for years.

Flexibility is an issue that is increasingly important for learners at a distance, or even for those learners who may be physically near traditional education and training institutions, but who prefer the flexibility provided by interactive learning systems that can be used anytime, anyplace. Comparative evaluations of most distance learning systems with traditional classroom instruction indicate equivalent effectiveness, but the criteria of great flexibility and accessibility tip the scales for the distance approaches (Moore & Kearsley, 1996; Schlosser & Anderson, 1994).

Yet another important criteria for comparative evaluation is efficiency. A consistent finding from the research literature on interactive learning systems has been a 25 percent or more savings in the amount of time learners take to complete a given set of instructional objectives using interactive learning systems over traditional classroom approaches (Hall, 1997; Reeves, 1988; Rosenberg, 2000). These results make sense if you think about group pacing versus individualized pacing. In the former, all learners proceed at the rate determined by the instructor, whereas in interactive approaches, learners often proceed at their own speed. Thirty learners in an hour-long lecture take an average of 60 minutes each to complete instruction. The same learners using computer-based training may take from 20 to 80 minutes to complete instruction, but their average time may only be 45 minutes.

How can alternative learning systems be described?

As noted above, evaluators have often relied upon traditional empirical evaluation methods that compare the effectiveness of an instructional innovation with some other approach, but the results of these types of studies have been disappointing (Clark, 1992). A major weakness in comparative approaches to evaluation is that the systems being compared (e.g., interactive multimedia versus classroom instruction) are assumed to be cohesive, holistic entities with meaningful differences. Berman and McLaughlin (1978) as well as Cooley and Lohnes (1976) have illustrated the fallacy of assuming that there are meaningful differences between two programs just because they have different names. Given the great variance in implementation of various instructional methods, there may be more differences among methods with the same name than between differently labeled methods. It is imperative to open up the "black boxes" of alternative learning systems and reveal the relevant pedagogical dimensions they express if an evaluation is to be meaningful and useful.

Reeves and Harmon (1994) describe a set of 14 pedagogical dimensions that can be used to analyze multimedia as an interactive learning system. Figure 8.6 is an example of a rating form using 10 of those dimensions that may be used to analyze the pedagogical differences between two different instructional approaches within a comparative evaluation. It is important to note that this instrument is a descriptive rather than a prescriptive one. Each of the ten dimensions in this instrument is presented as a two-ended continuum with contrasting values at either end. Of course, the world is rarely dichotomous, and there is more complexity involved in learning than any one of these dimensions represents. The individual dimensions themselves are not as important as the arrays across the ten dimensions that represent the instructional designs of various interactive learning systems. A particular array of ratings is not guaranteed to yield an effective interactive learning system. This instrument is to be used to identify the pedagogical similarities and differences between two programs you intend to subject to a comparative evaluation. A description of each dimension follows.

Pedagogical philosophy

The debate between instructivist and constructivist approaches to teaching and learning continues throughout education and training (Duffy & Jonassen, 1992; Kafai & Resnick, 1996). At the risk of over-simplifying this issue, the "pedagogical philosophy" dimension ranges from a strict instructivist structure to a radical constructivist one. Instructivists stress the importance of objectives that exist apart from the learner. Once objectives are identified, they are sequenced into learning hierarchies, generally representing a progression from lower to higher order learning. Then, direct instruction is designed to address each of the objectives in sequence. Little emphasis is put on learners per se, who are viewed as passive recipients of instruction or treated as relatively "empty vessels" to be filled with learning. (Or so constructivists claim.)

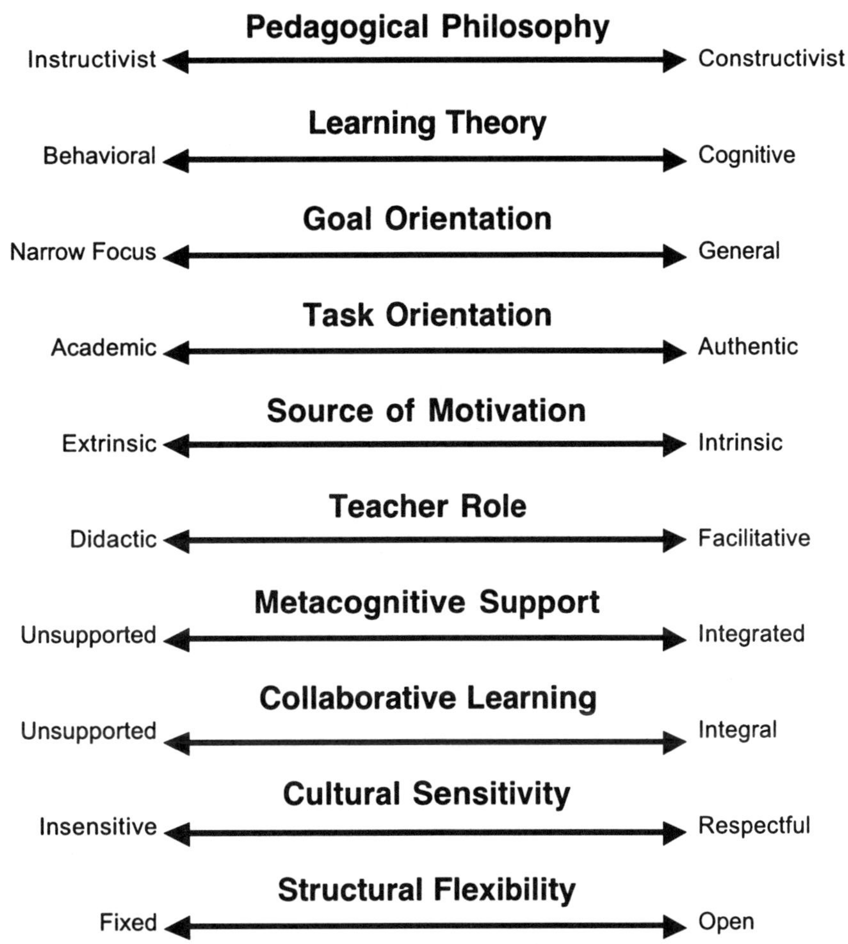

Figure 8.6. Pedagogical dimensions of interactive learning systems.

Instructivists espouse an objectivist epistemology that defines knowledge as separate from knowing. They believe that reality exists regardless of the existence of sentient beings; humans acquire knowledge about this reality in an objective manner through the senses; learning consists of acquiring truth; and learning can be measured precisely with tests. Examples of interactive learning systems grounded in an instructivist pedagogy abound, especially in the form of computer-based training used in industry and popular computer-based tutorials used in schools.

By contrast, constructivists emphasize the primacy of each individual learner's intentions, experiences, and cognitive strategies. According to constructivists, any given learner constructs different cognitive structures based upon his or her previous knowledge and what he or she experiences in different learning environments. It is paramount for constructivists that learning environments be as rich and diverse as possible. The learner is regarded as an individual replete with pre-existing knowledge, aptitudes, motivations, and other characteristics that are difficult to assess, much less accommodate. Direct instruction is replaced with tasks to be accomplished or problems to be solved that have personal relevance for each learner.

With regard to epistemology, constructivists believe that knowledge does not exist outside the minds of humans, and that what we know of "reality" is individually and socially constructed based on prior experience. Rather than truth, learning consists of acquiring viable strategies that meet one's objectives, and at best, learning can be estimated only through observation and dialogue. Wilson (1996) describes numerous examples of interactive learning environments that function primarily as resources for learners engaged in constructing their own knowledge representations.

Learning theory

The design of interactive learning systems should be based upon sound learning theories. Although there are other useful learning theories, two that dominate instructional design are behavioral and cognitive psychology. These two theories are often juxtaposed, and thus the "learning theory" dimension has behavioral psychology at one end of the continuum and cognitive psychology at the other. Behavioral psychology continues to underlie most interactive learning systems. According to behaviorists, the critical factors in learning are not internal states, but observable behavior. Behaviorist instruction involves shaping desirable behaviors through the arrangement of stimuli, responses, feedback, and reinforcement. A stimulus is provided, usually in the form of a short presentation of content. Next, a response is demanded, often via a question. Feedback is given as to the accuracy of the response, and positive reinforcement is given for accurate responses. Inaccurate responses result in a repetition of the original stimulus or a modified (often simpler) version of it, and the cycle begins again.

Cognitive psychologists, by contrast, place more emphasis on internal mental states than on behavior. As described above, a typical cognitive taxonomy of internal learning states includes simple propositions, schema, rules, general rules, skills, general skills, automatic skills, and mental models (Kyllonen & Shute, 1989). Cognitivists claim that a variety of learning strategies, including memorization, direct instruction, deduction, drill and practice, and induction, are required in any learning environment depending upon the type of knowledge to be constructed by the learner. Interactive learning systems can be grounded in behavioral learning theory, cognitive learning theory, or a blend of both.

Goal orientation

The goals for education and training can range from sharply focused ones (e.g., following medical trauma protocols) to general, higher order ones (e.g., developing patient rapport). Similarly, the goal orientation dimension of an interactive learning system can vary in degree of focus from sharp to broad. Cole (1992) maintains that some knowledge "has undergone extensive social negotiation of meaning and might most efficiently and effectively be presented more directly to the learner" (p. 29). In such cases, direct instruction, perhaps in the form of an interactive tutorial, may suffice. Other knowledge is so tenuous, creative, or of a higher level that a constructivist learning environment supporting inductive learning is much more appropriate (Wilson, 1996). Advanced learning environments might include a blend of direct instruction with opportunities to use technology as a cognitive tool (Jonassen & Reeves, 1996).

Task orientation

A basic tenet of adult learning theory (andragogy) is that the context of learning is enormously important to adults (Beder, 1989; Merriam, 1993). Contemporary cognitive learning theories also emphasize the importance of context (cf. Brown, Collins, & Duguid, 1989). The "task orientation" dimension has academic tasks at one end and authentic tasks at the other. Most interactive learning systems still employ academic tasks, but interactive learning can be designed to focus on authentic tasks relevant to learners. Consider the design of educational software for adult literacy. An academic design would depend heavily on having the learners complete traditional academic exercises such as identifying parts of sentences. By contrast, an authentic design would engage the adults in practical activities such as preparing job applications, thereby situating practice and feedback within realistic scenarios. Cognitive learning theory indicates that the ways in which knowledge, skills, and attitudes are initially learned affect the degree to which these abilities can be used in other contexts. If knowledge, skills, and attitudes are learned in a context of use, they will be used in that and similar contexts. Otherwise, it is left up to learners to generate connections between problems and solutions. Whenever transfer to real-world contexts is of primary concern, situating interactive learning in relevant contexts may be advantageous, although the research support for this is still weak.

Source of motivation

Motivation is a primary factor in any theory or model of learning. Every new educational technology promises to be intrinsically motivating, and interactive learning systems are no exception. Consider the hype about the Internet as a vehicle for interactive learning (cf., Perelman, 1992). The "source of motivation" dimension ranges from extrinsic (i.e., outside the learning environment) to intrinsic (i.e., integral to the learning environment) (Malone, 1981). Intrinsically motivating instruction is elusive regardless of the delivery system, but some proponents seem convinced that multimedia motivates learners automatically, simply because of the integration of music, voice, graphics, text, animation, video, and a user-friendly interface. Actually, multimedia studies indicate that some learners tire of these media elements (Reeves, 1993a). It is obvious that motivational aspects must be consciously designed into an interactive learning system as rigorously as any other pedagogical dimension.

Teacher role

Interactive learning systems can be designed to support different roles for teachers, e.g., the traditional didactic role of the instructor as "sage on the stage" or the facilitative role as "guide on the side." Accordingly, the "teacher role" continuum ranges from didactic to facilitative. Over a quarter century ago, Carroll (1968) told us that "By far the largest amount of teaching activity in educational settings involves telling things to students..." (p. 4). Little has changed since then, despite much discussion of a shift in the teacher's role from a didactic one to that of a facilitator. Part of the problem is that educational technology research continues to be focused on how the computer can be used to present information and judge learner input (neither of which computers do well) while asking learners to memorize information and later recall it on tests (which computers do with far greater speed and accuracy than humans). It is time to assign cognitive responsibility to the part of the learning system that does it best, i.e., the learner (Jonassen & Reeves, 1996).

Well-designed interactive learning systems may be the ideal vehicle for this transformation. The learner should be responsible for recognizing and judging patterns of information, organizing data, constructing alternative perspectives, and representing new knowledge in meaningful ways, while the computer should perform calculations, store information, and retrieve it upon the learner's command. For example, when multimedia is used by learners as a cognitive tool for representing their own knowledge, the teacher can be a coach or even a collaborator in the knowledge construction process.

Metacognitive support

Metacognition refers to a learner's awareness of objectives, ability to plan and evaluate learning strategies, and capacity to monitor progress and adjust learning behaviors to accommodate needs (Flavell, 1979). In short, metacognitive skills are the skills one has in "learning to learn." The "metacognitive support" dimension has unsupported at one end of the continuum and integrated at the other. Imagine an interactive learning system designed to challenge learners to solve complex problems such as troubleshooting electrical circuit boards. Metacognitive support integrated into such a program could provide learners with recapitulations of their troubleshooting strategies at any point in the problem-solving process. Much research and development remains before interactive learning systems regularly include sophisticated metacognitive support, but the potential is enormous.

Collaborative learning

Interactive learning systems can be designed to ignore or promote collaborative learning, i.e., some programs require cooperative learning whereas others make no provision for its support. The "collaborative learning" dimension ranges from a complete lack of support for collaboration to the inclusion of collaborative learning as an integral feature. Cooperative and collaborative learning refer to instructional methods in which learners work together in pairs or small groups to accomplish shared goals. When interactive learning is structured to foster collaborative learning, learners can benefit both instructionally and socially. Given an appropriate instructional design, two or more learners working together may accomplish more than a single learner because the interactions between the learners may be just as important for learning as the interactions between the learners and the interactive program.

Cultural sensitivity

All instructional systems have cultural implications. For example, whereas constructivist pedagogy advocates questioning on the part of learners, "why?" questions may be inappropriate in some cultures. Although it is unlikely that an interactive learning system can be designed to adapt to every cultural norm, programs should be designed to be as culturally sensitive as possible. The "cultural sensitivity" dimension ranges from insensitive to respectful. Few interactive learning systems have been developed in which cultural sensitivity is integral to their design, whereas more than a few are culturally insensitive. For example, multimedia that uses icons such as a pointing hand to indicate direction may violate a cultural taboo by representing a dismembered body part in certain African cultures. At the very least, interactive learning systems should accommodate the diverse ethnic and cultural backgrounds among the learners expected to use it. Better yet, these systems should build upon the diversity in the populations where these programs will be used so that the overall learning environment is enhanced.

Structural flexibility

Interactive learning environments can be "fixed" or "open" with respect to time and/or place. "Fixed" systems, still dominant in U.S. education, are usually limited to specific places, e.g., a classroom or laboratory, at specific times, e.g., the ubiquitous 50-minute class period. "Open" systems can be used by the learner independent of time and/or place constraints, e.g., print-based independent study materials mailed to learners. Interactive learning systems can provide opportunities for more open (asynchronous) learning. Major questions remain about whether or how interactive learning systems can be used to break the hegemony of fixed instructional modes that limit pedagogical innovation in traditional academic settings. To date, most of the interactive learning systems developed for education and training simply supplement traditional "fixed" approaches to teaching and learning. However, the rapid growth of the Internet and the high bandwidth capabilities of the World Wide Web mean that interactive learning can be designed for delivery anytime, anywhere to anyone with a personal computer and a high-speed modem.

Applying the Pedagogical Dimensions Analysis Tool

The *Jasper Woodbury Problem Solving Series* (CTGV, 1992) was created in an academic environment within the context of a research and development program. Its use was initially confined to a few dozen schools in the southeastern U.S., but it is now commercially available. The *Jasper Series* (delivered via interactive videodisc) is regarded as an example of a well-designed interactive learning system because it provides students with opportunities to develop mathematical problem-solving skills through high-interest simulated adventures. Students discover the need to develop mathematical skills within the context of flying ultra-light planes and operating motor boats to solve challenging dilemmas. Numerous studies have been conducted using the *Jasper* series of programs (cf., Bransford *et al.*, 1990).

The *Jasper* series is an example of what Hannafin (1992) calls a "generative" learning environment, i.e., a program that requires students to construct or generate their own knowledge as opposed to one that requires them to select knowledge from prepackaged options. Knowledge constructed in generative environments is more likely to transfer than the inert knowledge that is acquired in traditional passive learning environments (CTGV, 1992). Figure 8.7 presents a profile of the *Jasper* programs using the 10 pedagogical dimensions described above. These ratings are based on seeing demonstrations of the programs at professional conferences, reading several extensive reports about the programs (cf., Bransford, Vye, Goldman, Hasselbring, & Pellegrino, 1991), and limited first-hand experience with the programs themselves. This analysis reveals that the *Jasper* programs are grounded in constructivist and cognitivist foundations. Teachers are integral facilitators in implementing *Jasper*, and they are encouraged to modify it according to their local needs. Collaborative learning is strongly supported in these programs. Special attention appears to have been paid to cultural aspects of the populations likely to use these programs.

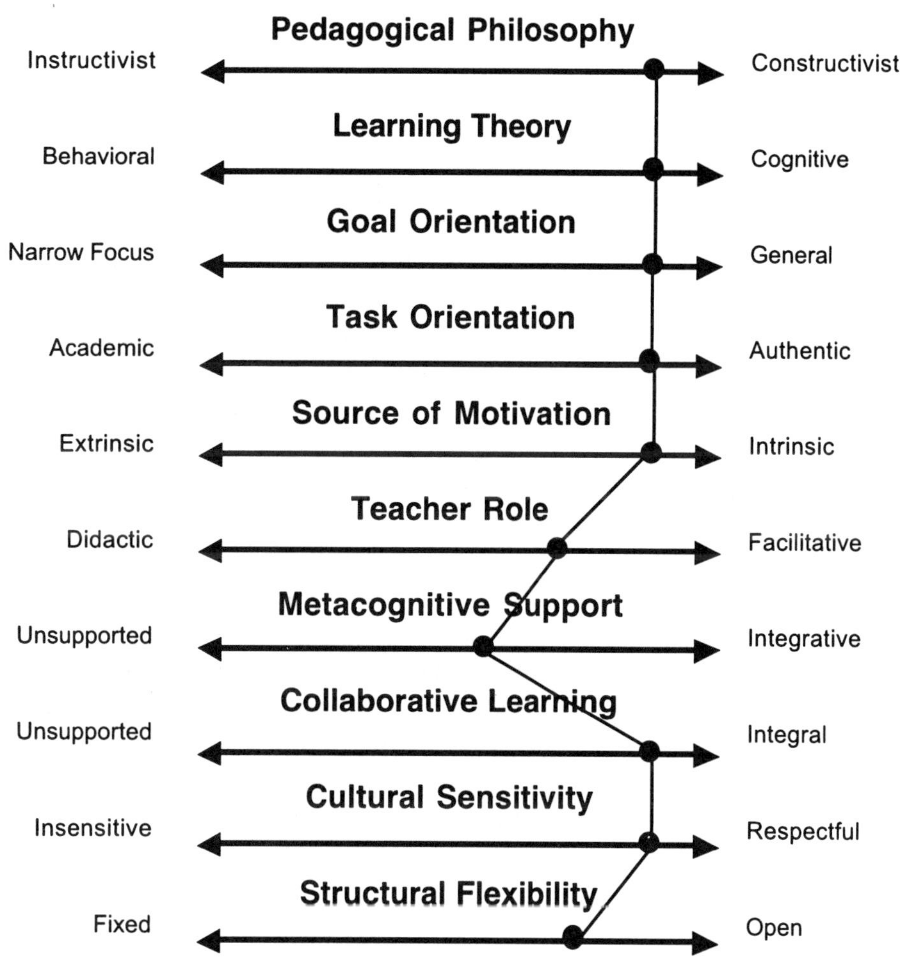

Figure 8.7. Pedagogical analysis of Jasper Woodbury programs.

If we were asked to conduct a comparative evaluation of the *Jasper* programs with an alternative approach to teaching mathematical problem-solving skills, one of the first things we would want to do is to analyze the pedagogical similarities and differences between the two programs using a version of the pedagogical analysis tool. This would be our first step because we know that it is the mix of pedagogical dimensions, i.e., the instructional design of the programs, that is more important than the particular delivery systems used to implement them, electronic or otherwise. The failure to focus on pedagogical differences and the tendency to over-emphasize technological ones are perhaps the greatest flaws we see in attempts to evaluate (as well as to conduct research with) interactive learning systems.

What are some examples of actual effectiveness evaluations?

We have conducted numerous effectiveness evaluations, some quantitative and others more qualitative. Most often, our designs are eclectic, using a blend of quantitative, qualitative, and even critical methods.

Military example

In the mid-80s, the U. S. Navy began to investigate the use of interactive videodisc technologies to deliver emergency care training to Naval Corpsmen (medics) through the CAMIS (Computer Aided Medical Instruction System) program. A prototype interactive learning system was developed to address several emergency care procedures that had been taught via four hours of lecture and demonstration supplemented by an illustrated text within the context of the overall Corpsman training program. We were asked to conduct a comparative evaluation of the two approaches. Accordingly, a quantitative, experimental approach was adopted whereby 500 sailors were randomly assigned to use the new CAMIS materials, and another 500 sailors were assigned to attend the traditional lecture/demonstration classes. Standardized tests were used to compare the outcomes of the two groups, and the results indicated that the trainees using the interactive learning system scored an average of 84%, whereas the traditionally-trained corpsmen scored an average of 80%. These differences were statistically significant, and the Navy officers promoting the new technology were quite pleased with the findings (Reeves, Marlino, & Strub, 1989).

However, we had concerns about the small size of the gain, regardless of its statistical significance. We wondered if it was educationally significant, especially in relation to the extra costs involved in the new technology. Fortunately, we supplemented our quantitative design by interviewing samples of corpsmen in both treatments, in person immediately after the training and via telephone three months after graduation from the Corpsmen school. These interviews provided data, albeit "soft" in the eyes of the Navy officers, that the interactive videodisc scenarios used in the interactive learning system had been very motivating, and that the procedures learned through those simulations seemed to be more durable than those learned in the lectures. We also interviewed instructors at the Corpsman school and were able to report that they were very much in favor of the new interactive simulations.

Corporate example

The effectiveness of the *Macintosh Fundamentals* interactive videodisc training system mentioned earlier in this chapter was evaluated several different ways (Gustafson, Reeves, & Laffey, 1990). For example, with the cooperation of Apple's Training Support Group in Cupertino, California, several graduate students from The University of Georgia enrolled in two-day training sessions at selected training sites, unbeknownst to the local trainers. As participant observers, these students were able to provide a firsthand perspective on the implementation of the programs. They were also able to talk about the perceived effectiveness of the interactive modules with other trainees during breaks and meals.

At other training sites, we used both paper-and-pencil tests and performance exercises as more direct measures of effectiveness. For the latter, after a trainee had completed a particular module, e.g., one on linking peripheral devices with a Macintosh, we would invite the trainee into another room where he or she would be asked to assemble a typical computer system including several peripherals such as printers and external hard drives right out of the shipping boxes. We also conducted exit interviews with numerous trainees once they had completed *Macintosh Fundamentals*. We were able to report to the Training Support Group at Apple Computer that *MacFun* (as it came to be known) was seen as an effective training system by both trainees and trainers, and that test results indicated significant improvements in learning knowledge and skills before and after the training. Because of the commitment Apple had already made to interactive training using their own computers, it did not make sense to conduct a traditional comparative evaluation between the interactive videodisc training and the previously used leader-led course.

How should effectiveness evaluations be reported?

— WEB LINK —
For an example of a Web-based evaluation report, go to:
http://it.coe.uga.edu/~treeves/RSUSeval/

The results of effectiveness evaluations can be presented in a number of formats, including formal and informal written reports, multimedia presentations, online databases, or Web sites. The type of report(s) you produce will depend on the information needs of your clients and the other relevant audiences that will be given access to the effectiveness findings. It is generally advisable to provide multiple reports using different formats so that your effectiveness data can be widely shared. Of course, this may not always be possible, depending on the nature of your relationship with your clients. We have found that using a focus group approach wherein we present the results of the evaluation to a group of clients in person, and then solicit their reactions is an especially powerful way of communicating the results of effectiveness evaluations. The discussion that evolves in these focus groups helps to ensure that the results will actually influence decision making.

Summary

The bottom line with respect to effectiveness evaluation can be summed up as follows:

- Never use a test unless you are certain it is reliable and valid.
- Evaluate the implementation of an interactive learning system as carefully as outcomes.
- Triangulate effectiveness, studying it from many different perspectives.

In the next chapter, we present strategies for evaluating the impact of interactive learning environments.

References

Angelo, T. A., & Cross, K. P. (1993). *Classroom assessment techniques: A handbook for college teachers* (2nd ed.). San Francisco: Jossey-Bass.

Beder, H. (1989). Purposes and philosophies of adult education. In S. B. Merriam & P. M. Cunningham (Eds.), *Handbook of adult and continuing education* (pp. 37-50). San Francisco: Jossey-Bass.

Berman, P., & McLaughlin, M. (1978). *Federal programs supporting education change. A model of education change, Vol. VIII: Implementing and sustaining innovations.* Santa Monica, CA: Rand.

Bransford, J. D., Sherwood, R. D., Hasselbring, T. S., Kinzer, C. K., & Williams, S. M. (1990). Anchored instruction: Why we need it and how technology can help. In D. Nix & R. Spiro (Eds.), *Cognition, education, and multimedia: Exploring ideas in high technology* (pp. 115-141). Hillsdale, NJ: Lawrence Erlbaum Associates.

Bransford, J. D., Vye, N., Goldman, S. R., Hasselbring, T. S., & Pellegrino, J. W. (1991, April). *The design of environments that support meaningful, generative learning: An introduction to the mathematics problem solving series, The Adventures of Jasper Woodbury.* Paper presented at the Annual Meeting of the American Educational Research Association, Chicago, IL.

Brown, J. S., Collins, A., & Duguid, P. (1989). Situated cognition and the culture of learning. *Educational Researcher, 18*(1), 32-41.

Carroll, J. B. (1968). On learning from being told. *Educational Psychologist, 5*, 4-10.

Clark, R. E. (1992). Media use in education. In M. C. Alkin (Ed.), *Encyclopedia of educational research* (pp. 805-814). New York: Macmillan.

Cognition and Technology Group at Vanderbilt. (1992). The Jasper experiment: An exploration of issues in learning and instructional design. *Educational Technology Research and Development, 40*(1), 65-80.

Cole, P. (1992). Constructivism revisited: A search for common ground. *Educational Technology, 32*(2), 27-34.

Converse, J. M., & Presser, S. (1986). *Survey questions: Handcrafting the standardized questionnaire.* Thousand Oaks, CA: Sage.

Cooley, W. W., & Lohnes, P. R. (1976). *Evaluation research in education.* New York: Irvington.

Duffy, T. M., & Jonassen, D. H. (Eds.). (1992). *Constructivism and the technology of instruction: A conversation.* Hillsdale, NJ: Lawrence Erlbaum Associates.

Exploring the Nardoo. (1996). Project Manager: B. Harper, Instructional Design: B. Harper, J. Hedberg, R. Wright, G. Farr, & C. Brown (An interactive multimedia CD-ROM produced in collaboration with NSW Dept of Land and Water Conservation). Canberra, Australia: Interactive Multimedia.

Fink, A., & Kosecoff, J. B. (1998). *How to conduct surveys: A step by step guide.* Thousand Oaks, CA: Sage.

Flavell, J. H. (1979). Metacognition and cognitive monitoring: A new area of psychological inquiry. *American Psychologist, 34*, 906-911.

Fowler, F. J. (1995). *Improving survey questions: Design and evaluation.* Thousand Oaks, CA: Sage.

Gronlund, N. E., Linn, R. L., & Davis, K. M. (1999). *Measurement and evaluation in teaching* (8th ed.). Englewood Cliffs, NJ: Prentice-Hall.

Gustafson, K. L., Reeves, T. C., & Laffey, J. M. (1990, April). *The experience and outcomes of interactive videodisc orientation training for sales personnel.* Paper presented at the Annual Meeting of the American Educational Research Association, Boston, MA.

Haladyna, T. M. (1999). *Developing and validating multiple-choice test items.* Mahwah, NJ: Lawrence Erlbaum Associates.

Halford, G. S. (1993). *Children's understanding: The development of mental models.* Hillsdale, NJ: Lawrence Erlbaum Associates.

Hall, B. (1997). *Web-based training cookbook.* New York: John Wiley & Sons.

Hall, B. (2001). *Learning management systems 2001: How to pick the right one for your organization.* Sunnyvale, CA: Brandon-Hall.com.

Hannafin, M. J. (1992). Emerging technologies, ISD, and learning environments: Critical perspectives. *Educational Technology Research and Development, 40*(1), 49-63.

Hedberg, J. G., Harper, B. M., Brown, C., & Corderoy, R. (1994). Exploring user interfaces to improve learner outcomes. In K. Beatie, C. McNaught, & S. Wills (Eds.), *Interactive multimedia in university education: Designing for change in teaching and learning* (pp. 15-29). Amsterdam: Elsevier.

Henderson, J. (1991). Designing realities: Interactive media, virtual realities, and cyberspace. *Multimedia Review, 1*(2), 47-51.

Investigating Lake Iluka. (1993). Project Manager: B. Harper, Instructional Design: B. Harper, J. Hedberg & C. Brown (An interactive multimedia CD-ROM produced in collaboration with Apple Computer). Canberra, Australia: Interactive Multimedia.

Jonassen, D. H., & Reeves, T. C. (1996). Learning *with* technology: Using computers as cognitive tools. In D. H. Jonassen (Ed.), *Handbook of research on educational communications and technology* (pp. 693-719). New York: Macmillan.

Kafai, Y., & Resnick, M. (Eds.). (1996). *Constructivism in practice: Designing, thinking, and learning in a digital world.* Mahwah, NJ: Lawrence Erlbaum Associates.

Kirkpatrick, D. L. (1998). *Evaluating training programs: The four levels* (2nd ed.). San Francisco: Berrett-Koehler.

Kyllonen, P. C., & Shute, V. J. (1989). A taxonomy of learning skills. In P. L. Ackerman, R. H. Sternberg, & R. Glaser (Eds.), *Learning and individual differences: Advances in theory and research* (pp. 117-163). New York: W. H. Freeman.

Loewenthal, K. M. (2000). *An introduction to psychological tests and scales.* London: Psychology Press.

Malone, T. (1981). Towards a theory of intrinsically motivating instruction. *Cognitive Science, 4*, 333-369.

Merriam, S. B. (Ed.). (1993). *An update on adult learning theory.* San Francisco: Jossey-Bass.

Moore, M. G., & Kearsley, G. (1996). *Distance education: A systems view.* Belmont, CA: Wadsworth.

Morris, L. L., Fitz-Gibbon, C. T., & Lindheim, E. (1987). *How to measure performance and use tests.* Newbury Park, CA: Sage.

Newby, A. C. (1992). *Training evaluation handbook.* San Diego, CA: Pfeiffer.

Patton, M. Q. (1997). *Utilization-focused evaluation: The new century text* (3rd ed.). Thousand Oaks, CA: Sage.

Perelman, L. J. (1992). *School's out: Hyperlearning, the new technology, and the end of education.* New York: William Morrow.

Reeves, T. C. (1988). Effective dimensions of interactive videodisc for training. In T. Bernold & J. Finkelstein (Eds.), *Computer-assisted approaches to training: Foundations of industry's future* (pp. 119-132). Amsterdam: Elsevier Science.

Reeves, T. C. (1993a). Research support for interactive multimedia: Existing foundations and future directions. In C. Latchem, J. Williamson, & L. Henderson-Lancett (Eds.), *Interactive multimedia: Practice and promise* (pp. 79-96). London: Kogan Page.

Reeves, T. C. (1993b). Pseudoscience in computer-based instruction: The case of learner control research. *Journal of Computer-Based Instruction, 20*(2), 39-46.

Reeves, T. C., & Harmon, S. W. (1994). Systematic evaluation procedures for interactive multimedia for education and training. In S. Reisman (Ed.), *Multimedia computing: Preparing for the 21st century* (pp. 472-505). Harrisburg, PA: Idea Group Publishing.

Reeves, T. C., Marlino, M. R., & Strub, P. (1989). The evaluation of the emergency medical conditions (EMC) interactive videodisc system case simulations. *Proceedings of the Eleventh Annual Conference on Interactive Videodisc in Education and Training*. Warrenton, VA: Society for Applied Learning Technology.

Rosenberg, M. J. (2000). *E-learning: Strategies for delivering knowledge in the digital age*. New York: McGraw-Hill.

Salter, G. (1995). Quantitative analysis of multimedia audit trails. *Proceedings of the 12th Annual Conference of the Australian Society for Computers in Learning in Tertiary Education* (pp. 456-461), Melbourne, Victoria, Australia.

Schlosser, C. A., & Anderson, M. A. (1994). *Distance education: Review of the literature*. Washington, DC: Association for Educational Communications and Technology.

Schwier, R. A., & Misanchuk, E. R. (1993). *Interactive multimedia instruction*. Englewood Cliffs, NJ: Educational Technology Publications.

Simon, H. A. (1987). Computers and society. In S. B. Kiesler & L. S. Sproul (Eds.), *Computing and change on campus* (pp. 4-15). New York: Cambridge University Press.

Westgaard, O. (1999). *Tests that work: Designing and delivering fair and practical measurement tools in the workplace*. San Francisco: Jossey-Bass/Pfeiffer.

Wiggins, G. P. (1998). *Educative assessment: Designing assessments to inform and improve student performance*. San Francisco: Jossey-Bass.

Wilson, B. G. (Ed.). (1996). *Constructivist learning environments: Case studies in instructional design*. Englewood Cliffs, NJ: Educational Technology Publications.

Wright, R., Harper, B. M., & Hedberg, J. G. (1999). Visual support for authoring. In J. van den Akker, R. Branch, K. Gustafson, N. Nieveen, & T Plomp (Eds.), *Design approaches and tools in education and training* (pp. 205-214). Dordrecht, The Netherlands: Kluwer.

CHAPTER 9

Impact Evaluation

Objectives

After reading Chapter Nine, you should be able to:

- identify decisions involved in evaluating the impact of interactive learning systems;
- specify questions that should be answered before making decisions related to the impact of interactive learning systems;
- identify the information needed to answer questions about the impact of interactive learning systems; and
- decide how to collect and report information so that the impact of interactive learning systems can be judged.

Why should you conduct impact evaluation?

The overall purpose of impact evaluation is to determine whether the knowledge, skills, and attitudes (KSAs) learned via interactive learning systems transfer to the intended context of use, e.g., the work place. As illustrated in Figure 9.1, different types of decisions must be made concerning the adoption, dissemination, or certification of interactive learning systems. These are critically important decisions that should be informed by reliable and valid answers to the types of questions that can be addressed through impact evaluation.

Impact evaluation is the fifth facet or function of the evaluation model presented in this book. Evaluating whether learners actually apply the knowledge, skills, and attitudes they learn via interactive learning systems "on the job" or in another learning environment is rarely easy. There is usually some aspect of an impact evaluation that remains ambiguous. In fact, impact evaluation may well be the greatest challenge faced by evaluators, regardless of the context or the type of interactive learning system being evaluated. Not surprisingly, it is also the most neglected facet of evaluation.

Decisions	Example Questions
Should workers who have completed an e-learning program be certified?	Do trainees transfer knowledge, skills, and attitudes to the workplace?
Should this interactive learning system be adopted?	What evidence supports the impact of this program on sales and profits?
Should workers be given bonuses for completing this e-learning program?	Is the safety record in the workplace improved by this program?
What price should be charged for this ILS?	How does the impact of this program compare to alternatives?

Figure 9.1. Typical decisions and questions in an impact evaluation.

When should you conduct impact evaluation?

Impact evaluation provides answers to the questions that most people ultimately ask about the results of using interactive learning systems or any other sophisticated (and costly) information technologies, such as knowledge management systems. Impact questions are related to "the bottom line" in business and industry. Typical questions include: Does an interactive learning system increase sales, reduce complaints, or save lives? In education, impact questions are related to the long-term effects of a learning environment. For example, does an interactive learning system enhance literacy, encourage minority students to pursue careers in engineering, or promote lifelong learning habits? Or does interactive training have undesirable social costs (Meyrowitz, 1985)?

Although an interactive learning program may have "production value" that is comparable to broadcast video or commercial film, if the program doesn't increase profits, enhance client loyalty, decrease accidents, or significantly influence the lives of students, it has no real value. After all, an interactive learning system is not an end in itself, but a means to ends such as higher motivation, better learning, enhanced performance, greater profitability, or in some cases, even corporate survival.

In Kirkpatrick's (1998) well-known evaluation model, there are four levels of evaluation (see Figure 8.2 in Chapter Eight). The last two levels in Kirkpatrick's model, "Behavior" and "Results," fit within the facet of evaluation we call "Impact." We have not separated behavior from results because we know from experience how complex it is to detect evidence of the impact of education or training in any form. Thus we promote an approach that consists of gathering as much evidence as possible in different formats to build a convincing case for impact. In our experience, there are plausible alternative explanations for most "results." Hence, we advise against putting too much effort into any single type of evaluation strategy if you think that it alone will allow you to definitively attribute results to a specific interactive learning system. Triangulating evaluation results, i.e., collecting data from multiple sources using multiple methods, is essential in impact evaluation.

What kinds of decisions can you anticipate?

Evidence of impact influences a wealth of decisions, some of which can affect your career as a developer of interactive learning systems. An interactive learning system is not the solution to every problem, but its ultimate value as a solution cannot be established without impact data. In a corporate environment, interactive learning systems compete with other problem "solutions," such as changing incentives, modifying managerial structures, and increasing employee participation in decision making. At some point, managers must make difficult decisions about how to increase productivity, save costs, or improve safety. Should more or less interactive training be provided? Should interactive learning systems be developed in-house or contracted to external vendors? Should workers' pay and/or benefits be increased to bolster corporate morale, or should motivational e-learning programs be provided on each worker's desktop computer? Should dangerous equipment in the workplace be replaced, or should safety training be intensified? These and other realistic decisions will be affected by information you can provide about the impact of interactive learning systems in business and industrial settings.

The comprehensive implementation of interactive learning systems in education is still rare, and thus it is more difficult to define the type of decisions that should be anticipated in schools and universities. However, one decision we would like to see erased from any list is whether teachers should be replaced by interactive learning systems. The best evidence is that, instead of replacing teachers, interactive learning systems generally increase the importance of teachers (Coley, Cradler, & Engel, 1997). Instead of teacher obsolescence, what is likely to happen is that teachers will find themselves in different roles, e.g., changing from primary deliverers of information to facilitators and mentors within a more effective, more efficient, and more complex learning environment (Jonassen & Reeves, 1996; Pittinsky, 2003; Roblyer, 1999).

Although we firmly believe that instructors can be empowered by new technologies, it must be acknowledged that others have predicted more drastic changes. In 1992, Perelman predicted that "In the wake of the HL [hyperlearning] revolution, the technology called 'school' and the social institution commonly thought of as 'education' will be as obsolete and ultimately extinct as the dinosaurs" (p. 50). More recent predictions have been made about enormous changes in higher education. Although he himself does not advocate this future vision, James J. Duderstadt (1999), former president of the University of Michigan in the USA, described business people and educators who believe that the:

> ... emerging domestic market for educational services could be served by a radically restructured enterprise consisting of fifty thousand faculty "content providers," two hundred thousand faculty "learning facilitators," and one thousand faculty "celebrities," who would be the stars of the commodity learning-ware products. The learner would be linked to these faculty resources by an array of for-profit service companies handling the production and packaging of learning-ware, the distribution and delivery of these services to learners, and the assessment and certification of learning outcomes. (p. 12).

Whether such predictions come to be will be determined to a large extent by the willingness of educators to conduct rigorous evaluations of present and future interactive learning systems in realistic contexts. In the absence of better evaluations that yield credible impact data, external attempts to reduce the role of instructors may be more likely to succeed.

What questions should be answered before making decisions?

Questions about the impact of training and education programs are concerned with examining the transfer of knowledge, skills, and attitudes (KSAs) from the context of education and training to that of performance. Do health care workers follow federally mandated safety procedures? Do assembly line workers actively participate in quality circles? Is work place morale high? Has industrial recycling increased? Are profits up? Do students have greater self-esteem? Are more females pursuing careers in science and mathematics? Have scores on standardized tests increased? These are the types of questions addressed by impact evaluation. It should be obvious immediately that these types of questions are not easy to answer.

The challenge of evaluating impact is further complicated by the fact that many impact questions raise political issues in the school, community, or workplace. School system administrators and politicians who have invested heavily in classroom technologies may not support rigorous, in-depth investigations concerning the ultimate benefits of their pet innovations. In business and industry, relations between unions and management often add complications. For example, one of us was once asked to evaluate the effectiveness and impact of an interactive multimedia program used to train workers at a large U.S. auto manufacturing corporation to read hazardous chemical safety management data sheets. The training was mandated by the Occupational Safety and Health Administration (OSHA) of the U. S. federal government. However, the United Auto Workers (UAW) union would not permit their members to be tested on their ability to read and interpret these data sheets. Further, the management of the auto company did not want the workers to be interviewed during the time when they should be working. In the end, no impact data could be gathered, and the only implementation data that could be collected was the time a worker signed onto the interactive system and the time the worker signed off!

What kinds of information do you need to answer questions?

In business, impact data can range from the testimonials of front line supervisors about how their workers' morale has improved to the profit figures generated by the accounting department. As a developer and/or evaluator of interactive learning systems, you may often feel isolated from what others characterize as the real action centers of business, e.g., production, marketing, sales, and/or service. This is not an unusual position for training or human resources development (HRD) personnel. In the face of this marginalization, you are advised to take a responsible attitude and a proactive stance. Collecting and reporting impact data about sales, customer satisfaction, worker morale, safety records, and similar aspects of the business environment is critical to success. You can't expect to "prove" in a scientific sense that you caused positive changes, but failing to build a case that there is a relationship between your training program and these bottom line criteria could make you an easy target when budget cuts are considered within a corporation.

There have been numerous predictions about the role of training in the 21st century (Cohen, 1991; Kemske & Weingarten, 1989; Rosenberg, 2000). One that appears again and again is that trainers will be held responsible for the *effects* of training, not just its delivery. Increasingly, training departments are being held accountable for their impact on the bottom line. This pressure is unlikely to disappear, so you must learn to deal with it. If interactive learning systems are to have a place in the corporate world, then you must attempt to demonstrate impact on the kinds of indicators that executives, stockholders, and others in power accept as ultimately important, e.g., profits.

— WEB LINK —
For examples of educational technology evaluation reports provided by the U.S. Department of Education, go to: http://www.ed.gov/Technology/reports.html

Similarly, in education contexts, the technology honeymoon is over (Cuban, 2001), and the impact of interactive learning systems in technology-infused schools must be demonstrated if these systems are to enjoy continued support (Reeves, 1992). Political enthusiasm for school reform via technological innovations will evaporate quickly if the impact of interactive learning systems and related technologies cannot be demonstrated. As difficult as it is to collect impact data in the business world, the challenge is even greater in education. Nonetheless, you must try to estimate impact. The standardized test data commonly collected within educational contexts is rarely an adequate indicator of impact. Instead, you must attempt to collect data about the quality of life experienced by students after they leave school, their aspirations and motivations, and the opportunities they perceive as well as the careers they pursue. Long-term, follow-up data are required. This may seem especially daunting in light of what, at times, seems like a steady decline in educational indicators (drop-out rates, achievement scores, international comparisons, etc.), while critics grow increasingly shrill in their condemnations of public education (Gross, 1999; Sykes, 1996). However, if you believe, as we and others do (diSessa, 2000, Kallick & Wilson, 2000; Means, 1994; Papert, 1993), that interactive learning systems can be the vehicles for pedagogical reform, then it is critical to track long-term indicators of educational impact.

How should impact information be collected?

Impact evaluation should begin with a well-specified evaluation plan. The real challenge in evaluating impact is establishing causal relationships between interactive learning systems and various types of desirable outcomes. In the corporate world, you should not expect to establish unassailable causal links between your e-learning programs and results, such as higher profits, greater safety, and improved efficiency. There are many other factors that will influence the bottom line, such as advertising, market shifts, government mandates, and the general economy. But you should be able to build a case that supports the benefits of e-learning programs designed to influence performance and results.

In the absence of direct causal links, triangulation of data sources is the best strategy for evaluating impact. Triangulation involves seeking to compensate for the imperfections inevitable in any single type of measure by using multiple methods that may give you a clearer estimation of what you are evaluating (Mark & Shotland, 1987).

Suppose you want to assess the impact of sales training on profits for a large toy company. An innovative interactive multimedia sales training system has been placed in each of the toy company's regional offices, and your online data collection indicates that 93% of the sales force has completed the new program. Accounting indicates that sales figures are up in both quarters since introduction of the program. Can you conclude that this interactive learning system has had a beneficial impact on sales? Probably not without arguments from other business sectors. The marketing department wants a share of the credit for its national television advertising campaign. Marketing insists that its tie-in with a major motion picture aimed at children has attracted most of the new business. Sales managers claim that modifications in bonus structures deserve the credit, and so on.

Obviously, you will need other data sources to support your claims about the value of interactive training. A prerequisite, of course, is to establish the degree of relationship between the contents of the training and specific business results (Brethower, 1989), a process that depends heavily on the quality of the initial needs assessment conducted for the program (see Chapter Six). Where can you get additional data to support your case that the program deserves credit for the sales increase? You might interview sales personnel, sales managers, and customers to gather data about impact. It would help to build your case if you could report that sales persons are saying, "This e-learning taught me a new technique that helped me to close sales with formerly reluctant customers." What if you could provide evidence of customers claiming that what convinced them to buy your product was "the amount of competitive information the salesperson was able to give me about the other brands of toys?" Your argument would be enhanced if competitive sales information was stressed in your interactive training program.

You can conduct observations to provide valuable evidence of impact. Although it may be difficult to observe sales procedures, observations of other types of performance are more feasible to observe, e.g., the safety practices of workers on an assembly line. In education contexts, observations are sorely needed to determine the impact of interactive systems on the learning and socialization of students. There remains a dearth of understanding about how interactive learning systems are actually being used by teachers within school computer labs and classrooms.

1 Role of the evaluator-observer.

Full participant observation	Partial observation	Onlooker observation as an outsider

2. Portrayal of the evaluator role to others.

Overt observations: Program staff and participants know that observations are being made and who the observer is	Observer role is known by some, but not by others	Covert observations: Program staff and participants do not know that observations are being made or that there is an observer

3. Portrayal of the purpose of the evaluation to others.

Full explanation of real purpose to everyone	Partial explanation of real purpose	Covert explanation: No explanation given to staff or participants	Fake explanation: Deceive staff and/or participants

4. Duration of the evaluation observations.

Single observation of limited duration, e.g., one hour	Long-term, multiple observations, e.g., months

5. Focus of the observations.

Narrow focus: Single element in the program is observed	Broad focus: Holistic view of the entire program is sought

Figure 9.2. Dimensions of classroom observation (Patton, 1990).

Observing classroom performance (or any type of workplace performance) may sound like a straightforward, relatively simple process, but there are practical, technical, and even ethical considerations that must be taken into account before beginning actual observations. Patton (1990) has described five dimensions that characterize the different approaches to observations (see Figure 9.2).

It is useful to review these dimensions before undertaking an observation in an instructional context. In addition to considering the general dimensions shown in Figure 9.2, it is also useful to think about concepts or categories that might be used to direct your observations. Figure 9.3 lists seven factors that are relevant to the task of observing applications of interactive learning systems (or other forms of instructional technology, such as teleconferencing) in the context of education or training.

There are several things to remember when preparing to conduct observations:

- You can't observe everything.
- What you see and how you interpret it are influenced by your entire life's experience.
- You need to be sensitized to the goals of the observation and your relationship to those you are observing.

Setting – Where are you? A classroom? A lab? An auditorium? What does it feel like to be there? Is the space amenable to the technology? Are people comfortable in this space?

Objectives – Why are people here? Who is in charge (if anyone)? Are activities self-directed? Who maintains goal directed behavior? To what degree are people on task?

Implementation – Are things going as planned? Does the technology work? Who handles problems? Are people confident in their use of technology?

Interactions – How do people interact among themselves? Is the atmosphere formal? Informal? Friendly? Unfriendly? How are you viewed?

Nonverbal Behavior – What does body language tell you about this product or program? Are people interested? Going through the motions? Intimidated?

Unobtrusive Factors – What areas of the setting are heavily used? What areas are less used? Dusty? Cluttered? Can people hear? Air-conditioning?

Unexpected Things – Have you seen anything you didn't expect? What surprised you? What delighted you? What depressed you?

Figure 9.3. Seven factors relevant to classroom observation.

Before going onsite to conduct observations, it is useful to write down your expectations. Try to describe any biases or prejudices that might affect your observations. Having these expectations on record before observing provides you with a better basis for interpreting what you actually saw when you observed. Figure 9.4 provides a brief example of such a statement.

> I am going to observe high school sophomores using an interactive multimedia science program in a rural area. I expect the school to be old fashioned in construction because I heard that it has been around for 60 years. This technology-based science program is probably the pride of the school. The interactive systems in that school will look like space shuttles parked in a barn. The teachers will probably be intimidated by the technology. The students may be too, but there are probably a few "whiz kids" who are really into it. I doubt that the interactive video is closely coordinated with the rest of the science program. It may be viewed as a privilege to get to use the interactive video. I am a little nervous about being in a high school again. After all, it has been a long time. I wonder if I can relate to the students? Will the teacher feel that I am a threat?

Figure 9.4. Sample expectations statement for classroom observations.

There are several guidelines for recording your observations in an educational context:

- Collect field notes. This is not optional! Don't trust everything to your memory.
- Don't try to write down everything. You can't! Record your notes in some sort of outline or shorthand style that fits your experience and skills. Flesh out your notes with more details as soon as you can.
- Make your notes as descriptive as possible. Don't try to interpret what you are seeing at the same time you are describing it. Try to separate description from interpretation.
- Add interpretations and your own feelings later.

Separating observations from interpretations is not easy. Figure 9.5 provides a poor example and a good example of descriptive field notes.

> **Poor Notes**
>
> *- The classroom was a warm and friendly place. The teacher loves her students.*
>
> **Better Notes**
>
> *- bright walls - like the colors*
>
> *- some noise, but teacher doesn't seem bothered*
>
> *- students very busy - cooperative within groups - some competition*
>
> *- well-used bulletin boards - look fresh - lots of student work shown*
>
> *- teacher very active - helping kids - standing - sitting on floor - doesn't use her own desk during whole period*
>
> *- students are eager to demonstrate their work to me, the teacher allows me complete freedom to explore this classroom*

Figure 9.5. Poor and better field notes from classroom observations.

As soon as possible after you have completed your observations, you will want to do a "mind dump" (writing down everything you can recall) concerning what you have observed. It takes practice to develop good descriptive skills, and you are encouraged to work at developing these skills. Figure 9.6 provides an example of elaborated field notes written after observations have been conducted.

> The classroom walls are painted in pleasant colors rather than traditional institutional beige or green. Indirect lighting is used to soften the room. I feel very comfortable here. The bulletin boards feature student work, presented in an attractive manner. They have obviously been updated recently. The teacher's desk has an aquarium on it and there are lots of plants in the room. The teacher moves around the room a lot, getting close to the students. She even sat on the floor with some of them during part of the time. The teacher seems to have real rapport with these students. The students are talking among themselves, but the noise level is acceptable. The students appear to be including each other in the work to be done. No one seems unengaged in the tasks at hand. There is some competition, but it does not seem adversarial.

Figure 9.6. Example of detailed field notes written after observations.

One of the major problems with evaluations occurs when development team members are the only people who observe its use in the field. As honest as they might be, it is difficult for people to be objective about their expectations for the success of what they themselves have created. It is not bad practice to involve developers in such evaluations, but their work should be supplemented with external evaluators as well.

In addition to observations, anecdotal record forms, logs, and diaries can be used to evaluate impact. Supervisors may be asked to keep anecdotal records of unusual incidents related to the long-term outcomes of training. Workers or students themselves may be asked to keep logs or diaries of their activities related to what they are supposed to have learned and applied as a result of using an interactive learning system. The good news about anecdotal records, logs, and diaries is that they can provide pearls of evidence that an interactive learning program has had real impact. The bad news is that people need to be constantly reminded and rewarded if you expect them to keep these types of records.

Interviews are frequently used to collect evidence of impact. Telephone interviews can be used to follow up with trainees to find out if they are using the knowledge, skills, and attitudes from an interactive program on the job. The interviews can be conducted with the trainees, their supervisors, or even their clients or customers. Unfortunately, due to the frequency with which people are subjected to telemarketing today, some respondents may be reluctant to be interviewed via telephone.

Also, interviews can be conducted online, especially if the respondents are not expected to key in long responses to complex questions. Many workers have access to e-mail today. Therefore, if face-to-face interviews are not feasible and telephone interviews are too difficult to schedule, you might consider conducting interviews about program impact via e-mail or other Internet tools, such as chat or discussion forums.

– WEB LINK –
For information about surveys, and including survey software, go to: http://www.amstat.com/sections/SRMS/index.html

Questionnaires and other forms of survey can be used to collect impact data. Although the mails continue to be the dominant mode of distributing surveys, distribution through e-mail and the Web is increasing and is an alternative worth exploring (Dillman, 1999; Nesbary, 1999). There are some potential disadvantages to e-mail surveys (e.g., sample is limited to those people with e-mail, difficult to guarantee confidentiality, and limitations in question formatting), but there are many advantages (Thach, 1995). Distribution of electronic surveys is usually inexpensive, and the results are easy to edit and analyze because the responses are already online. The turn-around time is often much quicker, and the response rates may be higher than for a mailed interview. Surveys can also be conducted via the Web using interactive forms that, in turn, send the data to an address for analysis. As more people become Internet proficient, the utility of using the Internet for surveys is enhanced. A number of commercial companies now exist to support Web-based survey methods. The SphinxSurvey software program is one example of software that can assist in the design and implementation of surveys.

Yet another approach to estimating the impact of training or education, particularly popular in corporate settings, is "return on investment" (ROI) evaluation (Reeves & Carter, 2001). Training personnel are sometimes called upon to carry out ROI studies to demonstrate that the resources expended on training programs have yielded profits or benefits that exceed their costs. This is difficult, but not impossible. Medsker and Roberts (1992) describe a unique ROI study conducted by a large company whose business is delivering packages overnight. This company relies upon an accurate, highly motivated staff. Before sending them out into the field, new delivery personnel complete an intensive and expensive two-week training course. To demonstrate the value of the training, the training department managers conducted a risky experiment.

They allowed 20 new employees who had only been given a brief safety training program to start delivering packages without the two-week training program. They compared their performance with that of 20 new employees who had completed the training and with 20 veteran delivery personnel. They found that the trained new employees made far fewer mistakes than the untrained workers, and that the savings resulting from their lack of errors more than made up for the costs of the training program. (Ironically, they also found that the veteran employees made almost as many mistakes as the novices, indicating a need for retraining!)

Another way of looking at impact involves consideration of the costs of training in relationship to effectiveness and benefits (Kearsley, 1993). In many contexts, cost-effectiveness and cost-benefit studies will involve complex and controversial methodologies. These studies are difficult to conduct and defend because whenever you begin to attach actual monetary figures to various effects and benefits, your calculations will be challenged by others who have a stake in a different set of values.

It is also difficult in many contexts to calculate the actual costs of developing and implementing interactive learning systems. In the business world, some training departments are included as an overhead cost charged to all departments, whereas in others there is an internal charging system whereby various units pay for training within the company. Increasingly, large and small corporations are contracting outside vendors for training development, but there are still costs within the corporations in terms of managing these outside contractors.

If the costs of developing and implementing interactive learning systems are hard to track, the monetary values that can be attached to various effects and benefits are even more difficult to calculate. If sales go up in a retail organization, that type of effect is relatively easy to detect (although often difficult to attribute directly to a training program). However, what monetary value should be attached to improved morale on the assembly line? How do you assess the value of a life that may have been saved as a result of a new e-learning program about workplace safety?

– WEB LINK –
A free *Cost Analysis Handbook* can be obtained from the Flashlight Project at: http://www.tltgroup.org/programs/fcai.html

Monetary values are even more difficult to attach to the effects and benefits of educational programs (Newman, 1990). What is the ROI on an innovative, but controversial, sex education program that reduces pregnancies among unwed teenagers? We are convinced of the wisdom of the bumper sticker that reads "If you think education is expensive, try ignorance." However, we would be cautious in undertaking a cost-effectiveness evaluation of an interactive learning environment that is supposed to have long-term effects, such as improving problem-solving skills, encouraging intellectual curiosity, and promoting a positive attitude toward lifelong learning. The complexity of attaching unambiguous figures to these types of outcomes should be obvious.

Despite the difficulties, there is great interest in investigating the cost-effectiveness of interactive learning systems. Initial investments in interactive learning systems may be driven by a desire to be on the "cutting edge" or by the persuasive powers of dynamic individuals within an organization, but over the long haul, the cost-effectiveness of these systems will have to be supported through rigorous evaluation. Figure 9.7 presents a hypothetical cost-effectiveness comparison between two alternative methods of training flight attendants.

Problem: Alpha Airlines must provide 10,000 flight attendants with training every year to maintain certification by the Federal Aviation Administration (FAA).

Traditional Training Program: Flight attendants (10,000) are flown to the corporate base in Dallas twice a year for FAA-mandated safety training. Each day of training is leader-led with heavy use of airplane mock-ups. Costs per attendant per training session are listed below.

Travel Costs	$300
Hotel Costs	$100
Per Diem	$50
Average Training Costs	$50
Salary Paid to Attendant During Training	$150
Total	$650

Total Training Program Costs Per Year Based on Two Yearly Training Sessions for 10,000 Flight Attendants = $13,000,000

New Training Program: Flight attendants (10,000) are flown to corporate base in Dallas once a year for FAA-mandated safety training. The one day of training is leader-led with heavy use of airplane mock-ups. Costs per attendant per training session remain at $650. The other day of training is accomplished using e-learning systems distributed to all 25 Alpha Airlines bases around the country. Flight attendants accomplish the training objectives while waiting between flights. Travel, hotel, per diem, and salary costs are eliminated. E-learning development and implementation costs are listed below.

E-learning Development Costs	1,800,000
E-learning Delivery Systems Costs	500,000
E-learning Maintenance Costs	200,000
Total	$2,500,000

Total Training Program Costs Per Year Based on One Yearly Training Session Plus Dispersed E-learning Training for 10,000 Flight Attendants = $9,000,000

First Year Savings = $4,000,000

Figure 9.7. Hypothetical cost-effectiveness study.

If only we could reduce cost-effectiveness studies to the simplicity represented in Figure 9.7! And even when cost-effectiveness can be shown, experience indicates that other factors may influence decision making in unpredictable ways. For example, one of the U.S. military services conducted a series of studies that indicated that a self-paced interactive approach to electronics training was both efficient (saved training time) and cost-effective (saved money). However, the self-paced nature of the electronics training meant that some personnel were finishing what had been a 30-week training program at different times ranging from 20 to 35 weeks. The military system was not equipped to handle this individuality. It was deemed more important that classes graduate together. In fact, the local commanders believed that having personnel finish training at different times was bad for morale. As a result, despite the evidence in favor of the interactive approach, the training went back to the instructor-led, group-paced method.

How should impact studies be designed?

There are many ways that impact evaluations can be designed, but an especially important approach in today's financial climate is the ROI study. Such studies involve calculating the percentage of return for a dollar invested in training or another intervention. Phillips (1997) provides a simple formula for calculating ROI as:

$$\text{ROI (\%)} = \frac{\text{net program benefits}}{\text{program costs}} \times 100$$

– WEB LINK –
More information about ROI can be found at:
http://roi.astd.org/

How can Phillips' ROI formula be applied to interactive learning systems? Figure 9.8 illustrates an ROI study for a hypothetical Web-based training (WBT) program. In this example, the Omega Steel Company is confronting an absentee problem whereby employees are averaging 2.7 days away from work per month at a cost of $200 per day per employee. There are 5,000 employees in the company, so the annual costs of absenteeism exceed 32 million dollars. The training department produces a WBT program for all employees that stresses the effects of absenteeism on corporate profits and worker profit sharing rates. The primary goal of the program is to enhance employee motivation and lower absenteeism.

The costs of developing the WBT and providing the infrastructure to provide Web access to all employees are 3 million dollars. After only three months of usage, the absenteeism rate has fallen to 1.8 days per month. At first, this may not seem to be a significant outcome, but using Phillips' formula, the ROI for the first year would be 260% or, for every dollar spent on training, \$2.60 in benefits are realized. (Of course, the workers' commitment to showing up at work may not endure, and the company would need to do as much as possible to keep morale up and absenteeism down. If the absenteeism did not stay lower, then the ROI would decrease or disappear altogether!)

Problem: Omega Steel workers are averaging 2.7 days per month absenteeism rates. At an average cost of \$200 per day and 5000 workers, company losses exceed 32 million dollars per year.

Solution: WBT is provided to all employees to motivate them and lower absenteeism. Absentee rates fall to 1.8 days per month.

ROI Calculation: The first-year savings are projected at 10.8 million. The ROI formula requires calculation of net program benefits (10.8 million minus 3 million equals 7.8 million) and dividing by the program costs as illustrated below.

$$\text{ROI (\%)} = \frac{7{,}800{,}000}{3{,}000{,}000} \times 100$$

$$\text{ROI (\%)} = 260\%$$

First-Year Results = For each dollar spent on WBT, \$2.60 in benefits are realized.

Figure 9.8. Hypothetical ROI evaluation focused on WBT.

Other approaches to impact evaluation may involve long-term case studies (Merriam, 1998). Rigorous case studies as evaluations are relatively rare, perhaps because they require many hours of immersion in the context of learning and performance to yield robust interpretations of the impact of interactive learning systems on workplace performance and/or subsequent learning activities. Suppose you were asked to evaluate the impact of an online MBA program, such as the kind offered by UNext.com (http://www.unext.com/). With the cooperation of the clients at UNext, you could recruit some actual students to enroll in the online educational program so that they could carry out long-term participant observation case studies. Subsequently, you could interview graduates of the program at periodic intervals to find out how they perceive the impact of the program on their professional careers. You could also interview their supervisors and peers to get their opinions concerning the outcomes of the online program, especially in comparison to graduates of more traditional MBA programs. Through this triangulation of sources, you could build a case for the impact (or lack thereof) of the program being evaluated.

What are some examples of actual impact evaluations?

Phillips (1994) describes 18 case studies of ROI studies in corporate training contexts, although few involve interactive learning systems per se. These 18 case studies report ROI values ranging from 150% to 2,000% for training investments.

Unfortunately, ROI, cost-benefit, and cost-effectiveness studies are rare in K-12 and higher education. Perhaps the best known example of a technology impact study in education is the Apple Classroom of Tomorrow (ACOT) Project (Fisher, Dwyer, & Yocam, 1996). This study illustrated the enormous importance of implementation in efforts to infuse media and technology into classrooms. In 1985, Apple Computer, Inc. began a long-term collaboration with several widely-separated school districts around the U.S. Students and teachers were provided with computers and software for both school and home use, and research was conducted in the participating schools for over a decade. The ambitious research program focused on six major questions:

1) What kinds of collaborative environments and tools are most helpful in inquiry-based classrooms?
2) What happens when teachers and students have access to rich online resources and remote experts?
3) How can the computer's power to represent knowledge in multiple media support learning?
4) How can computers be used to support students in problem solving?
5) What happens to motivation and learning when students have the same access to the sophisticated tools that experts use?
6) How can the learning and competencies accomplished in a technology-rich environment be assessed?

Coley *et al.* (1997) summarized the results of the first decade of ACOT research:

ACOT students:

- Explored and represented information dynamically and in many forms.
- Became socially aware and more confident.
- Communicated effectively about complex processes.
- Used technology routinely and appropriately.
- Became independent learners and self-starters.

- Knew their areas of expertise and shared that expertise spontaneously.
- Worked well collaboratively.
- Developed a positive orientation to the future. (p. 37)

— WEB LINK —
The latest information about the ACOT evaluations can be found at: http://www.apple.com/education/research/

Some of the most interesting findings from the ACOT research concern teachers and implementation. ACOT researchers found that teachers had strong beliefs about their roles and efficacy as teachers which changed very slowly as their classrooms moved toward child-centered rather than textbook-driven education (Sandholtz & Ringstaff, 1996). Teachers had to make significant changes in their classroom management styles, giving up more control to technology and students. This also changed slowly. Initially, media and technology were primarily used within the context of traditional pedagogical methods, and most teachers required years of experience before they adopted more innovative strategies such as project-based learning. Finally, teachers struggled with fundamental incongruities between traditional assessment measures and the kinds of learning occurring in their classrooms. In fact, assessment problems proved to be the most resistant to solutions and many remained unresolved (David, 1996).

The bottom line of the ACOT Project is that pedagogical innovations and positive learning results did eventually emerge from the infusion of media and technology into schools, but the process took longer than most people imagined. Educational administrators who think that a summer workshop or a few after-school seminars by consultants will enable teachers to implement media and technology in their classrooms are mistaken (Cuban, 2001). Huge investments in time and support for teachers are especially needed when the adoption of constructivist pedagogies accompanies the infusion of new technologies (Duffy & Cunningham, 1996).

How should effectiveness evaluations be reported?

Impact data can be presented in various formats, such as print, video, or dynamic Web sites. Observational data requires special care in reporting. When you get ready to report observations, you should first go back over your original biases statement. Look at it in comparison to what you actually observed and how you interpreted what you saw. Before writing your final report of the observations, ask yourself these questions:

1) What happened as you thought it would?
2) What didn't happen?
3) What have you learned?

4) What can you conclude?
5) What recommendations would you make?

Few things tell the impact of an innovation as convincingly as a good story. Instead of preparing detailed technical descriptions, it is better to write in a style that anyone would be comfortable reading. Evaluations that tell stories or relate anecdotes portraying what an interactive learning system meant to real people are bound to be influential because people remember stories much more than they do facts and figures. Tracy Kidder, author of *Among Schoolchildren* (1990), is an award-winning writer with a story-telling style that can be emulated in evaluation reports.

Another important factor in reporting impact evaluation is providing the information in a timely manner while the important decisions that it should affect are still unresolved. Evaluation data become "stale" very quickly. Getting impact information out quickly to the important stakeholders and decision makers should be a primary concern.

Summary

The bottom line of impact evaluation is that it demands a creative effort to build a case in support of the value of your interactive learning system. The impact of these systems (or any other instructional technology) is rarely, if ever, established beyond a shadow of a doubt. Indeed, there will almost always be rival claimants for any successes that are realized (Swanson, 1989).

Training personnel, especially developers of interactive learning systems, may be accused of being somewhat isolated from the "trenches" of business. Similarly, educational technologists in schools, such as technology coordinators, may be considered peripheral to the main business of schooling, at least in the eyes of some administrators and teachers. You are advised to combat these prejudices proactively by undertaking the difficult job of evaluating impact.

– WEB LINK –
The *Program Evaluation Standards* can be found at: http://www.wmich.edu/evalctr/jc/

Estimating impact will never be easy, but you have an ethical responsibility to seek this kind of outcome data, even though your colleagues or associates may argue against it. A survey of 1,200 members of the American Society for Training and Development indicated that most tended to use training evaluation questionnaires much more than measures of outcomes and impact because the latter were viewed as "too time consuming, too expensive, and beyond their level of expertise" (cited in Sanders, 1989, p. 64). However, simply relying upon the ubiquitous "smilometer" for serious summative evaluation is no longer sufficient, if it ever was (Geber, 1995). Although you may not ever find the concrete evidence you desire to support the impact of interactive learning systems, you can build a credible case for interactive learning systems through the ethical application of the methods described above.

References

Brethower, D. M. (1989). Evaluating the merit and worth of sales training: Asking the right questions. In R. O. Brinkerhoff (Ed.), *Evaluating training programs in business and industry* (pp. 21-33). San Francisco: Jossey-Bass.

Cohen, S. L. (1991). The challenge of training in the nineties. *Training and Development, 45*(7), 30-35.

Coley, R. J., Cradler, J., & Engel, P. K. (1997). *Computers and classrooms: The status of technology in U.S. schools* (Policy Information Report). Princeton, NJ: Educational Testing Service.

Cuban, L. (2001). *Oversold and underused: Computers in the classroom.* Cambridge, MA: Harvard University Press.

David, J. L. (1996). Developing and spreading accomplished teaching: Policy lessons from a unique partnership. In C. Fisher, D. C. Dwyer, & K. Yocam (Eds.), *Education and technology: Reflections on computing in the classroom* (pp. 237-250). San Francisco: Jossey-Bass.

Dillman, D. A. (1999). *Mail and Internet surveys: The tailored design approach.* New York: John Wiley & Sons.

diSessa, A. A. (2000). *Changing minds: Computers, learning, and literacy.* Cambridge. MA: MIT Press.

Duderstadt, J. J. (1999). Can colleges and universities survive in the information age? In R. N. Katz (Ed.), *Dancing with the devil: Information technology and the new competition in higher education* (pp.1-25). San Francisco: Jossey-Bass.

Duffy, T. M., & Cunningham, D. J. (1996). Constructivism: Implications for the design and delivery of instruction. In D. H. Jonassen (Ed.), *Handbook of research for educational communications and technology* (pp. 170-198). New York: Macmillan.

Fisher, C., Dwyer, D. C., & Yocam, K. (Eds.). (1996). *Education and technology: Reflections on computing in the classroom.* San Francisco: Jossey-Bass.

Geber, B. (1995). Does your training make a difference? Prove it! *Training, 32*(3), 27-34.

Gross, M. L. (1999). *The conspiracy of ignorance: The failure of American public schools.* New York: HarperCollins.

Jonassen, D. H., & Reeves, T. C. (1996). Learning *with* technology: Using computers as cognitive tools. In D. H. Jonassen (Ed.), *Handbook of research on educational communications and technology* (pp. 693-719). New York: Macmillan.

Kallick, B., & Wilson, J. W. (Eds.). (2000). *Information technology in schools: Creating practical knowledge to improve student performance*. San Francisco: Jossey-Bass.

Kearsley, G. (1993). Costs and benefits of technology-based instruction. In G. M. Piskurich (Ed.), *The ASTD handbook of instructional technology* (pp. 16.1-16.19). New York: McGraw-Hill.

Kemske, F., & Weingarten, N. J. (1989). A memo from the future: Data training in 1999. *Data Training*, *8*(12), 14-22.

Kidder, T. (1990). *Among schoolchildren.* New York: Avon Books.

Kirkpatrick, D. L. (1998). *Evaluating training programs: The four levels* (2nd ed.). San Francisco: Berrett-Koehler Publishers.

Mark, M. M., & Shotland, R. L. (1987). Alternative models for the use of multiple methods. In M. M. Mark & R. L. Shotland (Eds.), *Multiple methods in program evaluation.* San Francisco: Jossey-Bass.

Means, B. (Ed.). (1994). *Technology and education reform: The reality behind the promise*. San Francisco: Jossey-Bass.

Medsker, K. L., & Roberts, D. G. (Eds.). (1992). *ASTD trainer's toolkit: Evaluating the results of training*. Alexandria, VA: American Society for Training and Development.

Merriam, S. B. (1998). *Qualitative research and case study applications in education* (2nd ed.). San Francisco: Jossey-Bass.

Meyrowitz, J. (1985). *No sense of place: The impact of electronic media on social behavior*. New York: Oxford University Press.

Nesbary, D (1999). *Survey research and the World Wide Web*. Boston: Allyn & Bacon.

Newman, D. (1990). Opportunities for research on the organizational impact of school computers. *Educational Researcher*, *19*(3), 8-13.

Papert, S. (1993). *The children's machine: Rethinking school in the age of the computer*. New York: Basic Books.

Patton, M. Q. (1990). *Qualitative evaluation and research methods* (2nd ed.). Newbury Park, CA: Sage.

Perelman, L. J. (1992). *School's out: Hyperlearning, the new technology, and the end of education*. New York: William Morrow.

Phillips, J. J. (1994). *In action: Measuring return on investment*. Alexandria, VA: American Society for Training and Development.

Phillips, J. J. (1997). *Return on investment in training and performance improvement programs*. Houston, TX: Gulf Publishing Company.

Pittinsky, M. S. (Ed.). (2003) *The wired tower: Perspectives on the impact of the internet on higher education*. Upper Saddle River, NJ: Prentice Hall

Reeves, T. C. (1992). Evaluating schools infused with technology. *Education and Urban Society Journal*, *24*(4), 519-534.

Reeves, T. C., & Carter, B. J. (2001). Usability testing and return-on-investment studies: Key evaluation strategies for Web-based training. In B. H. Khan (Ed.), *Web-based training* (pp. 547-557). Englewood Cliffs, NJ: Educational Technology Publications.

Roblyer, M. D. (1999). *Integrating technology into teaching*. Englewood Cliffs, NJ: Prentice-Hall.

Rosenberg, M. J. (2000). *E-learning: Strategies for delivering knowledge in the digital age*. New York: McGraw-Hill.

Sanders, N. M. (1989). Evaluation of training by trainers. In R. O. Brinkerhoff (Ed.), *Evaluating training programs in business and industry* (pp. 59-70). San Francisco: Jossey-Bass.

Sandholtz, J. H., & Ringstaff, C. (1996). Teacher change in technology-rich classrooms. In C. Fisher, D. C. Dwyer, & K. Yocam (Eds.), *Education and technology: Reflections on computing in the classroom* (pp. 281-299). San Francisco: Jossey-Bass.

Swanson, R. A. (1989). Everything important in business and industry is evaluated. In R. O. Brinkerhoff (Ed.), *Evaluating training programs in business and industry* (pp. 71-82). San Francisco: Jossey-Bass.

Sykes, C. J. (1996). *Dumbing down our kids: Why American children feel good about themselves but can't read, write, or add*. New York: St. Martin's Press.

Thach, L. (1995). Using electronic mail to conduct survey research. *Educational Technology*, *35*(2), 27-31.

CHAPTER 10

Maintenance Evaluation

Objectives

After reading Chapter Ten, you should be able to:

- describe the role of maintenance evaluation;
- use various tools to collect data which will be helpful in answering questions about the adequacy of an interactive learning system to continue meeting the objectives originally established for it; and
- utilize reporting strategies to increase the likelihood that maintenance evaluation will assist in decision-making.

Why should you conduct maintenance evaluation?

Maintenance can be defined as the act of keeping something in existence or keeping it working. Maintenance evaluation is the act of careful appraisal regarding whether something has been maintained appropriately. As illustrated in Figure 10.1, maintenance evaluation informs the revision and refinement of interactive learning environments. It enables the "prolonging of life of developed instruction while maintaining the original effectiveness and efficiency" (Tennyson, 1995, p. 52). This is an often-overlooked evaluation function.

The role of maintenance evaluation is to monitor the progress and the regular use of an interactive learning system so that decisions about support, modification, or reconceptualization can be influenced. Tennyson (1978) described this aspect of managing a technology-based learning environment by emphasizing the need to continually monitor the progress of an innovation, especially one dependent upon a complex technological infrastructure. Over time, many changes are likely to occur in an instructional system. As people move on and change roles, as equipment becomes obsolete and is replaced, maintaining the system becomes the key to ongoing effective use. It is also likely that the environment in which an interactive learning system is used will evolve, throwing the system's continued viability into question.

Decisions	Example Questions
Should an interactive learning project be reconceptualized?	Is the system still being used? Are its objectives still relevant?
Should the implementation plans for an ILS be modified?	How have teachers integrated a program into courses? What aspects of a program have been dropped?
Should a program be moved to another delivery system?	How has the computing environment changed? What is the quality of Internet access in the school?
Should video and other media aspects be updated?	Do the students perceive the program as current? Have styles changed dramatically since the first edition?

Figure 10.1. Typical decisions and questions in maintenance evaluation.

Consider, for example, an interactive learning program popular with teachers and students that was produced for an older Windows operating system. The school has just decided to replace all remaining computers with new Macintoshes. The software is machine specific and when the change is made, it will no longer run. Similarly, if the processes at a plant have been modified to reduce the number of steps in the manufacturing cycle, any associated computer-based training (CBT) programs will need to be modified to eliminate the production steps that are no longer relevant.

Alternatively, consider the training of a bricklayer. There is a need for bricklayers to understand construction plans. In the past, this was taught by teaching the novice bricklayer to draw a simple plan for a house or wall, and then to add the dimensions and other specific notations. Nowadays, building plans are usually drawn using a computer-aided design (CAD) package, and manual drawing skills in drafting are not required. If drawing by hand is still included in a vocational course for bricklayers, this should be examined with respect to its relevance and value. Of course, the skill of reading construction plans may still be important, but current practice requires bricklayers to learn something about how CAD programs are used. What is gained and lost when new technologies are integrated into practice must be continuously examined in reference to training. Keeping training up-to-date requires vigilance.

When should you conduct maintenance evaluation?

For effective maintenance evaluation, there must be continuous monitoring of the learning environment, delivery systems, and other resources so that they can be kept accurate and current. The purpose of maintenance evaluation is "to determine the contextual validity of the technology-based learning program"(Alexander & Hedberg, 1994, p. 242). As the context changes, maintenance evaluation becomes paramount.

In most presentations of instructional design models, the authors give the impression that the process is a linear and predictable one, when it is more often an iterative process, seeking ever closer approximations to learning outcomes. Viewing development tasks as a lockstep set of procedures, creativity may be ignored as a key component. We have presented an alternative model for instructional design wherein the relationships between the functions of development and the functions of evaluation are essential to the effective completion of a project (as illustrated in Figure 3.2 in Chapter Three).

Maintenance evaluation is a key function that informs the implementation of interactive learning systems and, in particular, their renewal. Data should be collected from multiple information sources using a variety of maintenance evaluation techniques to inform decisions about the need to revisit or rework interactive materials. This helps to ensure products are meeting current purposes and changing curriculum requirements. It is difficult to specify exactly when maintenance evaluation should be conducted simply because it is very challenging to predict how other aspects of the education and training environment will change. Few predicted the enormous changes currently underway in the online learning industry because even fewer people foresaw the rapid deployment of the Web around the globe (Khan, 1997, 2001). Many legacy education and training systems are being re-examined in light of the availability of high-speed Internet access in homes today. Whether the people doing these investigations actually think of their work as maintenance evaluation is doubtful, but the goals and tools are similar to what we recommend in this chapter.

Maintenance evaluation and instructional design

— **WEB LINK** —
More information about Tennyson's work can be found at: http://www.education.umn.edu/EdPsych/Faculty/Tennyson.html

The maintenance evaluation aspect of our evaluation model has been influenced by Tennyson's (1978) Fourth Generation Instructional System Development Model in which he identified four kinds of evaluation that should occur during the stages of an instructional design project. These are feasibility, formative, summative, and maintenance evaluation. The goal of maintenance evaluation is to "ensure quality control and currency of the material over time" (Ross & Morrison, 1995, p. 497). The target audience for Tennyson's model was instructional developers rather than evaluators.

Tennyson has updated this model (see Figure 10.2) and now calls the development phase "production" and justifies this "because of the increased use of electronic media as an integral part of instructional design" (Tennyson, 1995, p. 36). In the new model, Tennyson recommends that instructional developers design, implement, and operate a maintenance system for the learning environment. In what Tennyson calls his Fourth Generation Instructional System Development (ISD) Model, there is a much stronger focus on evaluation than in the previous models. In fact, Tennyson describes evaluation as taking on the central role "by becoming the interface between the author and the ID prescription in use" (p. 37). We concur with Tennyson's emphasis on the centrality of evaluation within ISD.

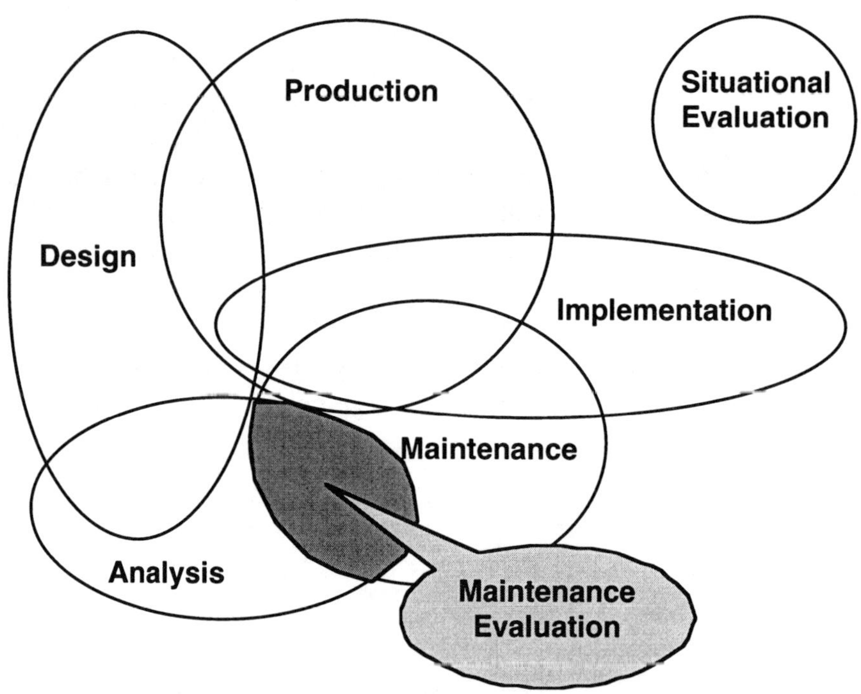

Figure 10.2. Fourth generation ISD model (Tennyson, 1995).

What kinds of decisions can you anticipate?

Two primary types of maintenance decisions involve the compatibility of different versions of software with various hardware platforms, and keeping interactive instructional systems updated on a regular basis. The rapidly changing specifications for Web-based e-learning make these decisions more complex than ever. Seemingly, hardly a month goes by without the introduction of a new Web-based media format (e.g., ever better streaming video) or a faster, easier Web authoring tool.

The challenge of different versions of software

Most interactive learning systems depend upon specific versions of software, e.g., effective operation may depend upon having the latest operating system or high-speed hardware. If these attributes are not present, the interactive learning system may not run, or it may be tediously slow and frustrating. It is a delicate balancing act to ensure that the development of the technical resources occurs along with the management of the software systems. Mismatches can be overlooked by instructors until the system grinds to a halt. The implementation of any system must include provisions for maintenance of the hardware and the software required to run on it. Sometimes, it is found that a very useful program can no longer run on new or upgraded hardware, so a new version must be purchased. The newer version may include new features, but often at a cost. This cost may take the form of an inability to do various tasks. Or the increased complexity of the software may mean that routine tasks are not as readily undertaken as previously.

As a developer, you may need to release new versions of software to correct bugs in earlier versions, to extend the instructional program to cover new content or teach new skills, or even to demonstrate a new range of features flowing from advances in hardware or software. Consider the arrival of Apple's QuickTime digital video technology; suddenly simple animations could be replaced with crude movies. Then, in rapid succession, new versions of the software were released and increasingly sophisticated movies (such as QuickTime Virtual Reality) could be incorporated into interactive learning environments. For users of earlier versions of QuickTime, movies seemed pixilated and slow by comparison with what was available a few months later (or they could not be played at all). Thus, sometimes the technology alone may drive the need for renewal. Often the change is unexpected. For example, a seemingly simple change in the equipment available in a computer laboratory might necessitate an upgrade or purchase of new versions of authoring software simply to continue working.

Sometimes the changes can be managed through automated procedures. Consider the use of a Web browser that can retrieve updated references by actually finding each page whenever it is updated by the owner. However, if your learning environment depends upon a set of resources being available on the Web, it can be difficult to keep the environment current if a Web server is given a new address and any links that you have developed are rendered useless. A requirement that learners work cooperatively with instructors and with each other on site maintenance tasks can circumvent this problem, but we are convinced that the problem of "dead links" will be a major challenge in maintaining complex learning environments on the Web in the foreseeable future.

Maintaining software

Maintenance evaluation is increasingly important in view of the array of options for delivering interactive learning available today. Imagine a simulation designed to help adults learn a second language by immersing them in a foreign scenario. There are a variety of delivery options for this interactive learning environment, including CD-ROM, digital videodisc (DVD), and the World Wide Web. Although each of these delivery systems is different, the programs could have the same mix of pedagogical strategies. For example, the learner could be interacting within the context of a real task (e.g., asking for directions in a foreign country) that would require him or her to listen to a native speaker, select the best response from a menu of choices, receive feedback, and subsequently be linked to remedial instruction as indicated by his or her success or failure in selecting the appropriate response within the simulation. Regardless of the instructional design, some delivery systems are easier to maintain than others. At the same time, some delivery systems are more secure or stable than others. There are always tradeoffs that must be considered.

Maintenance evaluation is a cost that few project managers anticipate. Since the time when mainframes were the primary delivery platforms, maintenance has often been ignored in the costing of software projects (Arthur, 1988; Martin & McClure, 1983; Sommerville, 2000). Software maintenance is considered to consist of: "The activities required to keep a software system operational and beneficial after it is accepted and placed into production" (Arthur, 1988, p. 235). Historically, it has usually been assumed to be a problem that developers could ignore.

In large software development projects, the costs of running a package would often only become evident after a system had been implemented, by which time it was too late to limit those costs because a large development investment had already been made. The importance of investigating the implementation and the ongoing maintenance of interactive learning systems cannot be underestimated. Several training and education systems have been developed by designers with good intentions who later found out that the required combinations of hardware and/or the software architecture were no longer being supported. In the past, whole systems have been scrapped because certain hardware was no longer available or because the authoring tools employed were no longer being supported by their vendors for use with a new hardware system or operating system.

The instability of today's hardware and software environments may mean that the ratio of development costs to maintenance costs can often be more like 1 to 2 rather than the 10 to 1 usually assumed. Initially the cost of maintenance is hidden, and yet it may represent up to 67% of overall costs for a large system (Zelkowitz *et al.* as cited in Martin & McClure, 1983). As software systems have evolved, maintenance has become more critical, especially when most companies seem to prefer investing in enhancing software so that they can issue a new release rather than in actually fixing bugs in the current version. Thus, the development of techniques to extract and monitor the ongoing costs of maintaining systems should be built into any evaluation process.

Nielsen's (1999) contention that new technologies like the Web are likely to be more cost-effective than older systems only if the new products integrate simple design concepts is worth remembering. There is little point in allowing programmers or developers to specify fancy Java-based applets to handle complex instructional interactions that in the grand scheme of things add little except gimmicks to a learning environment.

— WEB LINK —
More information about WebCT can be found at http://www.webct.com and about BlackBoard at http://www.blackboard.com

Course management systems and learning management systems present special maintenance challenges. For example, in higher education, several products are currently marketed to support Web-based courseware development, e.g., WebCT and BlackBoard (Pittinsky, 2003). Although these systems have strong capabilities, they should be selected and reviewed continually. It is easy to become too invested in a system that, in our rapidly changing world, may become a dinosaur incapable of being upgraded or maintained except by a band of expensive specialists.

Maintenance costs may be reduced through rapid responses to the need to change. Connell and Shaffer (1989) suggest that rapid maintenance can be useful in reducing costs. In other words, waiting to conduct maintenance evaluation until the need for fixing problems is critical may well prove more costly than a planned program of preventative maintenance evaluation would have been.

What questions should be answered before making decisions?

Project reconceptualization decisions have so many implications for developers and practitioners that many questions must be addressed before making these decisions. First, let's consider a real example. A few years ago, a sophisticated multimedia authoring system (which shall remain unnamed) had just begun to attract the attention of some of the best multimedia developers in the world when it was purchased by a larger corporation and shortly thereafter dropped as a viable product! It seems that the larger corporation engaged in little or no maintenance evaluation before making the drastic decision to drop the product. Maintenance evaluation could have addressed questions about the product that may have influenced a different decision. What was the number of designers who had adopted the product? What were they willing to pay for the product? If internationally recognized multimedia designers used the product, what did it mean for the future viability of the product when these same designers won design awards for programs developed with the software?

Second, let's consider a hypothetical example within a training context. Suppose a clothing manufacturer has been using computer-based training (CBT) delivered via CD-ROM for sales training for four years. Every salesperson carries a laptop computer whenever he/she is on the road, with travel averaging 15 days per month. In light of increasing bandwidth, high tech consultants recommend the development of a company Intranct for account tracking and sales management that would also enable the delivery of Web-based training (WBT). Before making the decision to move to WBT, a careful maintenance evaluation of the existing CBT should be conducted to address multiple questions. How widely used are the current CBT materials? How much does it cost to update and distribute CD-ROMs for this sales force? How would the sales personnel maintain easy access to the Intranet when they are on the road, e.g., waiting in airports or spending nights in hotels? What features of the CD-ROM CBT would be lost with Web delivery? What would be gained? These and other maintenance evaluation questions should be addressed carefully before making major decisions about reconceptualizing a training delivery system.

How should maintenance evaluation be conducted?

It is no longer acceptable for a development team or an instructional designer to implement a program and assume that it is finished. Just as in the software industry, the high costs invested in an interactive learning system indicate a need to support the program so that the end users can keep implementing it until a reasonable return on investment has been realized. Whether it is a DVD program or an online course, it will need continual maintenance evaluation until it becomes obsolete.

As noted above, the role of maintenance evaluation in a technology-based learning environment is to monitor the progress of the regular use of a product or system. Consider the following maintenance questions (as proposed by Tennyson, 1995, pp. 72-75):

1) Is the interactive learning system still meeting its goals and objectives?

Whether an interactive learning system continues to achieve its objectives is an issue at the core of maintenance evaluation. To address this issue in depth, consider questions such as:

- Do these materials/systems still produce the intended learning outcomes?
- Do learners view their learning experience positively?
- Is the system easy to manage and maintain?
- Are technical staff spending too much time to keep the system running?

2) Is the content current?

The content of some fields changes a great deal over a period of just a few years whereas other fields have more stable content. It is unlikely that interactive materials will remain useful in highly volatile curriculum areas for more than a few years. Consider questions such as:

- How is the curriculum changing in this domain?
- Are changes being required or mandated by other agencies (such as political, technological, or social groups)?
- If the materials are related to a specific product, is it still being sold or marketed?
- Have the prerequisite courses changed in content or approach?
- What new advances are being discussed and do they need to be added to the curriculum? What needs to be deleted?

3) What do the students think about the interactive learning system?

Surveying end users periodically is a critical method to review the curriculum and the instructional strategies used in the knowledge domain. Tastes and styles change over time, and often students will vote with their feet in taking or not taking courses they believe are poorly taught or uninteresting. It is a buyers' market in today's e-learning world (Pittinsky, 2003; Rosenberg, 2000). Conducting interviews or focus groups will provide valuable insights if a range of questions are asked, such as:

- What is the continuing motivation among students in using these materials?
- How up-to-date do the materials appear to the current population of learners?
- What alignment among the objectives, materials, and assessments do students perceive in the learning environment?

4) How is the target learner changing over time?

As students become more familiar with the use of technologies, not only will they find some older approaches too slow or boring, but also their skills and understanding might require access to new software tools. Modern software systems provide helpful adjuncts such as instant messaging tools that allows students to ask questions of instructors or peers on the fly or digital notebooks for students to make notes as they work through the material. These systems might also provide support for linking students to instructors, so that authentic learning communities can evolve (Palloff & Pratt, 1999, 2001).

The popularity of electronic games means that for many people the conventions of how a package can be navigated and manipulated are familiar. Recently, one of us finished a product that was designed as a learning game in which users were challenged to complete several tasks and problems. During the design phase, the client continually asked that detailed instructions be included about where to click to find information. There was an interesting standoff between the designers and the client because the changes the client was suggesting might have been appropriate for older users, but testing indicated too many instructions would ruin the product for the younger target audience.

There are many questions that should be addressed about how users may be changing, such as:

- What are the computing skills of the current population of target learners?
- What expectations do the new learners have for media elements such as digital video?
- How is the instructor population changing with respect to expertise and comfort with technology?

5) What is happening with the underpinning technology?

This last question is critical to the costs of maintenance in the brave new world of Web-based training delivery. For example, the U.S. Defense Department is establishing standards for e-learning products through its Advanced Distributed Learning (ADL) initiative that all new interactive training and education products must follow (Oehlert, 2001). The underpinning technology for interactive learning systems is also being affected by the rapid development of learning management systems (LMS) and learning content management systems (LCMS) (Schelin, 2001). To address this issue, you might ask many questions, but consultation with experts who have differing views is mandatory if you wish to avoid a technological dead end. Ask questions such as:

- When should the system be updated for a new platform?
- What seems to be happening to the technologies we are using?
- What are other groups (such as competitors) using to deliver this content or this instructional strategy?
- Can the system be moved to other technologies, and what is the cost?
- Can new media be integrated to extend the life of a program?
- Does the interactive learning system have to meet government and/or corporate standards?
- Does the interactive learning system have to be made compatible with various LMS or LCMS?
- Is there provision for updating instructor training?

Tools for maintenance evaluation

Asking the right questions informs the important decisions you and your clients must make, but you also must use the right tools to find the best answers. Consider some of the following tools and how they might inform better decision making.

Quick sources of ongoing data

Every system should have capabilities built into it for routinely collecting and collating data to identify important changes occurring over time. Each user of a package might simply be asked to complete a small card and deposit it in a "suggestions" box. Another simple method is to require that every user fill in a brief online questionnaire about the system or product. Consider the simple questionnaire in Figure 10.3.

Please answer the following questions to help us monitor this package.

- Please rate this package overall

  Poor 1 2 3 4 5 6 7 Excellent

Any comments?

- Were the objectives relevant to your studies? If no, why not? If yes, how?
- What are the best points about this package?
- Describe any problems you experienced with this package.
- What changes should be made and why?

Figure 10.3. Sample quick evaluation for routine package use.

Using automated data collection techniques

Information can be accumulated and analyzed in cost-efficient ways through the use of technology. This data can be used to obtain information about learning outcomes and can be manipulated as the learners interact with the materials. Several approaches have been used. For example, intelligent test scoring can provide feedback on student performance and yield an individual profile that can be reviewed by the instructor. If a diagnostic profile is collected, the student might be presented with options and choices based upon it. Alternatively, the package might suggest some options based upon artificial intelligence built into the software (Ross & Morrison, 1995).

Automated routines can help identify the location of strong and weak points in an interactive learning system. Reviewing data patterns can assist with modifying a system to produce the desired outcomes. Automated data collection can provide up-to-date and constant information about a program, e.g., by pointing to sections of an e-learning program that have had the highest change in traffic.

Automated systems can also determine if there are components that are constantly failing. For example, a Web server can provide a report giving information about access to a Web site. This information can determine when the server crashes, such as when a large number of people hit the server at the same time. This might occur the first time a new chat space is used. Automated systems can also provide information about which files are accessed frequently and which are not being used at all, thereby identifying files which might be removed to save space or accelerate access. Most proprietary learning management systems provide this kind of data, but the utility of the data must be questioned. For example, the frequency of use might mask other problems. Frequent access to a portion of an interactive learning system would seem at first glance to be desirable, but it might mean that those parts are so badly designed that they require inordinate amounts of time as learners try to fathom their meaning.

Developers can become overly dependent on the use of automated data, since it can be cheaper to obtain than asking direct questions of the users of a product. Interviews and other methods should be included in the evaluation plan to ensure that the interpretation is not simply a mechanical addition of meaningless numbers. Web servers often provide a numerical counter of hits on pages, thereby producing numbers, but the numbers are not always interpretable. For instance, a specific page can be set as the home page for a browser that automatically opens each time the browser is launched. Such hits are therefore meaningless unless they are linked to something that can provide indications of type of use.

There are numerous online courses available, and as with all information on the World Wide Web, their validity and utility must be questioned. Fortunately, by their very nature, Web-based courses can be modified easily, provided you have good data upon which to base changes. Maintenance evaluation of a Web course or even a Web page can start with simple observations of users. Or brief evaluation forms can be included within a Web site to collect feedback from users. If users report minor problems, updates can be quickly and efficiently completed.

If more sophisticated automated tools such as profile analysis and intelligent tutors are needed, the cost of setting up the maintenance evaluation system will be considerably higher. Currently there remains a large gap between the theory of "intelligent" advice and how it should be provided and the development of interactive tools for the application of this artificial intelligence theory (Shute & Psotka, 1996).

Automated systems produce large amounts of data. Unless collection of such data has been carefully thought out so that data can be analyzed efficiently and accurately, the data may not be useful. Sampling of the data to identify critical incidents or patterns may make the data more useful. Several methods have been suggested, but all have problems and each produces only part of the picture. Evans (1994) and Fritze (1994) have suggested several approaches. Figure 10.4 demonstrates the use of visual mapping techniques to represent the path of a student through a package. Note that a single student can produce quite a complex plot, and each student will produce a unique trace. Comparisons and generalizations using this type of data are not trivial tasks.

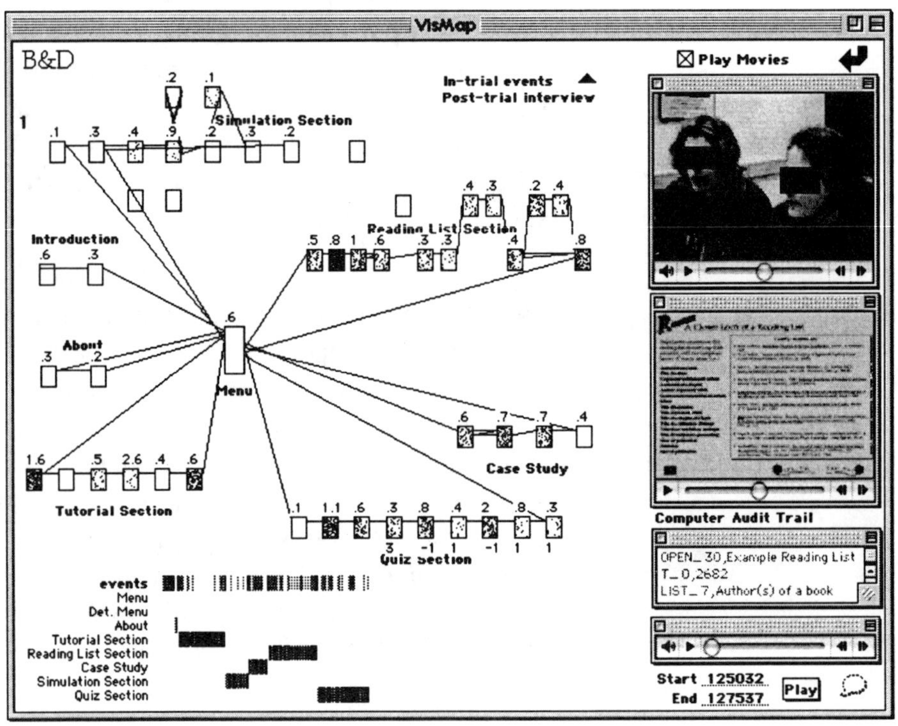

Figure 10.4. Displaying automated data collected to view use of a program.

Critical incidents

Most organizations have routine methods of data collection. They may be as innocuous as the collection of ideas through a suggestion box or the monitoring of reports of accidents on the plant floor. Provided that the culture of an organization supports the routine collection of such data, it can prove invaluable in determining if related interactive training products need to be redesigned. Consider the standard safety programs that most organizations hold regularly. If the number or type of accident reports seem to vary, rise, or fall, then something has occurred and should probably be investigated. Training may no longer be adequate.

Collection of other routine data, such as absenteeism, attrition, popularity of certain interactive materials, or number of hits on a Web page can also inform decisions providing they are monitored and interpreted. Critical incidents, such as a shop floor accident, or informal insights shared by a typical user, can be important in instigating the review of a project.

Unobtrusive measures

Depending upon the type of context and the way interactive learning systems are implemented within an organization, you might consider "unobtrusive" ways of obtaining maintenance data. You might even collect useful data from the custodial staff. For example, in evaluating interactive kiosks, the volume and frequency of cleaning the dust from interactive displays may give you an indication about the interest in particular kiosks. Suppose you want to know if your Web-based learning environment is encouraging students to go beyond the content provided in the course text. You could ask your librarian or school media specialist if there has been an increase in the rate that materials are checked out related to the topics in the interactive learning course. Although unobtrusive data will rarely tell a complete story and inferences must be made, such data can be usefully triangulated with evidence collected via more traditional methods.

Other methods

Several common methods might be employed in the collection of data about the ongoing use of an interactive learning system. In the evaluation of a school-based interactive learning system, data can be collected from administrators and office staff as well as from parents, teachers, and students who use the system. Often training departments collect routine reports and surveys about student comments. Taken over a period of time this might indicate a trend in certain training courses the department runs. This will certainly be the case if the course is a pre-packaged one with the same series of activities and exercises. Over time, you will begin to hear coffee-break stories about interactive products, such as "the content is not really relevant now," or "the training needs have changed since the courseware was written."

Serendipitous events may be overlooked, but they should be documented if the ongoing viability of interactive learning systems is being monitored. Casual comments in the corridor might lead to great insights. After all, recognizing that the mold growing on a glass dish could kill germs led to a great medical advance (penicillin); such things may occur in education and training contexts (although they are unlikely to have an analogous degree of impact). A great challenge facing the often scaled-down training operations today is the fact that training courses are often not monitored, and consequently no one within the organization is aware of the adequacy of the match to current training needs. If you have the responsibility to contract training or monitor career development processes for an organization, then you will need to design a documentation trail that will provide insights into the current utility of the courses and packages you are purchasing or managing.

What are some examples of actual maintenance evaluations?

In the following cases, we present ideas of how some systems have been developed to capture data about ongoing utility. Read each case and consider how the principles might be applied to other contexts, or best of all, to situations similar to the ones you have experienced.

Library catalogs

At most institutions, the library search catalog systems have automated data-collection functions embedded in the software. These functions provide details of the paths each user takes in his or her search for information, with the aim of improving and simplifying access to the database. This data is used to evaluate the system so that periodic decisions can be made to improve the design of the system. How can you employ these ideas within an instructional system?

Instructor reporting procedures

Most schools employ systems for recording and reporting student assessments. At one school, the system was modified in light of a number of critical incidents. In this school, teachers depended on other teachers to complete a section of a report card before the next section could be completed. Difficulties arose and reports were delayed when a number of teachers had difficulty reading files on their classroom computers. After interviewing the teachers, it was found that there were not only a number of different word processing packages being used, but also a number of versions of each package within the school. The software employed by each teacher was the version that was bundled with the computer he or she received when hired. Inevitably as new computers were purchased, later software versions were provided. Consequently, there were many problems throughout the school with people unable to read the files sent to them by others. Once the problem was identified, standard software was provided to ensure compatibility. All versions were updated by making a bulk purchase of word-processing software to be used on all machines for reporting and assessment. Can you envisage similar collaborative systems that might provide learners with an understanding of what they have learned and what gaps there are in their knowledge?

A student and course administration system

The "Mirage" administration system was designed for K-12 schools. After it had been used for five years to meet the requirements of school administration, there was an updating initiative within the school district. A number of teachers were given time away from their schools to assist in revising the package. These teachers were self-taught programmers with a teaching and school administration background. Many software "bugs" were discovered in the revised package as it was implemented. These errors were particularly difficult to fix because of the way the package was coded. In addition, the documentation was not prepared to commercial software standards.

The original software was developed for a particular machine and a specific operating system, which meant it wouldn't run on the new hardware and operating system being purchased in the district. The costs for maintenance were high and began to outweigh the advantages of the computerized data. Eventually a new version was developed, tested in three schools, and then rolled out to the other schools in the district after an evaluation was completed and some of the bugs were remedied. Unfortunately, staff had to be retrained, as there was a new screen design, and several frequently used features of the old system were not included in the new version. Maintenance evaluation strategies should have been utilized at an earlier point to reduce the types of problems encountered in this situation. Ongoing maintenance might have determined that the "Mirage" package needed updating or modification, or that a completely new system was needed. What processes should be put in place to collect this type of data for e-learning systems?

How should maintenance evaluations be reported?

Maintenance data reports are usually much less formal than the reports associated with other evaluation functions. The main concern for reporting in a maintenance evaluation context is that any data indicating problems with the implementation of interactive learning systems or the need to fix or enhance these systems must be put into the hands of decision makers as quickly and unambiguously as possible. A combination of Web-based reports and e-mails concerning critical data may be an efficient approach to reporting the results of maintenance evaluations. Having maintenance data accessible via the Web from a dynamic database may be a good approach to providing information rapidly.

Summary

Maintenance evaluation can be extremely influential in driving the implementation and redesign of interactive learning systems. The key questions this evaluation function seeks to answer are related to the continued relevance of delivery systems and products, and whether or not strategic decisions need to be made about the continuation or renewal of these systems and products. Several approaches can be undertaken to collect data, but simple routine data collection and records of critical events occurring over the use of the system will be most useful in indicating the need for specific changes, or when complete overhauls should be made. There is an old saying that goes: "If it isn't broke, don't fix it." However, this maxim is only meaningful if you know whether something is still working or not!

References

Alexander, S., & Hedberg, J. G. (1994). Evaluating technology-based learning: Which model? In K. Beattie, C. McNaught, & S. Wills (Eds.), *Interactive multimedia in university education: Designing the change in teaching and learning* (pp. 233-244). Amsterdam: Elsevier Science.

Arthur, L. J. (1988). *Software evolution: The software maintenance challenge*. New York: John Wiley and Sons.

Bunderson, C. V., Inouye, D. K., & Olsen, J. B. (1989). The four generations of computerized educational measurement. In R. L. Linn (Ed.), *Educational measurement* (3rd ed.). New York: Macmillan.

Connell, J. L., & Shaffer, L. B. (1989). *Structured rapid prototyping*. Englewood Cliffs, NJ: Prentice-Hall.

Edmonds, G. S., Branch, R. C., & Mukherjee, P. A. (1994). Conceptual framework for comparing instructional design models. *Educational Technology Research and Development*, *42*(4), 55-72.

Evans, P. (1994). Investigating the use of interactive hypermedia learning systems. In K. Beattie, C. McNaught, & S. Wills (Eds.), *Interactive multimedia in university education: Designing the change in teaching and learning* (pp. 259-271). Amsterdam: Elsevier Science.

Fritze, P. (1994). A visual mapping approach to the evaluation of multimedia learning materials. In K. Beattie, C. McNaught, & S. Wills (Eds.), *Interactive multimedia in university education: Designing the change in teaching and learning* (pp. 273-285). Amsterdam: Elsevier Science.

Khan, B. H. (Ed.). (1997). *Web-based instruction.* Englewood Cliffs, NJ: Educational Technology Publications.

Khan, B. H. (Ed.). (2001). *Web-based training.* Englewood Cliffs, NJ: Educational Technology Publications.

Martin, J., & McClure, C. (1983). *Software maintenance: The problem and its solution.* Englewood Cliffs, NJ: Prentice-Hall.

Nielsen, J. (1999). *Designing Web usability: The practice of simplicity.* Indianapolis, IN: New Riders.

Oehlert, M. (2001). ADL unites government, industry and academia. *E-Learning, 2*(3), 18-19.

Palloff, R. M., & Pratt, K. (1999). *Building learning communities in cyberspace: Effective strategies for the online classroom.* San Francisco: Jossey-Bass.

Palloff, R. M., & Pratt, K. (2001). *Lessons from the cyberspace classroom: The realities of online teaching.* San Francisco: Jossey-Bass.

Pittinsky, M. S. (Ed.). (2003) *The wired tower: Perspectives on the impact of the Internet on higher education.* Upper Saddle River, NJ: Prentice-Hall

Rosenberg, M. J. (2000). *E-learning: Strategies for delivering knowledge in the digital age.* New York: McGraw-Hill.

Ross, S. M., & Morrison, G. R. (1995). Evaluation as a tool for research and development: Issues and trends in its applications in educational technology. In R. Tennyson & A. Barron (Eds.), *Automating instructional design: Computer-based development and delivery tools.* Berlin: Springer-Verlag.

Shute, V. J., & Psotka, J. (1996). Intelligent tutoring systems: Past, present, and future. In D. H. Jonassen (Ed.), *Handbook of research for educational communications and technology* (pp. 570-600). New York: Macmillan.

Schelin, E. (2001). LMS and LCMS! *E-Learning, 2*(6), 22-24.

Sommerville, I. (2000). *Software engineering* (6th ed.) New York: Addison-Wesley.

Tennyson, R. D. (1978). Evaluation technology in instructional development. *Journal of Instructional Development, 2,* 19-26.

Tennyson, R. D. (1994). The big wrench vs. integrated approaches: The great media debate. *Educational Technology Research and Development, 42*(3), 15-28.

Tennyson, R. D. (1995). Instructional system development: The fourth generation. In R. Tennyson & A. Barron (Eds.), *Automating instructional design: Computer-based development and delivery tools.* Berlin: Springer-Verlag.

Tennyson, R. D., & Barron, A. (Eds.). (1995). *Automating instructional design: Computer-based development and delivery tools.* Berlin: Springer-Verlag.

Tucker, S. A. (1993). Evaluation as feedback in instructional technology: The role of feedback in program evaluation. In J. V. Dempsey & G. S. Sales (Eds.), *Interactive instruction and feedback.* Englewood Cliffs, NJ: Educational Technology Publications.

Zelkowitz, M. V., Shaw, A. C., & Gannon, J. D. (1979). *Principles of software engineering and design.* Englewood Cliffs, NJ: Prentice-Hall.

CHAPTER 11

Evaluation Reporting

Objectives

After reading Chapter Eleven, you should be able to:

- identify which elements should be included in an evaluation report;
- identify several strategies for reporting evaluations in print and other media to enhance the utility of evaluations; and
- identify criteria that can be used to judge the utility, feasibility, propriety, and accuracy of evaluations.

Reporting the story

Throughout this book, we have tried to emphasize that the role of the evaluator in the development of interactive learning systems is critical. After all, it is the evaluator who provides the information that project managers and other team members need to guide critical decisions throughout a project. Of course, information provided by evaluators will only influence decisions if it is provided to decision makers and others in formats that are appropriate and efficient. In this chapter, we suggest a range of ideas about how to present what you have found through evaluation to maximize your influence.

In presenting your evaluation results, remember that most readers want more than "just the facts." They expect you to explain how you have collected the data and how you arrived at the interpretations and recommendations in your report. The reporting task can be summarized simply as telling the story of the evaluation in the following order:

1) Describe the context of the project or system that was evaluated.
2) Explain the methods you used in reference to specific questions.
3) Report the data or evidence you have collected.

4) Summarize your conclusions and make recommendations.

Although we encourage you to consider other reporting formats such as video and Web pages, the reality is that most evaluations are still reported as written documents. A final written report should contain all the elements that will make it useful to the decision makers and other stakeholders. Most reports include an executive summary, which summarizes the findings and presents the recommendations along with a brief rationale for each recommendation. In addition, most evaluation reports include appendices that provide greater detail about various aspects of the evaluation such as instruments and transcripts of data. A list of the sections of a typical evaluation report appears in Figure 11.1.

1. Title
2. Table of Contents
3. Executive Summary
4. Overview and Background (includes description of what was evaluated and delineation of the purpose of the evaluation)
5. Decisions (intended to be influenced by the evaluation) and Questions (that were addressed)
6. Methodology (including complete description of the design and any instruments that were adapted or developed)
7. Results (possibly organized by methodologies, e.g. interviews, questionnaires, observations, or by the major questions)
8. Recommendations and Discussion
9. References
10. Appendices

Figure 11.1. Sections of a typical evaluation report.

Components of a typical evaluation report

The following sub-sections describe issues and options that can contribute to an effective final evaluation report. The type of report described in these sub-sections is a traditional one. Less traditional ways of reporting evaluation results are described later in this chapter.

Executive Summary

Figure 11.2 provides an abbreviated example of an executive summary for an evaluation report. The structure of the executive summary emphasizes the major recommendations and provides minimal explanation when required. This section of an evaluation report may be the most important simply because it may be the only part that most busy executives and managers ever read.

Executive Summary: E-Learning Evaluation

Introduction

In response to a mandate from the central administration to evaluate all new e-learning units developed by the organization, the Safety First Unit was evaluated during this month using three primary methods: (1) questionnaires completed by a representative sample of learners who have completed the Unit, (2) interviews with the Unit developers, and (3) focus groups conducted with three groups of workers who had not yet completed the Unit.

Overview of Results

The Safety First Unit is generally effective in enhancing workers' commitment to safe work practices and minimizing accidents. However, the Unit is still only available via the company intranet to those workers with their own workstations or those who can find time to come to the training lab. Many workers, especially those in some of the more accident-prone jobs, are not availing themselves of this important e-learning program.

Focus on Accessibility

It is recommended that the Unit be made available over the Web so that workers can more easily access the training at home or at a public library. Additional incentives for Unit completion are highly recommended so that all personnel will complete the Safety First Unit within a three-month timeframe.

Targeted Investments To Enhance Training Capacity

It is recommended that future training labs be established in locations closer to the production, assembly, and packaging lines within the company.

Figure 11.2. Sample "Executive Summary" of an evaluation report.

Above all, the executive summary should be succinct and clear, and it should highlight exactly what needs to be done in response to the evaluation. An executive summary may begin with a brief overview of the key questions addressed as well as a short description of the methods used in the evaluation. This should only take one or two paragraphs. The next sections in the executive summary usually take the form of recommendations with one-paragraph explanations of the rationale for each recommendation. The explanation might include some brief recounting of evidence if the recommendation is somewhat contentious or requires further explanation.

Overview and Background

This section is where the ability to write a good narrative (tell a story) can be extremely useful and efficient in getting the message across. The questions your report should answer for the reader are:

1) What is the interactive learning system that was evaluated? What is its physical location? How is it used or accessed? Are there physical constraints that make it effective or ineffective? Screen captures from the program can help readers unfamiliar with the program better understand its functions and look and feel.
2) Who are the users (real and potential) of the interactive learning system being evaluated? What is unique or important about them? Are there other people (e.g., instructors) who need to be considered and for what reason? Who participated in the evaluation? With respect to the last question, it is important to distinguish among the clients (people or agencies paying for the evaluation), audiences (people or agencies interested in the evaluation results), participants (those from whom evaluation data was collected), and evaluators (the people who actually conducted the evaluation).
3) What is the purpose of the evaluation? Is it a review, needs assessment, formative, effectiveness, impact, maintenance, or some sort of hybrid evaluation? Most evaluations have multiple purposes, e.g., effectiveness or impact evaluations may also include a formative component to collect data that can be used to enhance the program or product.
4) What was the starting point for the evaluation? Who asked for it and why? Most evaluations have "political" aspects, and it is better to describe these issues openly rather than to leave them hidden (Ryan & DeStefano, 2000). Needless to say, writing this section requires sensitivity to the unique views of various stakeholders.
5) What was the starting point for the interactive learning system and why was the project begun? Is there a historical background that should be described? Who started it? What are its objectives or goals? Interactive learning systems and other technological innovations are often the brainchild of a single "evangelist" within an organization. It is important to describe the origin of the vision for a new product as well as its current support.

6) How does the product fit within the organization? How is it configured to work with other components of the organization? Does it require special equipment? Why and how were changes made? What implications does it have for the organization's personnel systems? Interactive learning systems may disempower some groups and empower others within an organization.

Many of the above questions also have a cost element, and thus the background section might include some description of the budget allocated for the product. There may be many other elements that should be included in the overview and background section of your report, and you can include additional details in appendices. The driving issue in this section is to provide a complete picture through words and illustrations of what the interactive learning system is and why it was evaluated.

Decisions and Questions

A fundamental principle of our evaluation model is that evaluation should be conducted to provide the information people need to make better decisions. Accordingly, it is important to remind the readers of your report of the anticipated decisions and the questions that essentially drove the evaluation. These should be reported in a form that clearly illustrates the relationships between anticipated decisions and the questions that were asked to inform the decisions. Figure 11.3 is an example.

Decisions	Questions
How should access to the Web-based training (WBT) system be priced?	What is the audience for the WBT? What are the prices of competing products?
What learning styles should be accommodated by the WBT?	What are the individual characteristics of the target audience? What learning styles can be accommodated by the design of WBT?
How will the content be maintained for currency and accuracy?	How stable is the content? Do subject matter experts consider the product content an accurate representation of the state-of-the-art of expertise in the area?
How will learners be tracked for registration, completion, and assessment purposes?	How does the product align with certification procedures? What is the variance in test results?

Figure 11.3. Decisions and questions summary for final report.

Keeping decisions at the forefront of an evaluation report is not always easy or popular. After all, the results of the evaluation may lead to recommendations to make decisions that affect the careers and livelihoods of real people involved in the design or utilization of interactive learning systems. We know of a few evaluations where final reports were never shared beyond the immediate clients, who decided to "hide the evidence" rather than make tough decisions. In one case, one of us was repeatedly told by the primary client that our work was exemplary throughout an evaluation and that we could expect lots of future work from the client's organization. But when we provided a final report that showed negative findings for one of the client's pet projects, the report was buried, and we never got another request to provide more evaluation services for that organization. Evaluating innovations is always a political process (House, 1974, 1993; Kirkpatrick, 1998).

Methodology

Methodology is essentially about the design of the evaluation. This section should describe the time frame and sequence of data collection activities undertaken. It is important to link the methodology to the theoretical perspective or paradigm upon which the evaluation was based. Whatever is written should be consistent with the overall approach. Occasionally, an evaluator might claim to have adopted one approach and then reviews the data from a different perspective. For example, an evaluation that is supposedly designed from an interpretivist perspective intended to reveal the perspectives of multiple stakeholders should not shift into the voice of a critical theorist with "all the answers."

As you describe each method, include information about response rates and any unexpected things that happened during data collection. This helps the reader in linking the narrative and the veracity of each method.

Several issues should be addressed:

1) Reiterate the purpose and questions of the evaluation and clarify how the methods chosen provided reliable, valid answers to the questions.
2) Describe how the data sources (samples) were chosen and how the participants responded and reacted to the data collection activities.
3) Describe the exact nature of the instruments used or how case studies or other methods were conducted. Include copies of instruments and protocols in appendices.
4) Discuss any problems that occurred or limitations that should be acknowledged, and how these may affect data interpretation.

Results

A good presentation of data from an evaluation will not overwhelm the readers with technical details. After all, the intent of an evaluation report is to inform people, not to impress them with your technical expertise (Patton, 1997). If your recommendations are to have strength, the links among recommendations and sources of data must be clearly delineated. Present the data you have collected clearly, and employ summary formats (such as tables) to make comparisons possible.

Reporting should be done ethically. Huff's (1993) classic book about unethical reporting is titled *How to Lie with Statistics.* Huff describes techniques that can be employed to influence people's interpretation of evaluation or research results. For instance, a change in the scale of the axes within a graph can make it appear that a small variation is actually a major change. In Figure 11.4, the graph on the right suggests that the audience for a new product is rising dramatically, while the left-hand graph indicates slow growth and even a flattening out over time. Whenever graphs or other figures are used, you should strive to illustrate the findings as fairly and unambiguously as possible.

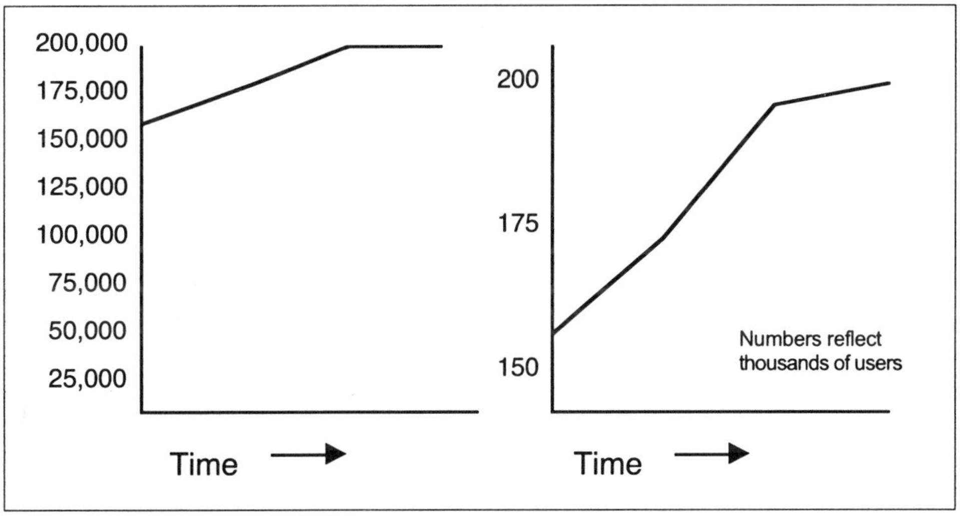

Figure 11.4. Illustration of "How to lie" with graphs.

Sometimes, the reverse of lying with statistics occurs when the report writer provides no interpretation of the data, but simply presents a series of numbers that are accurate, but difficult to interpret. A number often means very little unless it is explained and linked to other concepts. Most readers are interested in what the numbers imply rather than seeing the numbers per se. Your goal in presenting results is to guide the thinking of the readers while supplying enough information to ensure that they believe that you have substantiated the interpretations you are suggesting through your narrative and illustrations.

Recommendations and Discussion

The links between the decisions and questions that have driven the evaluation and the recommendations that stem from the answers should be clear. It might sound too obvious to state, but providing useful recommendations based upon appropriate evidence requires you to have deep insight into the effective workings of the system being evaluated. This is a skill that takes experience to build. Make sure that you address each issue and provide practical information that the developers, potential purchasers, and users of the interactive product can utilize to inform the decisions they must make.

In preparing recommendations, don't forget that sometimes there are unintended outcomes that might have been overlooked in the set of initial questions. Useful evaluation reports describe unexpected, as well as expected, issues that were revealed by the evaluation that managers and stakeholders should consider carefully in their decision-making.

Your recommendations should be pragmatic. Creating a list of unrealistic recommendations that will fail when implemented because they lack relevance to the context is just as useless as not providing any recommendations at all. Try to show how each recommendation addresses specific issues and why it is a practical solution to the problems or challenges inherent in the issue. Your awareness of what types of changes and actions are acceptable within a given context will ensure that your evaluation report will influence decision-makers to the fullest extent possible. For example, if you know that your clients have invested heavily in a specific interactive delivery option and that they are not in a position to change delivery systems, recommending that they move from one delivery system to another would be unwise in most situations.

In our experience, no aspect of an evaluation report is given more attention than the recommendations. Patton (1997) provides the following ten guidelines for making practical and useful recommendations:

1) The format and nature of the final report should be negotiated with stakeholders and evaluation funders.

2) Recommendations should clearly follow from and be supported by the evaluation findings.

3) Distinguish different kinds of evaluations (e.g., primary and secondary or formative and summative).

4) Some decision makers prefer receiving several options rather than recommendations advocating only one course of action.

5) Insofar as possible, when making recommendations, particularly major ones involving substantial changes in program operations

or policies, evaluators should study, specify, and include in their reports some consideration of the benefits and costs of making the suggested changes, including the costs and risks of not making them.

6) Focus on actions within the control of the intended audiences and clients.

7) Exercise political sensitivity in writing recommendations.

8) Be careful and deliberate in wording evaluations.

9) Allow yourself sufficient time to do a good job of writing the recommendations.

10) Develop strategies for getting recommendations taken seriously, e.g., help clients assign responsibility to various people for follow-up actions in response to each recommendation.

Alternative forms of reporting

Although many clients prefer to receive traditional print reports (Rudner & Schafer, 1999), we have found that our clients and other audiences are increasingly open to alternative forms of evaluation reports. In addition to innovative forms of print reports, evaluation reports can be reported via other media, such as video, the Web, and/or CD-ROM.

One alternative printed document approach that we have used successfully with numerous clients is a simple "two-page format." These evaluation reports are composed of a number of two-page sections, each one focused on a major question addressed or an issue revealed by an evaluation. One advantage of this format of report is that clients can pull the report apart and grapple with the implications of a few two-page sections at a time in face-to-face meetings or via electronic forums.

As illustrated in Figure 11.5, each two-page section of this form of report has four subsections. The first subsection is an attention-grabbing headline that is intended to motivate the reader to focus on the issue or problem addressed in the specific subsection. The headline can be an abbreviated version of the results (e.g., "Implementation of the 'Be Here or Else' Web site has lowered absenteeism by 80%."), a controversial statement made by a participant in the evaluation (e.g., "Interactive learning systems should replace textbooks!"), or a quote from another source related to the findings (e.g., "I know a false god when I see one." (Postman, 1995, p. 50).

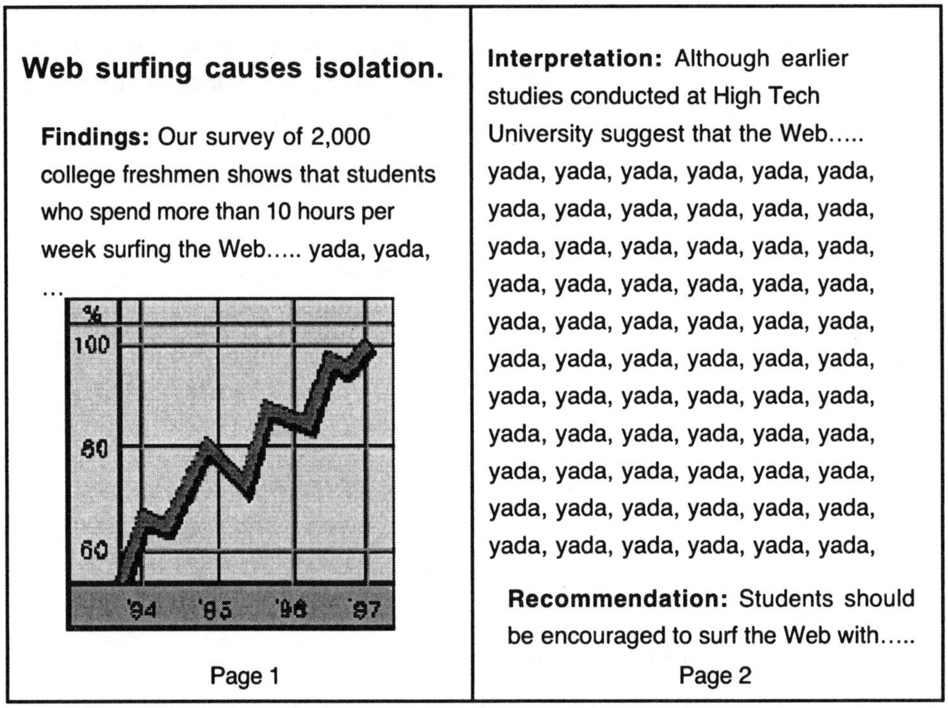

Web surfing causes isolation.

Findings: Our survey of 2,000 college freshmen shows that students who spend more than 10 hours per week surfing the Web..... yada, yada, ...

Page 1

Interpretation: Although earlier studies conducted at High Tech University suggest that the Web..... yada,

Recommendation: Students should be encouraged to surf the Web with.....

Page 2

Figure 11.5. Two-page format for evaluation report.

The second subsection contains the results or findings that are related to the issue highlighted in the headline. This section will often include tables or figures that summarize the findings. The data is generally reported in this section in as straightforward a manner as possible without subjective interpretation.

The third subsection presents a discussion, argument, or interpretation of the data. This portion is meant to communicate the evaluator's informed perspectives concerning the meaning of the data or results. This is usually the longest part of the two-page format.

The fourth and last subsection of this two-page report format presents a bottom-line recommendation concerning the issue. The two-page format starts by getting the audience to focus on the issue (e.g., the introduction of technology in the middle school has coincided with increased test scores); next it provides the data (e.g., test score patterns before and after the introduction of the technology); then it presents an interpretation or discussion (e.g., arguments for and against the premise that the improvements in test scores can be directly tied to the technology); and finally it leads to a bottom-line recommendation. The purpose of the bottom-line is to recommend a logical next step for using the results in making decisions (e.g., integration of the technology in the middle school should continue, but a more rigorous external evaluation should be commissioned to clarify the role of the technology in enhancing test scores).

— **WEB LINK** —
The George Lucas Educational Foundation Web site is: http://glef.org/

Another format we have used for evaluation reports is video. These reports usually consist of video of actual learners interacting with an interactive learning system, e.g., learners explaining their interactions via a think-aloud protocol. This may be interspersed with interviews with learners, expert statements, or video displays of the program with a voice-over explanation of the results. (A high-quality example of this type of report is the *Live and Learn* video produced by the George Lucas Educational Foundation.) We have found that corporate executives and high-ranking military personnel, as well as others who may not have the time or patience to read a print report, are more willing to watch a brief video report that illustrates the findings of an evaluation. Generally, video reports should not be longer than 15 to 20 minutes. The widespread availability of digital video editing software and screen capture hardware enables the production of sophisticated video reports highlighting problems with interface design and other usability issues related to interactive learning systems (Pearrow, 2000).

— **WEB LINK** —
To see a Web-based evaluation report, go to: http://it.coe.uga.edu/~treeves/RSUSeval/

The World Wide Web affords a new medium for the preparation of evaluation reports. Web sites are especially useful when the program or product being evaluated is a Web resource, given that there can be links from the report to the site itself. Several years ago, one of us evaluated an interactive Web-based learning environment focused on satellite imagery and hurricanes. The client preferred a Web-based report that could be easily reviewed by all members of the relevant stakeholder community. A Web-based report was the perfect vehicle. Goldman-Segall (1998) provides an innovative example of the integration of a print volume with a Web site that includes digital videos.

— **WEB LINK** —
The Center for the Study of Evaluation Web site is: http://www.cse.ucla.edu/

Alternatively, print-based reports can be made available through the Web by converting them to Adobe Acrobat pdf files for easy downloading. Several centers for excellence in evaluation, such as the Center for the Study of Evaluation at the University of California at Los Angeles (UCLA), provide free copies of their reports using the pdf format.

Another creative format for disseminating evaluation reports is a multimedia CD-ROM. This may be more desirable for clients who want an interactive capability in their reports, but do not wish their evaluation reports to be accessible to the public via the Web.

Regardless of the medium, effectively communicating the recommendations to the client of the evaluation is critical to the success and utility of the whole evaluation enterprise (Hopson, 2000). Good practice demands that you get several people (including, if possible, representatives of the audience for the evaluation) to review your draft reports to ensure that you have told the story as clearly and compellingly as possible and have argued for each of the recommendations with appropriate evidence.

You should be prepared to develop different forms of reporting for different audiences. For example, whereas the clients of an evaluation may expect or require a formal printed report, other audiences may be more receptive to alternative formats, such as the aforementioned two-page format or a Web site format. Videos are especially useful when you want to have a focus group reflect upon the evaluation findings. Web sites are useful when the findings of an evaluation must be frequently updated or widely disseminated. CD-ROMs are useful when you want to demonstrate interactivity, but maintain secure access to reports.

Meta-evaluation

As an evaluation professional, it is essential for you to examine the quality and utility of the evaluations you conduct and the reports you provide. This is a process known as meta-evaluation. Michael Scriven (1991), who created the concept of meta-evaluation, describes it as:

> the evaluation of evaluations – indirectly, the evaluation of evaluators – and represents an ethical as well as a scientific obligation when the welfare of others is involved. It can and should be done in the first place by an evaluator on his or her own work; although the credibility of this is poor, the results are considerable gains in validity.....[Because] the results of self-evaluation are notoriously unreliable, however, it is also desirable, wherever cost-justifiable, to use an independent evaluator for the meta-evaluation. (p. 228)

– WEB LINK –
The Program Evaluation Standards can be found at: http://www.wmich.edu/evalctr/jc/

What criteria should you use for meta-evaluation? The best starting point is the set of Program Evaluation Standards prepared by the Joint Committee on Standards for Educational Evaluation housed at the Evaluation Center at Western Michigan University in the USA. The Standards are divided into four sections relating to Utility, Feasibility, Propriety, and Accuracy.

Figure 11.6 provides a summary of the standards related to Utility. The utility standards are intended to ensure that an evaluation will serve the information needs of intended users. Standards U5 (Report Clarity) and U6 (Report Timeliness and Dissemination) are especially relevant to the reporting ideas we have expressed in this chapter.

Figure 11.7 provides a summary of the standards related to Feasibility. The feasibility standards are intended to ensure that an evaluation will be realistic, prudent, diplomatic, and frugal. The feasibility of recommendations included in an evaluation report is particularly important.

Utility Standards

U1 Stakeholder Identification: Persons involved in or affected by the evaluation should be identified, so that their needs can be addressed.

U2 Evaluator Credibility: The persons conducting an evaluation should be both trustworthy and competent to perform the evaluation, so that the evaluation findings achieve maximum credibility and acceptance.

U3 Information Scope and Selection: Information collected should be broadly selected to address pertinent questions about the program and be responsive to the needs and interests of clients and other specified stakeholders

U4 Values Identification: The perspectives, procedures, and rationale used to interpret the findings should be carefully described, so that the bases for value judgments are clear.

U5 Report Clarity: Evaluation reports should clearly describe the program being evaluated, including its context, and the purposes, procedures, and findings of the evaluation, so that essential information is provided and easily understood.

U6 Report Timeliness and Dissemination: Significant interim findings and evaluation reports should be disseminated to intended users, so that they can be used in a timely fashion.

U7 Evaluation Impact: Evaluations should be planned, conducted, and reported in ways that encourage follow-through by stakeholders, so that the likelihood that the evaluation will be used is increased.

Figure 11.6. Summary of Utility Standards.

Feasibility Standards

F1 Practical Procedures: The evaluation procedures should be practical, to keep disruption to a minimum while needed information is obtained.

F2 Political Viability: The evaluation should be planned and conducted with anticipation of the different positions of various interest groups, so that their cooperation may be obtained, and so that possible attempts by any of these groups to curtail evaluation operations or to bias or misapply the results can be averted or counteracted.

F3 Cost-Effectiveness: The evaluation should be efficient and produce information of sufficient value, so that the resources expended can be justified.

Figure 11.7. Summary of Feasibility Standards.

Figure 11.8 provides a summary of the standards related to Propriety. The propriety standards are intended to ensure that an evaluation will be conducted legally, ethically, and with due regard for the welfare of those involved in the evaluation, as well as those affected by its results.

Propriety Standards

P1 Service Orientation: Evaluations should be designed to assist organizations to address and effectively serve the needs of the full range of targeted participants.

P2 Formal Agreements: Obligations of the formal parties to an evaluation (what is to be done, how, by whom, when) should be agreed to in writing, so that these parties are obligated to adhere to all conditions of the agreement or formally to renegotiate it.

P3 Rights of Human Subjects: Evaluations should be designed and conducted to respect and protect the rights and welfare of human subjects.

P4 Human Interactions: Evaluators should respect human dignity and worth in their interactions with other persons associated with an evaluation, so that participants are not threatened or harmed.

P5 Complete and Fair Assessment: The evaluation should be complete and fair in its examination and recording of strengths and weaknesses of the program being evaluated, so that strengths can be built upon and problem areas addressed.

P6 Disclosure of Findings: The formal parties to an evaluation should ensure that the full set of evaluation findings along with pertinent limitations are made accessible to the persons affected by the evaluation and any others with expressed legal rights to receive the results.

P7 Conflict of Interest: Conflict of interest should be dealt with openly and honestly, so that it does not compromise the evaluation processes and results.

P8 Fiscal Responsibility: The evaluator's allocation and expenditure of resources should reflect sound accountability procedures and otherwise be prudent and ethically responsible, so that expenditures are accounted for and appropriate.

Figure 11.8. Summary of Propriety Standards.

Figure 11.9 provides a summary of the standards related to Accuracy. The accuracy standards are intended to ensure that an evaluation will reveal and convey technically adequate information about the features that determine the worth or merit of the program being evaluated.

Accuracy Standards

A1 Program Documentation: The program being evaluated should be described and documented clearly and accurately, so that the program is clearly identified.

A2 Context Analysis: The context in which the program exists should be examined in enough detail, so that its likely influences on the program can be identified.

A3 Described Purposes and Procedures: The purposes and procedures of the evaluation should be monitored and described in enough detail, so that they can be identified and assessed.

A4 Defensible Information Sources: The sources of information used in a program evaluation should be described in enough detail, so that the adequacy of the information can be assessed.

A5 Valid Information: The information-gathering procedures should be chosen or developed and then implemented, so that they will assure that the interpretation arrived at is valid for the intended use.

A6 Reliable Information: The information-gathering procedures should be chosen or developed and then implemented, so that they will assure that the information obtained is sufficiently reliable for the intended use.

A7 Systematic Information: The information collected, processed, and reported in an evaluation should be systematically reviewed, and any errors found should be corrected.

A8 Analysis of Quantitative Information: Quantitative information in an evaluation should be appropriately and systematically analyzed, so that evaluation questions are effectively answered.

A9 Analysis of Qualitative Information: Qualitative information in an evaluation should be appropriately and systematically analyzed so that evaluation questions are effectively answered.

A10 Justified Conclusions: The conclusions reached in an evaluation should be explicitly justified, so that stakeholders can assess them.

A11 Impartial Reporting: Reporting procedures should guard against distortion caused by personal feelings and biases of any party to the evaluation, so that evaluation reports fairly reflect the evaluation findings.

A12 Meta-evaluation: The evaluation itself should be formatively and summatively evaluated against these and other pertinent standards, so that its conduct is appropriately guided and, on completion, stakeholders can closely examine its strengths and weaknesses.

Figure 11.9. Summary of Accuracy Standards.

Summary

The development of an evaluation report is an important activity that often gets overlooked until the deadline is looming. This may explain why so many evaluation reports are left unread in the file drawers of bureaucrats. Good planning for reporting as well as the use of alternative formats and media can increase the likelihood that evaluation results will be given proper attention, and most importantly, that the results will be used to inform real decisions in a timely and accurate manner.

References

Goldman-Segall, R. (1998). *Points of viewing children's thinking: A digital ethnographer's journey.* Mahwah, NJ: Lawrence Erlbaum Associates.

Hopson, R. K. (Ed.). (2000). *How and why language matters in evaluation.* San Francisco: Jossey-Bass.

House, E. R. (1974). *The politics of educational innovation.* Berkeley, CA: McCutchan Publishing.

House, E. R. (1993). *Professional evaluation: Social impact and political consequences.* Newbury Park, CA: Sage Publications.

Huff, D. (1993). *How to lie with statistics.* New York: W. W. Norton and Company.

Kirkpatrick, D. L. (1998). *Another look at evaluating training programs.* Alexandria, VA: American Society for Training and Development.

Patton, M. Q. (1997). *Utilization-focused evaluation: The new century text* (3rd ed.). Thousand Oaks, CA: Sage Publications.

Pearrow, M. (2000). *Web site usability handbook.* Rockland, MA: Charles River Media.

Postman, N. (1995). *The end of education: Redefining the value of school.* New York: Alfred A. Knopf.

Rudner, L. M., & Schafer, W. D. (1999). How to write a scholarly research report. *Practical Assessment, Research & Evaluation, 6*(13). Available online: http://ericae.net/pare/getvn.asp?v=6&n=13.

Ryan, K. E., & DeStefano, L. (Eds.). (2000). *Evaluation as a democratic process: Promoting inclusion, dialogue, and deliberation.* San Francisco: Jossey-Bass.

Scriven, M. (1991). *Evaluation thesaurus* (4th ed.). Newbury Park, CA: Sage Publications.

CHAPTER 12

Enhancing the Worth of Evaluation

Objectives

After reading Chapter Twelve, you should be able to:

- identify long-term benefits of evaluation to education and training;
- understand the complex relationship between research and evaluation in the field of educational technology; and
- conduct your evaluations within the context of "development research" so that you can use your evaluation results to improve your practice and contribute to the field of educational technology.

A line in the sand

Several years ago, Utah State University Professor M. David Merrill, one of the foremost experts in the field of educational technology, drew a metaphorical line in the sand that called for anyone committed to serious learning technology research to join him and his associates in pursuing an empirical research agenda based upon the fact that instruction is a science (Merrill, Drake, Lacey, & Pratt, 1996). Professor Merrill also contended that instructional design is a technology derived from the science of instruction based on principles that could be verified by empirical data.

– WEB LINK –
More information about AERA can be found at: http://www.aera.net

Not everyone shares Professor Merrill's assessment of instructional design as a scientifically valid technology. Consider the following quote from Professor Lauren Resnick, a distinguished cognitive scientist from the University of Pittsburgh. These remarks were made at the 1999 Annual Meeting of the American Educational Research Association (AERA) in Montreal, Canada, when Dr. Resnick responded to a question from the audience about what kinds of people could do "design experiments" of the kind she was advocating to advance educational practice. Resnick said:

> We don't have a well-developed design field in education, as a design field. So in our work, we do lots of design. Who's doing it? Well, there are some people who've traveled in from research that are doing it. There are some people who came from the world of schools, therefore practitioners, who turn out to have a tremendous flair for getting it shaped and codified so that others, besides themselves or a small in-group, can do it. I've looked around at the field called instructional design in which people can get degrees, and so far have not been interested in hiring any of the people with those degrees who have crossed my path. Just doesn't look like they were going to add much. In an hour or so and across this week, I will be interviewing students from some of the people here and some others of you who are out in the audience who I don't think have the word design on their curriculum vitae, but who look pretty promising to be the kinds of people we're talking about. So the real issue has to do with what would a design field in education that would be serious actually look like.

There is an enormous gap between Merrill's identification of instructional design as a robust technology derived from the science of instruction and Resnick's conclusion that instructional design is a field that does not seem to contribute to the solution of educational problems. This debate is not limited to the Ivory Tower. The cover story in the April 2000 issue of *Training* magazine (Gordon & Zemke, 2000) is titled "The Attack on ISD." According to the authors, "The 'systems approach' to instructional design is the training industry's guiding light. Some of the best minds in the business now say it's leading us astray" (p. 43).

Reflecting similar doubts, Dr. Robert B. Kozma, serving as a discussant for a session on applications of instructional theory and design at the AERA conference in Montreal in 1999, stated that instructional technology as a field is inward and backward focused, too disconnected from research and development in other fields, and insufficiently influenced by significant advances in technology (Ross, 1999). Of course, many, if not most, fields of inquiry are beset with similar controversies. For example, in biology, one camp of scientists is laboring mightily to explain the nature of human behavior on the basis of genetic mapping, whereas another camp argues that human behavior will ultimately be explained more completely by the effects of nurture and culture. If educational technology can be regarded as a field of inquiry, then it too must have its controversies. One of the most obvious disputes is between those who view educational technology as a branch of science or technology and those who regard it as more akin to a craft or even an art (Clark & Estes, 1998, 1999; Estes & Clark, 1999).

Another controversy concerns whether educational technologists should conduct basic research to build generalizable theories or pursue applied research to solve specific problems. We are much more convinced of the value of applied research than of basic research within the context of a design field (Nelson & Stolterman, 2003) such as educational technology.

So what does all this have to do with you as an instructional designer, project manager, or evaluator within the context of interactive learning systems? In this chapter, we argue that people like you can do more than simply conduct evaluations; they can extend the reach of their evaluations and contribute to design principles regarding interactive learning systems through a process called development research (van den Akker, 1999). But first, it is important to explain why we believe that the current dominant approaches to research in this field are inadequate.

Problems with research in interactive learning systems

Calling attention to problems with the research literature in educational technology has occupied scholars for decades (e.g., Clark, 1983; Hoban, 1958; Mielke, 1968), but many problems persist. Three significant problems with the research literature are highlighted in this chapter. First, major misunderstandings exist about the differences between basic and applied research. Second, the quality of published research in the field of educational technology is poor (although no poorer than educational research in general). Third, syntheses of the research focused on interactive learning systems, such as literature reviews and meta-analyses, provide practitioners with insufficient or confusing guidance.

Basic versus applied research

Most evaluators, not unlike educators in general, hold a traditional one-dimensional view of research as ranging from "basic" (research aimed at extending fundamental understanding within a scientific field) to "applied" (research aimed at solving problems that confront an individual, a group, or society at large). Among educational technologists, there have long been arguments about the relative value of basic versus applied research (Merrill *et al.*, 1996). Evidence of the schism is seen in the division of one of the leading journals in the field, *Educational Technology Research and Development*, into separate research and development sections (Higgins, Sullivan, Harper-Marinick, & López, 1989).

Some people have a preference for basic research, regardless of whether it has any practical value, perhaps because basic research seems more scientific or because they believe that basic research will ultimately lead to more advances in the field than will applied research. Other people believe that the value of basic research to the field of educational technology, and more specifically, to the design of interactive learning systems, is very limited. These people argue that applied research, focused upon direct and clear implications for practice, will yield greater progress.

Other research scholars maintain that traditional notions of basic and applied research are too simplistic. In a book titled *Pasteur's Quadrant: Basic Science and Technological Innovation*, Stokes (1997) recommended a matrix view of research (see Figure 12.1). Where a research agenda is placed within this matrix depends upon whether or not researchers are seeking fundamental understanding *and* whether or not they are concerned about practical uses of research findings. To illustrate the placement, Stokes stated that the research conducted by Danish physicist Niels Bohr, who sought pure knowledge about the structure of the atom without concern for practical application, belongs in quadrant 1. The research conducted by American inventor Thomas Edison, who sought to solve practical problems through the development of innovative technologies while expressing no interest in publishing his research findings, belongs in quadrant 3. Stokes placed the research of French chemist Louis Pasteur, who sought fundamental knowledge within the context of solving practical problems, within quadrant 2.

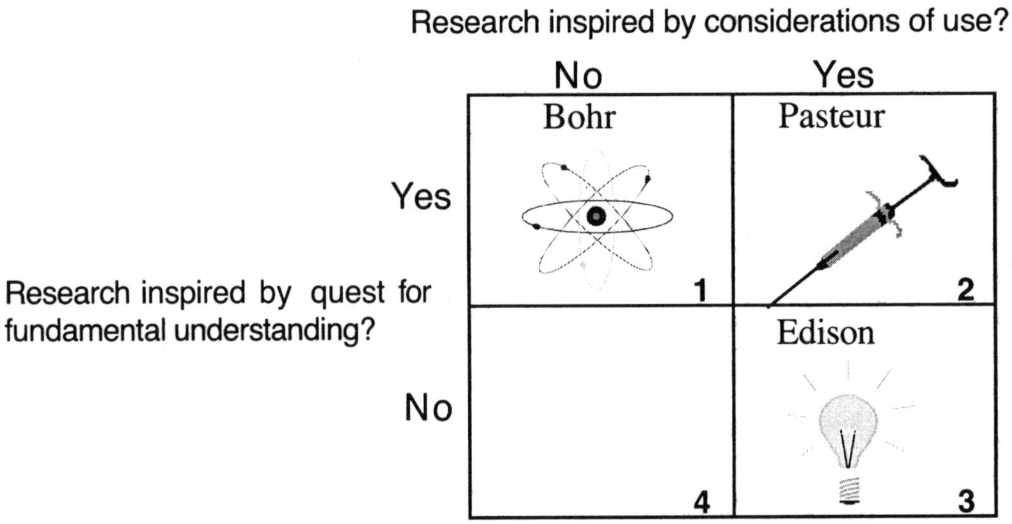

Figure 12.1. Pasteur's Quadrant View of Research (Stokes, 1997).

Although Stokes (1997) left blank quadrant 4, research that neither seeks fundamental understanding nor considers use, much of research conducted in the area of interactive learning systems (as well as educational research in general) belongs in this sterile quadrant. Such research is conducted and published solely to advance the careers of academics confronted with the mandate to publish or perish. (When Tom Reeves first arrived at The University of Georgia in 1982, several College of Education professors advised him to get his hands on a large set of data so that it could be mined for multiple publications. Hardly anyone pointed him toward solving the problems confronting what was then and remains one of the most educationally under-achieving states in the USA. A new assistant professor at another university, after reading an earlier draft of this chapter, wrote to say that this situation has not changed much.)

Stokes (1997) called for increased "use-inspired basic research" of the kind conducted by Pasteur. Stokes also called into question the assumption that pure basic research leads to the development of new technologies. He pointed out that in contemporary science, new technological developments often permit the advancement of new types of research, thus reversing the direction of the basic to applied model. For example, the development of powerful computers and sophisticated data analysis software led to the growth of computational modeling as a viable approach to research in scientific fields from astronomy to zoology (Ilgen & Hulin, 2000).

Poor quality of educational technology research

Although more educational technologists appear to be adopting qualitative or mixed methodologies than was the case just a few years ago, when quantitative studies dominated the research literature (Reeves, 1995), there is little evidence that the quality of research has improved. The Panel on Educational Technology of the President's Committee of Advisors on Science and Technology (PCAST) (1997) severely criticized educational technology research. The PCAST experts listed as one of its six major strategic recommendations that the government "initiate a major program of experimental research....to ensure both the efficacy and cost-effectiveness of technology use within our nation's schools" (p. 5). Unfortunately, the PCAST panelists failed to explain how this additional experimental research would be better than the previous decades of experimental studies that have failed to establish the advantages of technology-enhanced education over more traditional approaches (Cuban, 1986). Nonetheless, support for traditional research approaches persists as evidenced by a November 2002 report titled *Bringing Evidence-Driven Progress to Education* from the Coalition for Evidence-Based Policy and The Council for Excellence in Government in Washington, DC. The authors of the report claim that there has been no improvement in education over the last 30 years, despite a 90 percent increase in real public spending per pupil. As a solution, they promote the use of randomized controlled trials as used in medical research to prove which interventions really work in education.

Regardless of methodological preferences, the bulk of the educational technology research literature is generated by isolated researchers, most often doctoral students and new faculty members, who conduct individual studies that are rarely linked to a robust research agenda. These studies do not constitute basic research in the classic scientific sense, nor are the studies focused on enhancing practice in an unambiguous manner. The main criterion for success of this research is that papers about it are accepted for presentation at conferences largely attended by other researchers or published in academic journals that few people read. A detailed analysis of such studies (Reeves, 1995) found that most are riddled with problems, such as specification error, lack of linkage to theoretical foundations, inadequate literature reviews, poor treatment implementation, major measurement flaws, inconsequential learning outcomes for research participants, inadequate sample sizes, inaccurate statistical analyses, and meaningless discussions of results.

Although some may interpret this as an overly harsh critique of educational technology research, we must point out that educational research in general has been subjected to similar criticism (Lagemann, 2000). In the first week of August 1999, the headline on the cover page of *The Chronicle of Higher Education* proclaimed "The Failure of Educational Research" (Miller, 1999). During the past 20 years, similar articles have occasionally appeared in *Educational Researcher* and other education publications (Kaestle, 1993), but this was the first time such an indictment appeared on the cover of the weekly newspaper of record for academics in the USA. For those engaged in educational research, it stings to see it condemned in such a public manner for its lack of substance and influence. But ignoring such critiques is irresponsible.

Disappointing research syntheses

Given the poor quality of the inputs to research syntheses in the field of educational technology, it is little wonder that the literature reviews and meta-analyses yield disappointing results that provide practitioners with confusing guidance. Reviewers usually must reject 75 percent or more of the published studies to find a handful that are worthy of further review or inclusion in a meta-analysis (Hunt, 1999; Kulik & Kulik, 1991).

The problems with instructional technology research were demonstrated in two literature reviews published in the *Review of Educational Research*, a highly-respected AERA publication. Dillon and Gabbard (1998) reviewed the literature concerning hypermedia in education, and Fabos and Young (1999) reviewed the literature examining telecommunications in the classroom. After reviewing nearly 500 papers related to hypermedia and learning, Dillon and Gabbard identified 118 studies that appeared to meet their criteria for quantitative studies examining the effectiveness of hypermedia in education. From this pool, only 30 studies published between 1990 and 1996 met the minimal criteria of scientific merit for inclusion in the literature review. Their in-depth analysis of these 30 research reports yielded the following major conclusion: "Clearly, the benefits gained from the use of hypermedia technology in learning scenarios appear to be very limited and not in keeping with the generally euphoric reaction to this technology in the professional arena" (p. 345).

In a similar review, Fabos and Young (1999) critiqued the research on telecommunications in the classroom and concluded:

> Telecommunications exchanges are lauded by educational researchers and industry experts for enhancing writing and collaboration skills, increasing multicultural awareness, and expanding future economic possibilities. As we have seen, however, many of these expected benefits are inconclusive, overly optimistic, and even contradictory. Like much scholarship on educational technology, many researchers are quick to enter discussions about skill, social, and economic benefits without considering the scholarly, historical, or industrial context of their claims. With regard to skills, we need to extend the discussion of telecommunication exchange projects from overgeneralized and often nebulous claims about skill benefits, and focus on the content of particular projects, why they hold promise, and how they can be used to meet specific educational goals.... While distance learning activities may appear to be magical education experiences, all educators must first step back, critically evaluate the inevitably enthusiastic rhetoric, and attempt to understand the complex contextual framework behind the push for telecommunication exchange. (p. 254)

What are teachers, who are encouraged to integrate hypermedia modules into their K-12 lesson plans, or faculty members, who are pushed to develop Web pages for university courses, to do with the conclusions reached by Dillon and Gabbard (1998) and Fabos and Young (1999)? Frankly, it is highly unlikely that these literature reviews will ever be read by practitioners, so such a question will go unanswered.

Clarifying the goals of research in interactive learning systems

Researchers investigating interactive learning systems, especially novices, appear to have difficulty distinguishing between research goals and research methods. Evidence of this confusion is seen when a novice researcher states that he/she is only interested in conducting quantitative (or alternatively qualitative) studies without specifying the type of research goal he/she is pursuing. The research goals held by any given researcher are influenced by many factors, including the epistemological views of the investigator, his/her research training, and the dominant research paradigms within his/her line of inquiry. Six major types of research goals commonly pursued by educational technology researchers are described in the following paragraphs.

Theoretical goals

Researchers with theoretical goals are focused on explaining phenomena through the logical analysis and synthesis of theories, principles, and the results of other forms of research such as empirical studies. This type of research is relatively rare because it requires levels of synthesis, generalization, and theory construction for which most researchers have not been prepared. In addition, this type of research usually requires a long-term scholarly agenda that can be sustained for many years. One example of research with theoretical goals within the field of educational technology is the seminal work of Gagné (1997) to describe the basic conditions of learning and a theory of instruction.

Predictive goals

Researchers with predictive goals are focused on determining how education works by testing conclusions related to theories of teaching, learning, performance, assessment, social interaction, instructional design, and so forth. Researchers with this type of goal usually employ experimental (or quasi-experimental) methods to determine or predict the effects of some form or aspect of a technological innovation under controlled conditions. This type of research has dominated instructional technology for decades, but reviews reveal that it is often done poorly (Reeves, 1993). Its popularity stems from the fact that, until recently, it was the only goal graduate students and young researchers were encouraged to pursue. In addition, predictive studies using quasi-experimental methods take less time and logistical support than other approaches, and many research journals are more receptive to reports of predictive studies than other forms of research. Although most studies of this kind are flawed, there are examples of good predictive research, such as the investigation of cooperative learning and learning control conducted by Hooper, Temiyakarn, and Williams (1993) and the investigation of the influence of emotions and intentions on performance in a Web-based learning environment carried out by Martinez and Bunderson (2000).

Interpretivist goals

Researchers with interpretivist goals are focused on portraying how education works by describing and interpreting phenomena related to teaching, learning, performance, assessment, social interaction, innovation, and so forth. Learning systems researchers with interpretivist goals draw upon naturalistic research traditions borrowed from other sciences, such as anthropology and sociology. The popularity of conducting research from an interpretivist perspective has increased dramatically among educational researchers over the past 20 years, although this trend has not been as evident among educational technologists until recently. A backlash against qualitative research seems to be developing in some circles. *The Chronicle of Higher Education* cover story about educational research mentioned above (Miller, 1999) was especially critical of qualitative research for "yielding little that can be generalized beyond the classrooms in which it is conducted." "Too much useless work is done under the banner of qualitative research" said an expert interviewed for the article. A pioneering example of interpretivist research within the educational technology field is Neuman's (1991) naturalistic observations of learning disabled children using commercial courseware. A more recent example is Orrill's (2001) qualitative study of teachers as their professional development framework evolved with respect to building technology-based, learner-centered classrooms.

Postmodern goals

Researchers with postmodern goals are focused on examining the assumptions underlying contemporary educational programs and practices with the ultimate aims of revealing hidden agendas and/or empowering disenfranchised minorities. Although it is increasingly conducted by researchers with strong multicultural, gender, or political interests, research in the postmodern tradition is very rare within the educational technology field. There are several reasons for this, not the least of which is the fact that there are relatively few educational technologists capable of mentoring graduate students or young researchers in this approach. Also problematic is the difficulty postmodern researchers have in finding scholarly outlets for their papers. De Vaney's (1998) analysis of the field of educational technology in relation to race, gender, and power is a rare example of research with a postmodern perspective in this field.

Development goals

Researchers with development goals are focused on the dual objectives of developing creative approaches to solving human teaching, learning, and performance problems while at the same time constructing a body of design principles that can guide future development efforts. Development research, which is also referred to as design experiments or formative research, has recently received endorsements from leaders in the field of educational technology (Richey & Nelson, 1996). Van den Akker (1999) identifies a significant characteristic of development research as focusing on "complex, innovative tasks for which only very few validated principles are available to structure and support design and development activities" (p 7). One example of development research is the long-term agenda of the Cognition and Technology Group at Vanderbilt (1992) aimed at developing innovative solutions to complex mathematics and reading problems, while at the same time building theoretical models, such as "anchored instruction."

Action goals

Researchers with action goals are focused on a particular program, product, or method, usually in an applied setting, for the purpose of describing it, improving it, or estimating its effectiveness and worth. Sometimes called action research or evaluation research, research with action goals is similar to development research except that there is often little or limited effort to construct theory, models, or principles to guide future design initiatives. The major goal is solving a particular problem in a specific place within a relatively short timeframe. Some purists maintain that this type of inquiry is not research at all, but merely a form of evaluation. However, despite its primary focus on considerations of use for local practitioners, it can be regarded as a legitimate form of research, provided reports of it are shared with wider audiences who may themselves choose to draw inferences from these reports much as they would from reports of interpretivist research. One example of this research is an evaluation of a project-based undergraduate engineering course conducted by Reeves and Laffey (1999).

Selecting research methods

In evaluation, methods should not be selected until the evaluator is clear about the decisions and questions to be addressed. Similarly, research methods should not be selected until a researcher is clear about his/her research goals as well as the nature of the research questions to be addressed within a particular study. Educational researchers who identify themselves as quantitative researchers or qualitative researchers are somewhat misguided; this is analogous to builders identifying themselves as hammer carpenters or saw carpenters. Research methods are tools, and tools should only be selected once goals and tasks are clear.

– WEB LINK –
More information about research methods is at: http://trochim.human.cornell.edu/

There are more research methods than can possibly be described in this chapter. However, Figure 12.2 presents a simple taxonomy of six categories of research methods that can be used by educational technology researchers to address a range of research goals. It must be stressed that there is definitely not a one-to-one relationship between these six types of methods and the six research goals identified above. However, some types of goals tend to be addressed with specific types of methods, e.g., researchers with postmodern goals often employ critical theory methods. Other types of methods, e.g., literature review, are used by researchers with diverse goals.

Quantitative	experimental, quasi-experimental, correlational, and other methods that primarily involve the collection of quantitative data and its analysis using statistics, e.g., the analysis of variance in exam results among students in traditional courses and Web-based courses
Qualitative	observations, case-studies, interviews, and other methods that involve the collection of qualitative data and its analysis using ethnographic approaches, e.g., participant observation in a Web-based course
Critical Theory	deconstruction of "texts" or the technologies and systems that deliver them through the search for binary oppositions, hidden agendas, and disenfranchisement, e.g., a critical analysis of the "digital divide"
Historical	an objective and accurate reconstruction of the past based upon analysis of historical documents, interviews, etc., often in relation to the tenability of a hypothesis, e.g., that John Dewey was the originator of progressive education
Literature Review	various forms of research synthesis that primarily involve the analysis and integration of other forms of research, e.g., frequency counts and meta-analyses, often yielding support for a specific thesis, e.g., computer-based tutorials are most effective with less capable learners
Mixed-methods	research approaches that combine a mixture of methods, usually quantitative and qualitative, to "triangulate" findings, e.g., a pre-test, post-test quasi-experimental design integrated with classroom observations

Figure 12.2. Six types of research methods used by educational technologists.

Development research as "use-inspired basic research"

As noted above, Stokes (1997) called for more "use-inspired basic research" rather than either pure basic or applied research. "Use-inspired basic research" for educational technology researchers is what others have labeled "development research" (van den Akker, 1999), "design experiments" (Brown, 1992; Collins, 1992), or "formative research" (Newman, 1990). The critical characteristics of "design experiments," as described by Brown (1992) and Collins (1992) are:

- addressing complex problems in real contexts in collaboration with practitioners;
- integrating known and hypothetical design principles with technological affordances to render plausible solutions to these complex problems; and

- conducting rigorous and reflective inquiry to test and refine innovative learning environments as well as to define new design principles.

Van den Akker (1999) states that, "Methods of development research are not necessarily different from those in other research approaches" (p. 9). Although this is usually the case, there are major differences between the philosophical framework and goals of these different approaches. Figure 12.3 illustrates the differences between research conducted with empirical goals and that inspired by development goals.

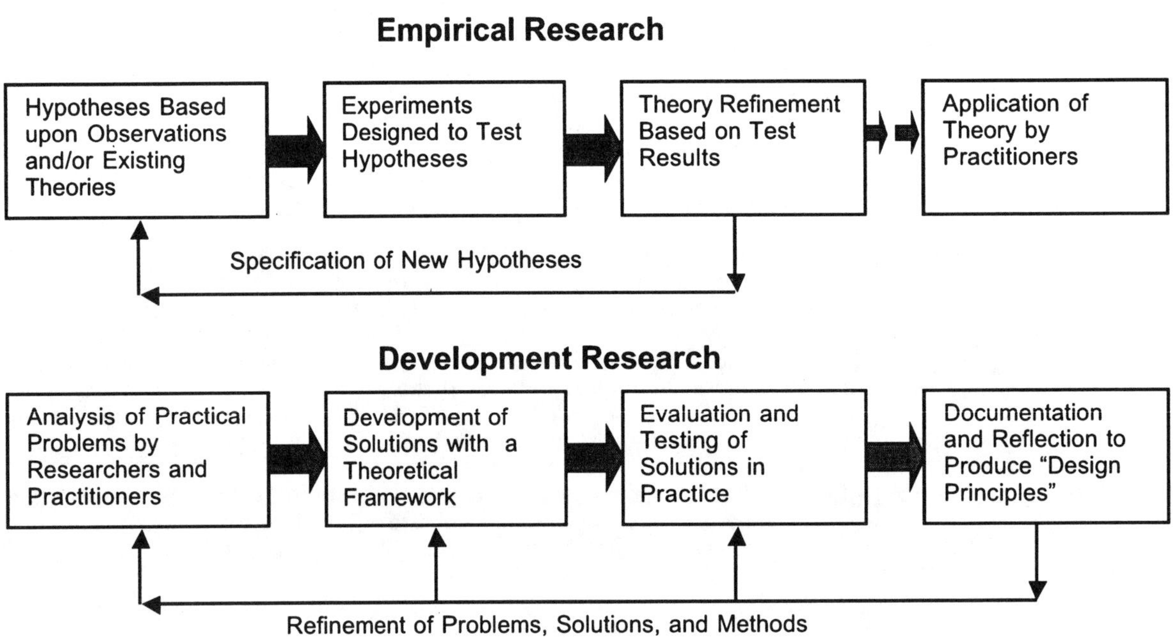

Figure 12.3. Empirical and development approaches to research in learning technologies.

Van den Akker clarifies the differences illustrated in Figure 12.3:

> More than most other research approaches, development research aims at making both practical and scientific contributions. In the search for innovative 'solutions' for educational problems, interaction with practitioners...is essential. The ultimate aim is not to test whether theory, when applied to practice, is a good predictor of events. The interrelation between theory and practice is more complex and dynamic: is it possible to create a practical and effective intervention for an existing problem or intended change in the real world? The innovative challenge is usually quite substantial, otherwise the research would not be initiated at all. Interaction with practitioners is needed to gradually clarify both the problem at stake and the characteristics of its potential solution. An iterative process of 'successive approximation' or 'evolutionary prototyping' of the 'ideal' intervention is desirable. Direct application of theory is not sufficient to solve those complicated problems. (pp. 8-9)

As illustrated in Figure 12.3, the influence of traditional empirical approaches to educational research on practice is based upon the optimistic assumption that practitioners can or will apply the theories derived from empirical investigations. If the theories have any merit, the persistence of significant problems in education suggest that this optimism is misplaced and that practitioners must be more directly engaged in the conduct of educational research. A basic tenet of development research is collaboration among practitioners, researchers, and technologists.

– WEB LINK –
More information about AECT can be found at: http://www.aect.org

Good examples of development research are difficult to find. The development activities of Jan Herrington and her colleagues at Edith Cowan University in Australia (Herrington & Knibb, 1999; Herrington & Oliver, 1999) are rare exemplars. In a doctoral dissertation study that won the 1999 YoungResearcher of the Year Award from the Association for Educational Communications and Technology (AECT), Herrington used a range of innovative investigative strategies, including video analysis of the dialogue between pairs of students engaged in multimedia learning. Her collaborators in this long-term effort to develop and apply a model of situated learning theory included other educational technologists, math educators, and teachers. She not only developed a model of the critical factors of situated learning and instantiated these factors in multimedia learning environments, but also she tested the model and the technological products in multiple contexts, including pre-service teacher education courses and K-12 schools. The research had value within the immediate context of its implementation, but also has yielded generalizable design principles. Her research agenda is still evolving, most recently focusing on the effectiveness of authentic activities in Web-based learning environments (Herrington, 2002).

Another fundamental tenet of development research is dedication to providing benefits to all stakeholders within the context of the research. Universities long ago established Human Subjects Review Boards to insure that researchers protect the welfare of the individuals who participate in their studies. Within a design field such as educational technology (and within education as a whole), we must go beyond concerns for the protection and safety of human subjects to examine the benefits to be derived from a particular line of research. A Human *Benefits* Review Board should review research plans with the intent of insuring that the research has some reasonable potential for solving problems that diminish the quality of life for individuals and groups. This is especially important within taxpayer-supported public research universities.

Such a proposal is likely to lead to protests among those who put academic freedom above all other concerns, including social responsibility. Critics will proclaim that without the right to pursue research independent of considerations of practical value, many of the most important discoveries in fields such as physics, chemistry, biology, and medicine would never have been made. We agree, and therefore would not support a Human Benefits Review for research in those fields. But education is a fundamentally different type of science, if it is a science at all, and educational researchers have never produced discoveries analogous to those in the physical and biological sciences. Educational researchers must confront the sterility of their labors and take radical steps to conduct inquiry in more productive ways. However, we do not agree with the call for more randomized controlled trials of educational interventions issued by the Coalition for Evidence-Based Policy (2002).

The prospects for change in research approaches

The history of research in interactive learning systems suggests that it is time to give graduate students and young researchers the guidance and support they need to pursue development goals that have been neglected in our field for too long. Decades of experimental research with theoretical or predictive goals have provided an insufficient foundation of theories and principles to guide practice, whether in K-12 schools, higher education, business training, or any other learning context.

Is development research the only viable approach to research related to interactive learning systems? Perhaps not, but there is little evidence that the increasing popularity of qualitative methods will improve the impact of the research on practice, especially given that the proponents of qualitative approaches make few claims to generalizability. Although research conducted from a postmodern perspective may alert educators and the public at large to the injustices inherent in various educational innovations, ultimately this line of research will be as sterile as interpretivist research with respect to improving the conditions for teaching and learning with technology. After all, postmodernists denounce the prescription of technical solutions to complex problems as misguided modernist thinking. Action research is and will continue to be important within local contexts, but it is too weak for solving more complex problems. Given the poor history of other approaches, we are increasingly convinced that if educational technologists want to contribute to meaningful educational reform, they should pursue development goals.

Of course, the probability of the establishment of a Human Benefits Review Board or the implementation of other radical reforms is extremely unlikely within today's academic climate. We can argue that educational technologists have a moral responsibility to pursue more development research, but the current focus on research for publication's sake will not change unless the reward systems in higher education are changed fundamentally, or unless the public demands more on the part of university faculty in terms of their productivity (Middaugh, 2000).

What can practitioners engaged in the development, implementation, and evaluation of interactive learning systems do with respect to advancing the state of design knowledge in the field of educational technology? Researchers with development goals focus on complex problems critical to human learning and performance. This type of research agenda requires intensive collaboration among researchers and practitioners. Rather than sticking to one preferred method, development researchers select methods as tools to accomplish specific tasks, and they engage in continual refinement of research protocols. There is considerable overlap between these activities and the activities in which you may be engaged as an evaluator of interactive learning systems.

Development researchers are also committed to constructing design principles and producing explanations that can be widely shared. This is not an activity in which practitioners typically engage. But there is little reason why you cannot take some time away from the hectic whirl of production schedules and evaluation activities to reflect upon what you have learned and how you might share "lessons learned" through presentations and publications. You don't have to be a university professor to produce evidence and ideas that are worth sharing with other professionals. After all, the best educational technologists are reflective and humble, cognizant that their designs, evaluations, and conclusions are tentative in even the best of situations.

Designers and evaluators of interactive learning systems who make time to engage in development research should share the results of their design experiments in multiple ways, including refereed and commercial publications, Web pages, conferences, and workshops. If you take up our challenge, you can expect to work a little harder. But we are confident that the long-term rewards with respect to your own professional development, as well as the general advancement of the field of educational technology, will make it all worthwhile.

Conclusion

Moving the educational technology community toward development research will not be easy because it requires fundamental changes in our epistemology and our mental models of the research process. It requires what Thomas Kuhn (1970) identified as a paradigm shift. Educational technology research and evaluation has long been dominated by positivist epistemology that regards learning theory apart from and above educational practice. The overall goal of research within the predictive tradition is to develop long-lasting theories and unambiguous principles that can be handed off to practitioners for implementation. Development research, on the other hand, requires a pragmatic epistemology that regards learning theory as being collaboratively shaped by researchers and practitioners. The overall goal of development research is to solve real problems while at the same time constructing design principles that can inform future decisions. In Kuhn's terms, predictive research and development research are different worlds.

Adding a reflective, development research orientation to your work as an instructional designer, project manager, or evaluator within the context of interactive learning systems may not require anything as dramatic as a paradigm change. But we believe that it can enhance your own professional development and the work that you and your colleagues accomplish. In addition, we are convinced that over time, such an orientation can contribute to the design knowledge upon which future advances in the educational technology field will be based. Stokes (1997) describes how Pasteur's research, although conducted in the context of solving practical problems, led to major advances in several fields. We may not attain the level of Pasteur's enormous impact, but together we can advance the state-of-the-art of the design and implementation of interactive learning systems.

References

Brown, A. L. (1992). Design experiments: Theoretical and methodological challenges in creating complex interventions in classroom settings. *The Journal of the Learning Sciences*, *2*(2), 141-178.

Clark, R. E. (1983). Reconsidering research on learning with media. *Review of Educational Research*, *53*(4), 445-459.

Clark, R. E., & Estes, F. (1998). Technology or craft: What are we doing? *Educational Technology*, *38*(5), 5-11.

Clark, R. E., & Estes, F. (1999). The development of authentic educational technologies. *Educational Technology*, *39*(2), 5-16.

Coalition for Evidence-Based Policy. (2002). *Bringing evidence-driven progress to education: A recommended strategy for the U.S. Department of Education*. Washington, DC: The Council for Excellence in Government.

Cognition and Technology Group at Vanderbilt. (1992). The Jasper experiment: An exploration of issues in learning and instructional design. *Educational Technology Research and Development*, *40*(1), 65-80.

Collins, A. (1992). Towards a design science of education. In E. Scanlon & T. O'Shea (Eds.), *New directions in educational technology* (pp. 15-22). Berlin: Springer.

Cuban, L. (1986). *Teachers and machines: The classroom use of technology since 1920.* New York: Teachers College Press.

De Vaney, A. (1998). Can and need educational technology become a postmodern enterprise? *Theory into Practice, 37*(1), 72-80.

Dillon, A., & Gabbard, R. (1998). Hypermedia as an educational technology: A review of the quantitative research literature on learner comprehension, control, and style. *Review of Educational Research, 68*(3), 322-349.

Estes, F., & Clark, R. E. (1999). Authentic educational technology: The lynchpin between theory and practice. *Educational Technology, 39*(6), 5-13.

Fabos, B., & Young, M. D. (1999). Telecommunications in the classroom: Rhetoric versus reality. *Review of Educational Research*, *69*(3), 217-259

Gagné, R. M. (1997). *The conditions of learning and theory of instruction*. New York: Holt, Rinehart, and Winston.

Gordon, J., & Zemke, R. (2000). The attack on ISD. *Training*, *37*(4), 42-53. Available online: www.trainingsupersite.com/publications/archive/training/2000/004/004cv.htm

Herrington, J. (2002). Designing authentic activities for Web-based courses. In M. Driscoll & T. C. Reeves (Eds.), *Proceedings of E-Learn 2002* (Montreal, Canada). Charlottesville, VA: Association for the Advancement of Computing in Education.

Herrington, J., & Knibb, K. (1999). Multimedia and student activity: An interpretive study using VideoSearch. *Australian Journal of Educational Technology*, *15*(1), 47-57.

Herrington, J., & Oliver, R. (1999). Using situated learning and multimedia to investigate higher-order thinking. *Journal of Interactive Learning Research*, *10*(1), 3-24.

Higgins, N., Sullivan, H., Harper-Marinick, M., & López, C. (1989). Perspectives on educational technology research and development. *Educational Technology Research and Development, 37*(1), 7-18.

Hoban, C. F. (1958). Research on media. *AV Communication Review*, *6*(3), 169-178.

Hooper, S., Temiyakarn, C., & Williams, M. D. (1993). The effects of cooperative learning and learning control on high- and average-ability students. *Educational Technology Research and Development*, *41*(2), 5-18.

Hunt, M. (1999). *How science takes stock: The story of meta-analysis*. New York: Russell Sage Foundation.

Ilgen, D. R., & Hulin, C. L. (Eds.). (2000). *Computational modeling of behavior in organizations: The third scientific discipline*. Washington, DC: American Psychological Association.

Kaestle, C. F. (1993). The awful reputation of educational research. *Educational Researcher, 22*(1), 26-31.

Kuhn, T. S. (1970). *The structure of scientific revolutions* (2nd ed.). Chicago: The University of Chicago Press.

Kulik, C.-L., & Kulik, J. A. (1991). Effectiveness of computer-based instruction: An updated analysis. *Computers and Human Behavior, 7*(1/2), 75-94.

Lagemann, E. C. (2000). *An elusive science: The troubling history of educational research.* Chicago: The University of Chicago Press.

Martinez, J., & Bunderson, C. V. (2000). Building interactive Web learning environments to match and support individual learning differences. *Journal of Interactive Learning Research, 11*(2), 163-195.

Merrill, M. D., Drake, L., Lacey, M. J., & Pratt, J. (1996). Reclaiming instructional design. *Educational Technology, 36*(5), 5-7.

Middaugh, M. F. (2000). *Understanding faculty productivity: Standards and benchmarks for colleges and universities.* San Francisco: Jossey-Bass.

Mielke, K. W. (1968). Questioning the questions of ETV research. *Educational Broadcasting, 2*, 6-15.

Miller, D. W. (1999, August 6). The black hole of educational research: Why do academic studies play such a minimal role in efforts to improve the schools? *The Chronicle of Higher Education,* A17-A18.

Nelson, H. G., & Stolterman, E. (2003). *The design way: Intentional change in an unpredictable world — Foundations and fundamentals of design competence.* Englewood Cliffs, NJ: Educational Technology Publications.

Neuman, D. (1991). Learning disabled students' interactions with commercial courseware: A naturalistic study. *Educational Technology Research and Development, 39*(1), 31-49.

Newman, D. (1990). Opportunities for research on the organizational impact of school computers. *Educational Researcher, 19*(3), 8-13.

Orrill, C. H. (2001). Building technology-based, learner-centered classrooms: The evolution of a professional development framework. *Educational Technology Research and Development, 49*(1), 15-34.

Planck, M. (1949). *Scientific autobiography, and other papers.* New York: Philosophical Library.

President's Committee of Advisors on Science and Technology. (1997, March). *Report on the use of technology to strengthen K-12 education in the United States* (http://www.whitehouse.gov/WH/EOP/OSTP/NSTC/PCAST/k-12ed.html). Washington, DC: The White House.

Reeves, T. C. (1993). Pseudoscience in computer-based instruction: The case of learner control research. *Journal of Computer-Based Instruction, 20*(2), 39-46.

Reeves, T. C. (1995). Questioning the questions of instructional technology research. In M. R. Simonson & M. Anderson (Eds.), *Proceedings of the Annual Conference of the Association for Educational Communications and Technology, Research and Theory Division* (pp. 459-470). Washington, DC: Association for Educational Communications and Technology.

Reeves, T. C., & Laffey, J. M. (1999). Design, assessment, and evaluation of a problem-based learning environment in undergraduate engineering. *Higher Education Research and Development Journal, 18*(2), 219-232

Richey, R. T., & Nelson, W. A. (1996). Developmental research. In D. H. Jonassen (Ed.), *Handbook of research for educational communications and technology* (pp. 1213-1245). New York: Macmillan.

Ross, S. M. (1999, April). *Current applications of instructional theory and design in technology.* Symposium presented at the Annual Meeting of the American Educational Research Association, Montreal, Quebec, Canada.

Stokes, D. E. (1997). *Pasteur's quadrant: Basic science and technological innovation.* Washington, DC: Brookings Institution Press.

van den Akker, J. (1999). Principles and methods of development research. In J. van den Akker, N. Nieveen, R. M. Branch, K. L. Gustafson, & T. Plomp (Eds.), *Design methodology and developmental research in education and training* (pp. 1-14). Amsterdam: Kluwer Academic Publishers.

Author Index

E

F

G

H

I

T

U

V

W

Y

Z

Subject Index

D

E

F

G

P

Q

R

S

T

U

V

W

About the authors

Thomas C. Reeves, Professor, The University of Georgia. Since receiving his Ph.D. at Syracuse University in 1979, Professor Reeves has developed and evaluated numerous interactive multimedia learning programs for education and training. In addition to many presentations and workshops in the USA, he has been an invited speaker in several other countries including Australia, Brazil, Bulgaria, China, England, Finland, Malaysia, New Zealand, Peru, Russia, Singapore, South Africa, Sweden, Switzerland, and Taiwan. He is a past president of the Association for the Development of Computer-based Instructional Systems (ADCIS), a former Fulbright Lecturer in Peru, and the former editor of the Journal of Interactive Learning Research. His research interests include: evaluation of instructional technology for education and training, mental models and interactive multimedia, electronic performance support systems, multimedia user interface issues, and instructional technology in developing countries. Dr. Reeves is a co-founder of the Learning and Performance Support Lab (LPSL) at The University of Georgia. His teaching areas include program evaluation, instructional design, project management, and research methods.

John G. Hedberg, Professor, National Institute of Education, Nanyang Technological University, Singapore. He also studied at Syracuse University and was awarded his Ph.D. in 1976. Prior to his current appointment he was Professor or Education and Director of the Educational Media Laboratory, at the University of Wollongong, Australia. During this period he led the production team which won a British Academy Award (BAFTA) for the CD-ROM *StageStruck.* His particular areas of teaching and research interest are cognitive strategies, interface design for learning with information and communications technologies, and implementation and evaluation of technology based learning. He has written widely and consulted on implementation and policy aspects of new technologies in education, especially in Australia and Asia, and is the editor-in-chief of *Educational Media International.* He has also been a frequent keynote speaker at conferences in North America, China, and Europe. In 2002, he was honored as one of the pioneers in educational technology in the *Educational Media and Technology Yearbook.*